THE GAME & THE GLORY

THE GAME & THE GLORY

**EDITED BY
JOE REICHLER**

Prentice-Hall Inc.,
Englewood Cliffs, New Jersey

THE GAME & THE GLORY
EDITED BY
JOE REICHLER

CREDITS

Design by:
Craven and Evans, Inc.

Hal Evans
Creative Director

Joel Weltman
Designer

Carmen Cavazos
Art Associate

Beth McNally
Art Associate

Hal Siegel
Art Director

John Monteleone
Associate Editor

Al Glossbrenner
Assistant Editor

Copyright © 1976 by Prentice-Hall, Inc.

Produced in association with Major League
Baseball Promotion Corporation.

Printed in the United States of America

Prentice-Hall International, Inc., London
Prentice-Hall of Australia, Pty. Ltd., Sydney
Prentice-Hall of Canada, Ltd., Toronto
Prentice-Hall of India Private Ltd., New Delhi
Prentice-Hall of Japan, Inc., Tokyo

Library of Congress cataloging in
   publication data.

Main entry under title:
The Game and the glory.

1. Baseball – – United States – – History – –
   Addresses, essays, lectures.

I. Reichler, Joe.
GV863.   A1G35   796.357'0973
   76-10707

ISBN 0-13-346072-X

CONTENTS

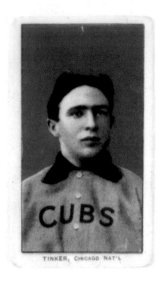

UNFORGETTABLE MOMENTS

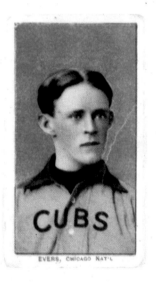

GIANTS OF THE GAME

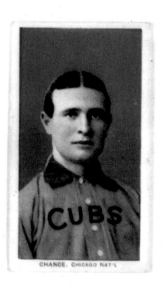

THE GLORY

THE HALL OF FAME

To the generations of fans
and players for their loyalty,
support and devotion
to the game.

INTRODUCTION

*From its great stars to its magnificent stadiums to the drama
of dramatic pennant races and World Series finishes, Baseball
has made a huge impact upon our lives.*

*There could be no more appropriate time to reminisce about
Baseball's past and glory in its present than in 1976, as
America observes its 200th birthday while the National League
celebrates its 100th anniversary and the American League its
75th.*

*THE GAME AND THE GLORY puts together the pieces of
Baseball's glorious traditions and places them into perspective
with the game today. The history and mood of Baseball in every
phase imaginable are here for the fan to digest and enjoy again
and again.*

*This impressive volume takes a look at a century of the game's
greatest heroes, teams and events, written by some of the
country's most accomplished writers and distinguished followers of the Baseball scene.*

*Baseball has much to be proud of, from its great traditions to
its magnetic appeal to Americans in all walks of life. THE
GAME AND THE GLORY does justice to baseball's stature,
in my opinion, by presenting its story in this book.*

*I hope you will spend many enjoyable hours absorbing the
charm and excitement that is Baseball.*

BOWIE K. KUHN
Commissioner of Baseball

THE
GAME

BY JAMES MICHENER

On a summer day in 1862, during the most tragic period of the Civil War, President Abraham Lincoln interrupted his duties long enough to take his son Tad to a baseball game.

Since that fateful day, baseball has been the chosen sport of the American people, the one game that most faithfully adheres to the great traditions of the people. It's a game that can be played in any pastureland, as I played it in my youth, traveling from one small village to the next. It's a game that can be played without fear of injury by kids of all ages and by men in their forties. It is leisurely and pastoral, yet exciting and requiring extreme skill.

It originated in rural areas and prospered there. I cannot remember a Fourth of July in my youth that was not marked by speeches in the morning and a baseball game in the afternoon. Farmers and townspeople gathered from miles around to watch the locals play traditional rivals, and whereas our team was always composed of simon-pure amateurs, we always suspected that the visitors relied upon imported professionals from New York or Philadelphia. (Of course, our heavy-hitting second baseman was paid a tidy sum for coming in from Baltimore, but since he came regularly, we thought of him as a hometown boy.)

But baseball reached its flowering only when it moved into the cities, finding a natural home among the workers there. It was then that the famous major-league loyalties were generated. It was then that workingmen began to applaud the stars of German, Irish, and Polish extraction, identifying with them as they would with players of no other sport. And it has been in the cities that baseball has prospered, especially when new-style black and Latin American heroes were invited to play.

I have been following baseball for the past sixty-two years and can still rattle off the lineups of the three radically different teams I rooted for: the Philadelphia Athletics of 1929–31, probably the finest all-around team I ever watched; the tragic Boston Red Sox of 1936–39, who often challenged for the league lead during the summer, only to fade before the Yankee onslaught in September; and the remarkable New York Giants of 1946–48, who once set a season's record with 221 home runs. What a terrifying row of sluggers they presented: Johnny Mize with 51 homers, Willard Marshall with 36, Walker Cooper with 35, and Bobby Thomson with 29. You'd have thought they'd sweep the pennant race by twenty games, but they finished fourth, thirteen behind, because their pitching was so poor.

It has always seemed to me that the allure of this magnificent game, its magnetic attraction for the true fan, was complex, grabbing the enthusiast from many angles and with many varied attractions. And I now believe that these manifold aspects ensure a long survival, for baseball speaks directly to certain traits in the American character.

Baseball is a game of great beauty. The field is harmonious, a bright green marked off by clean white lines, with the parabola of the base paths indicated in dark brown. The movements of the players are poetic, especially the staccato bursts of the short-to-second-to-first double play, or the long rhythmic lope of the center fielder as he moves back to drag down a long fly. There is extraordinary grace in the way a batter races to first on a well-hit ball, hits the bag with his inside foot, and turns in a tight, controlled arc so that he can speed on to second. I have always especially liked the play in which the right-handed batter slams a tremendous shot down the third-base line which Pie Traynor or Brooks Robinson takes with a miraculous backhanded stab. Then, steadying himself by digging in his right foot, he pivots and with one unbroken motion throws the ball to first in a low, flat trajectory just in time to nail the runner.

Baseball is a game of precision. I have always thought it miraculous that the early developers of the game settled upon the distance of ninety feet between the bases, for this permits many alternatives. The batter at

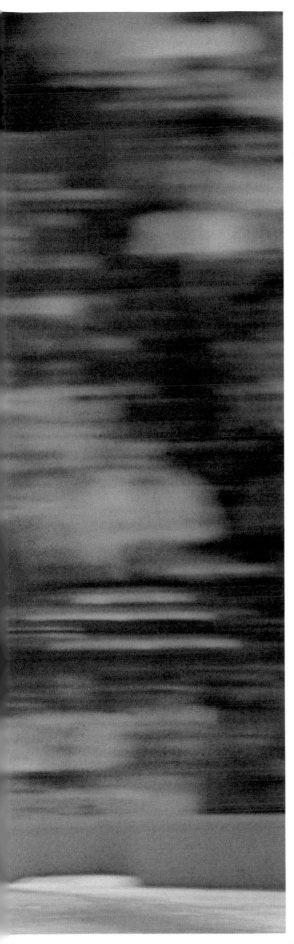

the plate hits a high bounding ball to short. If he can show a burst of speed going down to first, he can beat out the throw for a hit. If the shortstop is unusually skillful, trapping the ball and throwing in one motion, he can nip the runner for an out. A hard-hit ball to third, with a man on first, can be converted into a double play if the third baseman and the second baseman execute the play properly, but if they falter for even a second, the batter speeds safely to first. No play better illustrates the miracle of that ninety-foot distance than the steal. If the base runner gets exactly the right lead and proper start, he can just make it to second base ahead of the catcher's throw. But if he is a split second off, the catcher will nail him as he slides in. This same precision operates elsewhere than on the base paths. An outfielder, racing toward the distant wall after a lofty fly ball, can detect the warning track, take two more steps, and leap high against the wall, protecting himself with his bare hand while he spears the ball with his glove. If a catcher is swift and brave, he can just reach the high foul at the lip of the opposing dugout. It is this delicate precision that adds so much excitement to the game.

Baseball is a game of historical record. Many of us love baseball because it represents an unbroken tradition, with facts that can be quoted to settle arguments. Ted Williams batted .406 in 1941 and you can look it up in the book. There it is: at bat 456, runs 135, hits 185, average .406. And Ty Cobb had an incredible lifetime average of .367. You can look it up. There was the longest game ever played, Brooklyn-Boston, twenty-six innings, in 1920.

5

And Joe DiMaggio's hitting streak of fifty-six straight games in 1941. And Billy Wambsganss' unassisted triple play in the 1920 World Series; he snagged a line drive off the bat of Brooklyn pitcher Clarence Mitchell. And that memorable World Series inning in which the Philadelphia Athletics scored ten runs; it happened in the bottom of the seventh, on October 12, 1929, against the Chicago Cubs. And fat Wilbert Robinson's amazing record set in 1892 of collecting seven straight hits in one game, unmatched until the summer of 1975 when Rennie Stennett of the Pittsburgh Pirates also got seven straight.

The saddest statistic I can recall occurred on May 26, 1959, when slim little Harvey Haddix of the Pittsburgh Pirates pitched a perfect game against Milwaukee for nine innings, except that his team didn't score a single run for him. So he pitched a perfect tenth, and then the eleventh, and then the twelfth. In the thirteenth Milwaukee got to him for a run and Haddix lost 1–0.

These and a multitude of other records are what the true fan keeps stored in his head, the wonderful mileposts of the sport. Baseball is unique in that it provides so much exact data by which individual performances can be compared, and it is these almost sacred figures that enshrine and protect the game. I could go on reciting statistics that would bewilder the reader, figures that were significant to me when I was a boy and remain significant now as reminders of great days, but no statistic is more meaningful to me, in a nagging, gnawing way, than this: Of the original sixteen teams that made up the two big leagues, my team, the Philadelphia Phillies, have won the fewest World Series games: exactly one, back in 1915 when they finished 1 and 4 against the Boston Red Sox. A fact like that could make a strong man weep, and I did in 1950, when my team finished its second World Series 0 and 4 against the New York Yankees.

Baseball is a game of individual performance. Each player performs alone, in the full glare of the spotlight. Teamwork is important, but it is possible only if the individual player executes his part perfectly. And the important thing is that the fan knows whether the performance was good or not. No play requires more precise teamwork than a 6-4-3 double play. Man on first, batter slams a hard shot toward short. The shortstop grabs the ball and tosses it gently toward the empty second base. The second baseman appears out of nowhere, grabs the floating ball, tags second, pivots, and sees the base runner hurtling at him. He flinches, moves aside, then throws to first, too late to catch the batter. Everyone in the stands can see that the second baseman could have completed the double play if he had not been afraid to challenge that hurtling base runner. An outfielder makes a splendid backhand trap on a double to right, preventing an inside-the-park home run, but then throws to the wrong base, allowing the batter to stretch his double into a triple. Everybody in the park knows an error has been made, even though it will not show in the box score. This individual accountability is unique to baseball and explains in part why it has become our national game. We are a nation of individuals who can when needed function as a team. We prize individual action, individual responsibility, the willingness of the individual to stand alone and take the consequences. You had better not play baseball if you flinch at criticism when you goof.

Baseball produces durable heroes. Baseball, more than any other sport, creates heroic figures who are remembered and cherished. I think it extraordinary that year after year our stadiums can be filled by fans attending Old-Timers' Day. They pay to see their former heroes playing an abbreviated game, and the teams do not have to be composed of only the super-greats like Joe DiMaggio or Willie Mays. The fans delight to see the lesser men, too, the ones who held the teams together. No other sport would dare to bring the old-timers back to play an actual game. Some games are too rough. Others could be played by old-timers, but there is no interest in them. Other games require such massive equipment that they hide the personality of the player; a fan wouldn't remember what an old-time star looked like if, indeed, he ever knew. In other games the stars survived only briefly and had not the time to become commanding personalities. And in still others the mode of play was so intricate that no star could function without his complete supporting team. But in baseball the star was preeminent; he played a long time; he wore a uniform that allowed the fan to see him and know him; and whatever he did on the field could be recorded and analyzed and remembered. He developed individual characteristics that could easily be identified, and he was usually so colorful that he generated outrageous stories which would live permanently in the legends of the sport. He was a true hero, and now when he trots onto the field as an old-timer, he evokes vibrant memories of his greatness. Only a very few heroes in other sports achieve this perpetuity, because the games in which they specialized were not suitable for the creation of charismatic individual figures. In the Revolution of 1776 the United States rejected royalty, but we have never lost our hunger for the regal figure. Therefore, having no royal family to gloat upon, we bestow our affection on heroes from sport, and no game produces a better surrogate royalty than baseball.

Baseball is fun. We must not get too serious about this rollicking game. Not many superior ballplayers achieve the immortality Marv Throneberry did when he cavorted so hilariously for the inept New York Mets under Casey Stengel. A volume could be written about Marv's antics, but the story I like best, perhaps apocryphal, concerns the game in which he had committed various errors, enabling the other team to build a 3–1 lead. But in the ninth Marv redeemed himself. With two on and two out he blasted a screaming triple, which tied the score, and as he slid safely into third he shook hands with himself, only to see the first-base umpire signaling that he was out (which meant that no runs had scored) because he had failed to touch first. When Stengel ran screaming to protest, the umpire at second base walked up quietly and whispered to Casey, "Take it easy, Case. He didn't touch second, either."

The stories that accumulate around the game make it a joy. The hillbilly outfielders, the ungovernable left-handed pitchers, the sluggers with their phobias, the tyrannical managers, and the inventive sportswriters form a pantheon of frolic. I've had some great times in the ball park, none better than when I used to frequent the bleachers at Fenway Park in Boston, surrounded by the faithful. One truck driver took an intense dislike for me when he learned I was teaching at Harvard and he used to abuse me as "that softy from East Cup Cake, Vermont." But at the close of that crucial day when the Red Sox had lost the vital doubleheader to the Yankees, I saw him sitting alone, a man bereft. I was pretty well chopped up myself, so I went over to him in a gesture of conciliation and found that he was weeping. In a compulsive gesture he swept me into his capacious arms and sobbed, "It just seems we ain't never gonna make it."

I have often thought that the best entertainment dollar in America is a ticket to a twi-night doubleheader between two good teams. The beautiful park, the green grass, the clean figures moving with exceptional grace, the noise, the comradeship, the lights standing out against the dark sky, the sounds of the city distant and outside, the fun of the game. These are the reasons why baseball continues to allure. It's a bargain, and it's fun.

Baseball epitomizes many of the finest aspects of American life. No sport can survive and grow in acceptance if it does not contain elements that reflect the spiritual characteristics of the nation in which it is played. If it fails in this respect, it must not claim to be a national sport. In the burgeoning America of the post-Civil War period a spirit of optimism was essential, and it was well expressed in baseball's "The game is never over till the last man is out." This became an essential American belief, illustrated by a score of historical situations in which businesses made miraculous recoveries or political parties achieved last-minute victories. I have always preferred games like baseball and tennis in which victory is possible until the final second rather than those games that are governed by an implaccable clock and in which a team that is behind 36–7 with a minute to go has no possible chance. I want to hope. Perhaps I have been infected by those remarkable baseball games in which teams have made heroic recoveries after two were out in the bottom of the ninth. I prefer to trust in the American myth that preaches that salvation is always possible.

In the post-Civil War period baseball provided another service, which has often been overlooked. It was the only field in which the southern boy could find a good job in the North, and the camaraderie that developed on the ball field helped unite old enemies. Also, northern teams began training in the South, and this too helped.

Baseball also became a prime agency for the Americanization of vast numbers of immigrants who were coming to our cities, for it provided them with a focus for their loyalty. Belatedly, it became a major influence in public acceptance of the black into all channels of American life.

But its major contribution to our national life was its cultivation of a code of sportsmanship, hard play, and regional loyalties. It served as a truly national game, participated in by all segments of the nation, followed by citizens in all parts of the country and in all walks of life. I have constantly been amazed to find boys in Arizona who are red-hot supporters of the Boston Red Sox or the Detroit Tigers. I was not surprised when, during the broadcast of game four of the epic Mets-Orioles World Series of 1969, the television cameras caught former Chief Justice Earl Warren in the stands, keeping his scorecard up to date as the game moved into extra innings. Thousands of American men keep score at each game they attend, and thousands of others know the batting averages of their hometown teams, for baseball is an inherent

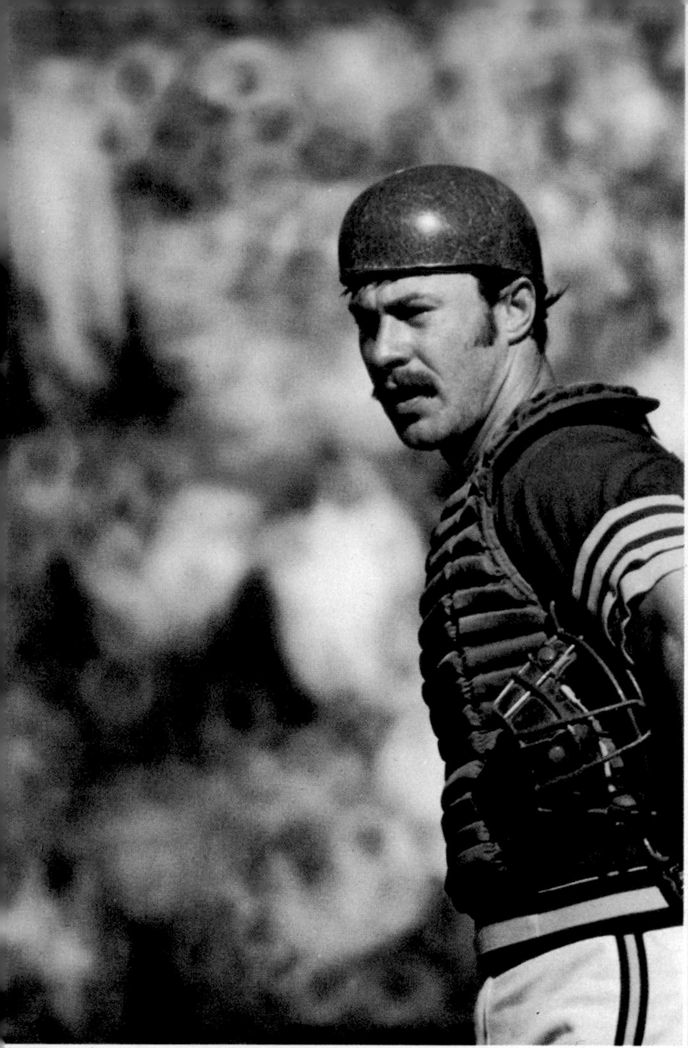

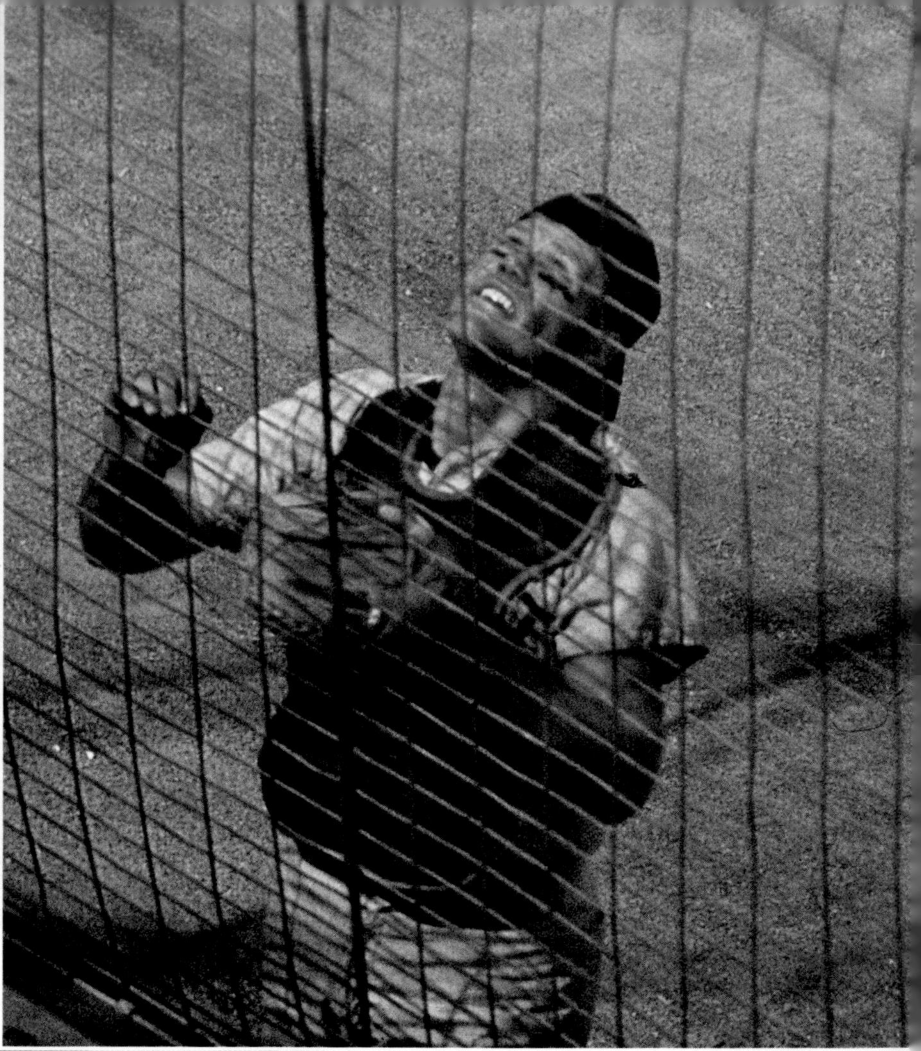

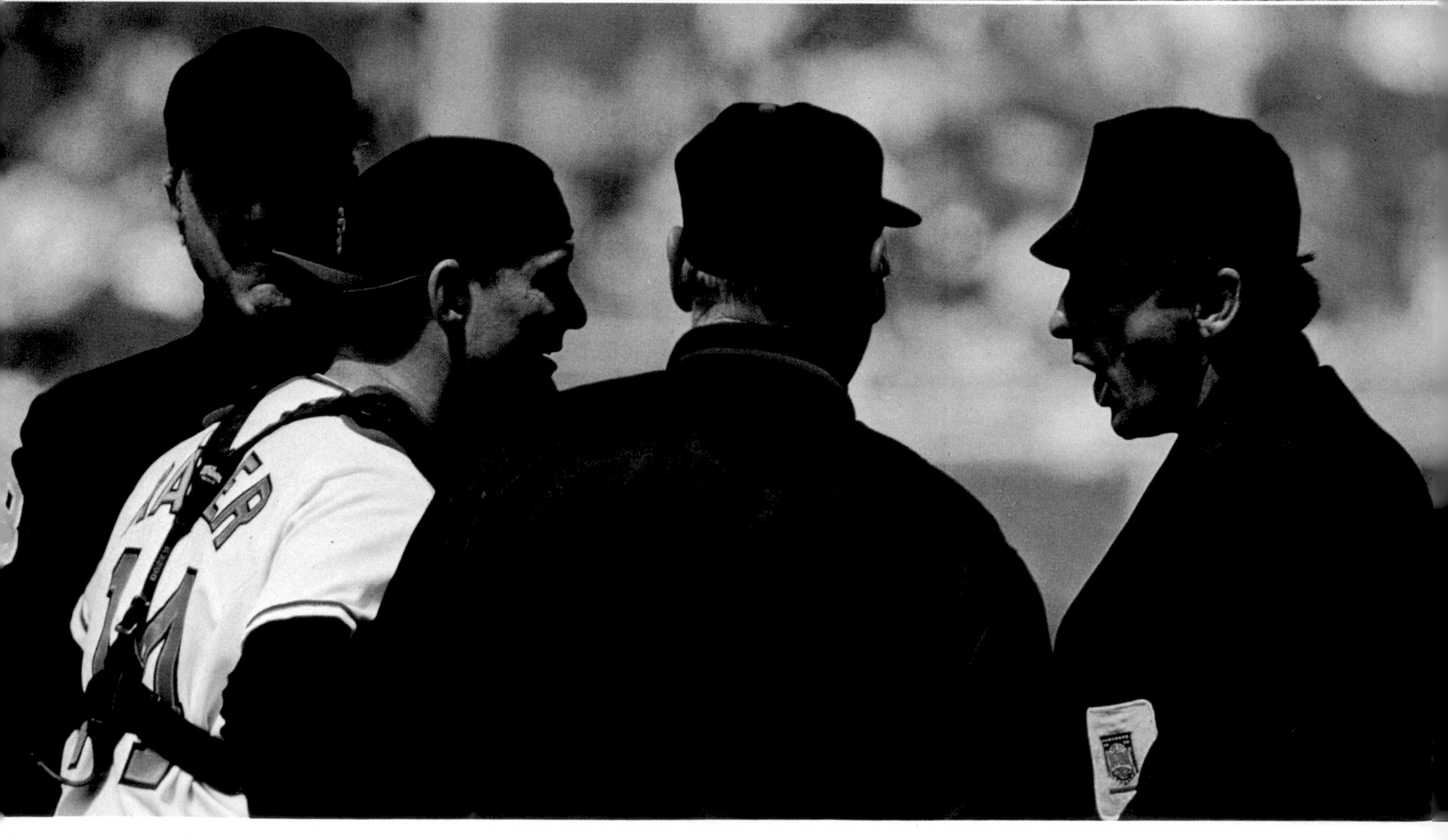

part of their culture.

As a writer, I have been impressed by the many words and phrases introduced into our language by baseball. No better example can be cited than that of the southern Baptist whose daughter married an Episcopalian from up north. The old man opposed the marriage, but as a gesture of conciliation he did attend one service in his son-in-law's church. He enjoyed the singing but was disturbed by the constant kneeling and rising, so when his daughter asked him how he liked the new service he replied, "The music and preaching were all right. But they had too many seventh innings."

A politician who makes an effective speech is said to have "hit a home run." But one who garbles things has "struck out."

When a young man is rebuffed by a pretty girl, he complains, "I never got to first base." And when he is faced by an unexpected bit of bad luck, he says, "They threw me a curve."

In business, when a man is given an inferior job, he tells his wife, "They put me out in right field." But if he perseveres he boasts, "I'm still in the old ball game." And if he really triumphs, he gloats, "I knocked it out of the park."

A salesman reporting to his main office says, "I made nine calls and struck out on six, but I closed three big sales, so I'm batting .333 and that's good enough to stay in the big leagues." I heard a friend say, after he had passed up a good opportunity, "I kept my bat on my shoulder and looked that one over, but I'm swinging at the next one."

I also heard a professor explain a sequence of bad luck, which had come in the wake of real success: "There I was, batting six for six, when I ran into this string of oh-fers." He was comparing himself to the hot slugger who suddenly goes 0 for 3, then 0 for 4, then 0 for 5. There is no more appropriate, yet encouraging, description of a man temporarily down on his luck than to say of him, "He's only in a slump."

Baseball terms crop up everywhere. I know a tennis bum who plays a mean psychological game of doubles. When a discombobulated opponent serves him a double fault, he cries, "Never walk the pitcher! Never put the weakest man on base." This can be especially unnerving when the man who has just double-faulted knows that the speaker is the best player on the court.

One of the most effective descriptions of failure is, "He struck out with the bases loaded," but the baseball phrase I recall most often was spoken by an elderly man to a brash young kid who had begun to cut corners where honesty was concerned: "Son, sooner or later you've got to learn. You can't steal first base."

I have written many words but realize with a pang of regret that none will live as long as certain ones uttered by baseball players. Dizzy Dean achieved immortality when he said over the radio, "He shoulda been out at second but he slud." Satchel Paige did the same with his remarkable summation of the human condition: "Don't never look back. Somethin' might be gainin' on you."

Some years ago, when other sports began to explode across the nation and find a valued place on television, some critics suggested that baseball, because of its adherence to tradition, might be doomed. They argued that Americans now preferred violence, that new games were destined to replace old, that customers would no longer pay to see the lovely, poetic, grace-filled spectacle that had for so long been our national game.

And temporary retreats at the ball park fortified these arguments. But any game as solidly rooted in American life as baseball would have to have lasting qualities and the ability to adjust to whatever general patterns the parent society took. And baseball had precisely those qualities.

It adjusted to new conditions, introduced new color, took necessary steps to hold on to its fans. Instead of declining, it developed new strength. Instead of being shoved off television, it built up a huge following. And instead of

losing its radio audience, it proliferated, reaching into all corners of the nation. In all aspects, it became stronger than before.

I like many of the newer sports, and in their proper seasons I watch them avidly. The success of football, basketball, hockey, and tennis proves that there is a place for them in the American scene, and I would expect them to continue to prosper. I would also expect innovations like lacrosse and volleyball to succeed in limited areas. Certainly, our culture is richer when we support a colorful variety of games, and the general sporting scene is stronger whenever a new sport establishes itself.

But I suspect that baseball, with its many unique qualities, will last as long as there is an America. When we look into the sources of our national strength, as many are doing today, we will generate a new loyalty to baseball. As our society becomes more nervous and violent, we will appreciate anew the comforting dignity of baseball. And as we discover the fun and excitement of newer games, we will come back to the established values of our traditional game, baseball ■

TODAY'S TEAMS

Introduction by
JOE REICHLER

There is a logical place for almost every kind of sport. Baseball started out at the very heart of our nation and will probably remain close to it. Personalities are and always have been an important part of baseball. But all too often, when we think of the game's personalities, we think only of individual players—their strengths and weaknesses, their personal records and accomplishments. We usually fail to remember that each ball club is also a personality, a unique blend of many characteristics that makes it separate and distinct from all others. Players, coaches, managers, front office staff, even the fans themselves—all play a role in shaping a team's personality. As with individual players, each club has its own history, high points, records, and standing. And each has its own place in the general scheme of things. Some teams are known for their strong defense, some for their power hitting, some for their speed and overall hustle, and some for their lack of any of these qualities.

Yet, whatever the situation may be in one season, you can be sure that it will somehow change in the next. Baseball teams have the luxury of being born again each spring. Promising rookies, players acquired through trades, yearlings who have matured in the previous season, old hands and veterans—the kaliedoscope turns each year and a new pattern clicks into place. The changes really begin during spring training, as all the various elements that make up a team begin to meld under the blazing southern sun. It is here that the hope is forged and the dream begins anew. This is part of what makes baseball so exciting. The renewal process continues, as it always has, from year to year, making it possible to guess, but *only* guess, which teams will come out on top at the end of the season. No one can ever know for sure what the summer will bring. There are simply too many variables. About all anyone can know in advance are the names of the teams involved, the backgrounds, and historical high points. Everything else is delightfully uncertain. And that, as all twenty-four of today's teams would agree, is as it should be.

17

Braves

As older baseball fans will remember, the team now known as the Atlanta Braves began their history in Boston. The nickname of the Braves was first given to the club at the suggestion of John Montgomery Ward in 1912. Before that, the team was known as the Doves because of its owners, the Dovey brothers. It was also known as the Beaneaters and the Red Caps. In 1936 the name was changed to the Bees as a result of a fan poll. Five years later the club readopted the nickname of Braves.

The Braves moved to Milwaukee in 1953 where over the next nine years the team won one World Championship (in 1957 over the New York Yankees) and two pennants. During that time the team won 802 and lost 586 games for a .572 percentage. No other club in the National League could match it.

After several disappointing seasons in the early sixties, the team headed for the sunny skies and warmer temperatures of Atlanta. The Braves played their first game in the Peach State capital on April 12, 1966, when they met the Pirates in Atlanta Stadium.

Carl Morton
Pitcher

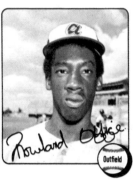

Rowland Office
Outfield

Darrell Evans
3rd Base

Phil Niekro
Pitcher

Since that time there have been some great moments and great stars who've filled the arena to the brim. There is, for example, that day in 1969 when Phil Niekro pitched the Braves to a win over the Cincinnati Reds, garnering the first N.L. Western Division Championship in history. "This place was like it's never been before," Niekro said. "People were here from all over the country just to watch us play. There was electricity in the air. It was one of the biggest thrills I've ever had."

Niekro responded by giving Atlanta a thrill too, this time in 1973. He was pitching on a Sunday afternoon against the San Diego Padres, and when the ninth inning rolled around Atlanta led, 9–0. San Diego meanwhile had no hits. Three heart-stopping outs later, Niekro had pitched the first no-hitter in the stadium's history.

Perhaps the greatest moment of all occurred on that chilly April night when the Braves played the Los Angeles Dodgers. Hank Aaron had gone through the winter with a total of 713 home runs, just one shy of Babe Ruth's great record. And then, in the first game of the season, he tied that mark against the Cincinnati Reds in Cincinnati.

So, on April 8, 1974, every eye was on Aaron. The 53,775 people in the stadium booed loudly when they watched Aaron walk on his first trip to the plate.

Then, on his second time at bat, Aaron lined the ball into left-center. It rose over the fence in left and into the glove of teammate Tom House waiting in the bullpen. It was homer No. 715.

The roar lasted forever. No one had ever seen anything like it in Atlanta. While dignitaries congratulated Aaron in special ceremonies on the field, House ran in with the ball and gave Aaron his special treasure. Al Downing, the victim of homer No. 715, watched glumly from the mound.

A marker has been erected in left field on the exact spot where House caught the home run. It'll stay there forever. No other park as young as Atlanta Stadium can boast such a famous memento.

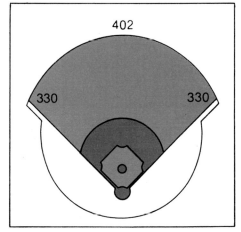

Atlanta Stadium
Seating Capacity: 52,870
First Game: April 12, 1966
Clockwise from left: Jimmy Wynn, Carl Morton, Phil Niekro, Darrell Evans

Baltimore and baseball have had a close relationship ever since the end of the Civil War, when a full twenty of the then ninety-one amateur Atlantic Coast ball clubs were located there. Originally known as the Marylanders (late 1860s) and later as the Lord Baltimores (1892), the city's teams first called themselves the Orioles (after the state bird) in 1883, making the nickname one of the oldest in the history of baseball.

The modern Orioles arrived in Baltimore by way of St. Louis in 1954. The team, preceded as it was by the unsuccessful St. Louis Browns, had something less than outstanding prospects. Everyone expected a last-place finish. Yet, despite 100 losses, the Orioles managed to avoid the basement that first season, just as they have every year since.

At the end of that first campaign, Paul Richards came to town as manager/general manager and began the serious work of building a winning ball club. By 1957, the Orioles had achieved parity for the first time (76–76), and since then no other major-league team has won as many games.

If the name "Robinson" seems synonymous with the Orioles, it is understandable. First there was Brooks Robinson, probably the greatest third baseman of all time. Brooks joined the organization as an eighteen-year-old in 1955 and has played all or part of the last twenty-one seasons in a Baltimore uniform.

As the Orioles' talent developed, there were two "near-misses," the first in 1960 and the second in 1964. Each time, however, the Baltimore bid was turned back by the powerful New York Yankees. As Brooks Robinson has often said, "We were a good ball club until we got Frank Robinson. He made us a winner."

He did, indeed. In 1966, Frank Robinson's first American League season, he won the "triple crown" and the Orioles won their first World Championship. In his six Baltimore seasons, the Orioles won four American League titles and two World Series.

With the two Robinsons plus big Boog Powell, the Orioles were a formidable force at bat, but pitching and defense have been the principal Baltimore trademark for the past several years.

Under the direction of Earl Weaver and his pitching coach, George Bamberger, the Orioles have produced fifteen 20-game winners in eight years. In 1971 alone, Baltimore had four 20-game winners, for only the second time in the history of the game. Both Dave McNally and Mike Cuellar contributed four 20-win seasons, and now Jim Palmer, whom Bob Feller recently described as "the best pitcher around today," has attained that level for a fifth time.

Brooks Robinson is, of course, the best known of all the Orioles defensively, but the Birds, who lead the majors in "gold gloves," have had many fine fielders, including people like Paul Blair (center field), Mark Belanger (shortstop), and Bobby Grich (second base), to name only those who are still active.

Strong arms, good gloves, timely hits, and one-run wins have been Baltimore's glorious past; more of the same is anticipated for the future.

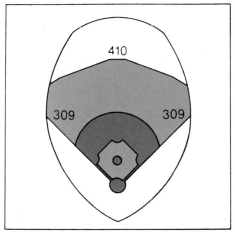

Memorial Stadium
Seating Capacity: 52,137
First Game: April 15, 1954
Clockwise from left: Brooks Robinson,
Mike Cuellar, Bobby Grich, Jim Palmer

The Boston Red Sox are a team rich in baseball tradition. It was with the Red Sox that Babe Ruth played his first major-league game, and it was the Red Sox who boasted one of the greatest outfields of all time in Tris Speaker, Harry Hooper, and Duffy Lewis. Both Cy Young, winner of more games than any pitcher who ever lived, and Ted Williams, the greatest of modern hitters, wore the Boston flannels.

The team entered the American League at its birth in 1901 as the Somersets. This was because of their owner, Charles W. Somers. At various times the team was also known as the Puritans, the Pilgrims, and the Plymouth Rocks. These history-based names failed to stick, however. In 1907 when the rival Boston Nationals discarded their traditional red stockings for white ones, John Irving Taylor, then president of the team, quickly capitalized on it. He had his team wear red stockings and changed the name of the team to the Red Sox.

The Red Sox first hit the jackpot in 1903, winning the pennant by $16\frac{1}{2}$ games and going on to beat Pittsburgh in the first of the modern World Series. Jake Stahl managed the 1912 team to a stupendous .601 percentage and a soul-satisfying victory over John McGraw's New York Giants.

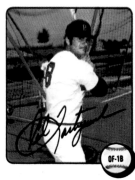   

Three years later, in 1915, former catcher Bill Carrigan's team beat out Detroit for the pennant and went on to take the World Championship from the Phillies in five games. Led by the pitching of Babe Ruth (23 wins), the Sox repeated in 1916. In that series Ruth defeated Sherry Smith of Brooklyn, 2–1, in fourteen innings, the longest World Series game on record.

A second-place finish in 1917 and another World Championship (over the Cubs) in 1918 were followed by the unsuccessful ownership of Harry Frazee and later a syndicate headed by Bob Quinn. Finally, in 1933, millionaire sportsman Thomas A. Yawkey purchased the club and began a franchise ownership that has lasted longer than any other in history.

It required both high-priced talent and the building of a farm system to put the team back on the track, but it all paid off with a pennant in 1946.

The next Boston high point occurred in 1967 when the "Impossible Dream" team became the first big-league team to ever jump from ninth to first place and a pennant in a single year. In 1972 the team again astounded baseball fans by bouncing back from a disastrous mid-season slump to come within twenty-four hours and half a game of winning the division title.

Sparked by the talents of players like Carl Yastrzemski, Luis Tiant, Bill Lee, Rick Burleson, Fred Lynn, Carlton Fisk, and others, the Red Sox overcame the Oakland A's in the 1975 play-off. They went on to play the Cincinnati Reds for the World Championship, losing 4–3 in one of the most exciting, action-filled Series in the history of baseball.

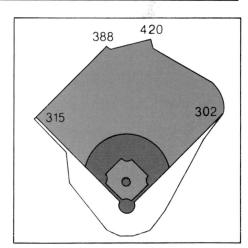

Fenway Park
Seating Capacity: 33,437
First Game: April 20, 1912
Clockwise from top: Jim Rice, Fred Lynn,
Carl Yastrzemski, Luis Tiant

23

The California Angels were born out of an interrupted romance between a singing cowboy and a baseball.

Gene Autry, whose budding diamond career gave way to a remarkable thirty-year reign atop the radio, recording, movie, and television industries, rekindled the flame when he acquired the Angels franchise at an American League expansion meeting late in 1960.

Autry went to the meetings merely as an interested observer. His Golden West Broadcasting flagship radio station, KMPC, had lost the rights to the transplanted Los Angeles Dodgers games, and he was anxious to negotiate with the owners of the neophyte American League entry. When prospective buyers balked, Autry reached for his pocket and pulled out his trusty checkbook. He and partner Bob Reynolds bought the team, naming it the Los Angeles Angels after the popular Pacific Coast League team that had departed when the Dodgers arrived from Brooklyn.

It was a whirlwind five months for Autry. He quickly hired Fred Haney as general manager and Bill Rigney as field boss; Haney and Rigney hastily accumulated an unlikely aggregation which the press termed "rejects and rookies who will be lucky to win fifty games." Well, as it turned out the young Angels didn't win fifty games—they won seventy their first year and startled the baseball world the following year by nailing down eighty-six. The Angels have won more games than any other expansion team, and the team's play has attracted a loyal following.

To escape the shadow of the Dodgers, whose park they shared from 1962 to 1966, the Angels moved to nearby suburban Orange County, where Anaheim Stadium was erected within the shadow of Disneyland. They became the "California Angels" at that time and have averaged more than a million fans per season ever since.

Pitching has been the strength of the organization from the very beginning. In 1964 there was Dean Chance, a Cy Young Award winner. More recently, it's been Nolan Ryan who has gained the Hall of Fame stature of Sandy Koufax in southern California.

Now, however, a new element has marked the Angels' play—speed. In 1975, for example, the Angels became the first team in fifty-seven years to steal more than two hundred bases, as they resorted to a style of play common in the 1920s, or about the time Autry wisely turned in his spikes and bat for spurs and a guitar.

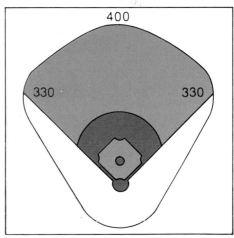

Anaheim Stadium
Seating Capacity: 43,204
First Game: April 19, 1966
Clockwise from left: Nolan Ryan, Dave Chalk, Frank Tanana, Ellie Rodriguez

The Chicago Cubs, who can trace their existence back to the year 1876, are the only team in the National League to hold continuous membership since its inception. This may be due in part to William A. Hulbert, who was both president of the club and president of the league from 1876 until his death in 1882.

Baseball's early years were marred by lack of organization and discipline. There was little control over scheduling, and players jumped from club to club at will. Hulbert realized that if baseball was to survive, some sort of reform was badly needed.

So, early in 1876, he persuaded seven other cities to form a new league. The organization was called the National League of Professional Baseball Clubs, and it adopted a written constitution and regulations to protect both players and management. The National League proved to be the solution, and, of course, is still going strong today.

After the 1915 season the Cubs were purchased from the Taft family of Cincinnati by a group of well-known Chicagoans. One of the group's first acts was to move the club to the site where it plays today. Three years later William Wrigley, Jr., bought out the other members of the original group and became the majority stockholder of the club. With the death of William Wrigley, Jr., in 1932, the majority stockholder position passed to his son Philip K. Wrigley.

To modern fans the club has always been known as the Chicago Cubs, but the team has borne three other nicknames. The team was originally called the White Stockings. Later, it became the Colts because its manager, Cap Anson, starred in a picture called *A Runaway Colt.* The nickname was discarded in 1898, after Anson's career came to an end, and the team was called the Orphans because of the passing of their longtime manager. In 1899 a Chicago newspaper held a contest to select a new name and the Cubs were born.

In one hundred National League seasons, the Cubs have won sixteen league championships. The first five were under the direction of Adrian "Cap" Anson, a man who ranks with John McGraw and Connie Mack for his long and notable career as a player and manager.

First Baseman/Manager Frank Chance, "the peerless leader," led the Cubs to pennants in 1906, 1907, 1908, and 1910. The team's 1906 record of 116 wins is unequaled in major-league history. Chance, of course, was a member of the Cubs' famed Tinker-to-Evers-to-Chance double-play combination. The Cubs won the Series in 1907 and 1908, both times against Detroit.

With Charlie Grimm as the manager, the Cubs won the pennant again in 1932, then repeated in 1935 with a spectacular twenty-one-game winning streak. In 1938 Gabby Hartnett became manager and took a personal hand in sewing up the flag with his famous "homer in the gloamin' " in the closing days of the season. Aided by a July deal that brought pitcher Hank Borowy from the Yankees, the Cubs won their sixteenth pennant in 1945 but lost the World Series in seven games to the Tigers.

The team has not won a National League pennant since, but in 1969, under Manager Leo Durocher, and led by "Mr. Cub" Ernie Banks, Billy Williams and Ron Santo, the team posted its best won-loss record (92–70) and finished second in the Eastern Division in the first season of baseball's divisional play.

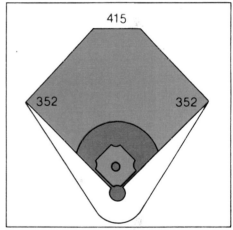

Wrigley Field
Seating Capacity: 37,741
First Game: April 20, 1916
Clockwise from top right: Rick Monday,
Bill Madlock, Rick Reuschel, Bill Bonham

27

The Chicago White Sox were founded by Charles A. Comiskey, the famous former first baseman and manager of the champion St. Louis Browns. Comiskey, who was just beginning to acquire his nickname of the "Old Roman," brought both the team and the American League into being in 1900.

The club was originally called the White Stockings, a name that had been used by the Chicago National League team several years earlier. But when the American League gained official status prior to the 1901 season, the team's name was changed to the Chicago White Sox.

White Sox Park, the oldest baseball stadium in the major leagues, was built in 1910 and named Comiskey Park after the team's founder. This was a perfectly natural choice, for from the very beginning the Old Roman played an active role in White Sox affairs. He managed the team to the league championship in 1900 and then moved to the front office, where he remained until 1931.

Outfield

Pitcher

2nd Base

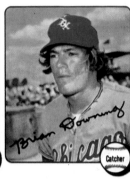

Catcher

During that period the club laid claim to four pennants, as well as the hearts and minds of thousands of fans. The 1906 pennant winners, the famous "Hitless Wonders," were typical. The team had the lowest batting average on the circuit (.228), yet it won ninety-three games, taking the title by three. The entire squad hit only seven home runs that year—but it stole 209 bases.

The World Series that year was also memorable. The White Sox defeated the Chicago Cubs four games to two, winning the only all-Chicago World Series in history.

The Sox downed the New York Giants in the same number of games in the 1917 Series. But they lost the 1919 Series to Cincinnati, five games to three, after which eight Sox were expelled from baseball for conspiring with gamblers.

There were many famous baseball personalities who wore the White Sox flannels in these early years, including Ed "20-Wins" Walsh, Clark Griffith, Harry Hooper, and Eddie Collins—all of whom were selected for the National Baseball Hall of Fame. Other superb Sox who later joined this group at Cooperstown—as well as Comiskey himself—are Ray Schalk, Urban "Red" Faber, Al Simmons, Ted Lyons, Early Wynn, and Luke "Mr. White Sox" Appling.

The club won its next pennant in 1959 by a comfortable five-game margin over the Cleveland Indians. The team, headed by Wynn, Nellie Fox and Luis Aparicio, literally ran the opposition into the ground. It led the league in stolen bases and in defense. But the Sox, despite a spectacular batting performance by Ted Kluszewski, who crashed three homers and drove in ten runs, lost the World Series to Los Angeles.

Some of the highlights of White Sox history include Charles Robertson's perfect game against Detroit (April 30, 1922), Bill Melton's home run crown (thirty-three) in 1971, and the club record set by Wilbur Wood when he registered his fourth straight season with twenty or more wins in 1974.

Since 1971 the White Sox have averaged over a million in attendance per season, outdrawing all Western Division foes. It's a record that would make the "Old Roman" Charles A. Comiskey very proud.

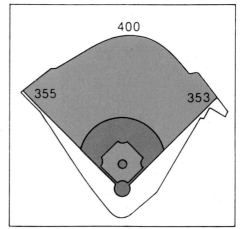

Comiskey Park
Seating Capacity: 44,492
First Game: July 1, 1910
Clockwise from right: Carlos May, Wilbur Wood, Rich Gossage, Bucky Dent

29

The Cincinnati Reds, whose nickname derives from the color of the original Queen City team's stockings, was the first professional baseball club in history. That was more than one hundred years ago, but a pace-setting team from the very start, today's Reds are also a team of the Now Generation.

It is a team of the 1970s, a team that has won more games in this decade (1970–75) than any other team in the major leagues. It is a team that has won the National League's Western Division four times in those six years and narrowly missed a fifth time. It has gone on to take the National League pennant three times and the World Championship once (1975).

The true story of the Cincinnati Reds, though, can be found in people, not in numbers. The team has had its share of heroes over the years, but when it comes to capturing the fans' imagination, no group has been more successful than the Big Four of Johnny Bench, Pete Rose, Joe Morgan, and Tony Perez.

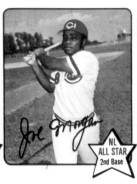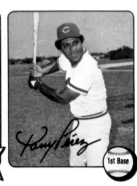

Bench began his major-league career at age nineteen. By the time he was twenty-five, he had twice been named Most Valuable Player in the National League and was annually among the major-league leaders in homers and RBIs. He has been hailed by many as one of the greatest catchers to ever play the game.

Rose, who has collected more than 2,500 hits, holds three National League batting championships and an MVP title. Morgan, the 1975 N.L. MVP, is credited with helping to change the image of the Reds from power to speed when he arrived in 1972. Despite his small stature (5'7" and 160 pounds), he averaged twenty homers and sixty stolen bases during his first four years with the Reds.

And last, but by no means least, there's Tony Perez. He has been Mr. Consistency on the Reds, knocking in ninety or more runs for the past nine years, the only active player ever to achieve that.

President Bob Howsam, who took over as general manager in 1967, built a farm system and supplemented it through trades to produce a fine collection of young talent to complement the Big Four: pitchers Don Gullett, Will McEnaney, and Rawly Eastwick; shortstop Dave Concepcion; and outfielders Ken Griffey, George Foster, and Cesar Geronimo.

These are the people who will join the many famous names of the Cincinnati past, names such as Johnny Vander Meer, the only man in baseball to pitch two consecutive no-hitters; Edd Roush, voted in 1969 as the Greatest Reds Player Ever for his hitting exploits that put him in Baseball's Hall of Fame with a .323 lifetime average; Ernie Lombardi, Bucky Walters, and Paul Derringer, who led the Reds to back-to-back N.L. titles in 1939–40; Ewell Blackwell, the side-wheeling pitching great of the forties; and fierce competitor Frank Robinson, who led the Cinderella Reds to the '61 pennant.

The Cincinnati Reds have given much to the game of baseball, including the very idea of getting paid to play (they formed the first professional team in 1869). And few contributions have had more impact on the modern game than an event that took place at Crosley Field on May 24, 1935—the first night game in major-league history. The Reds were also the first major league team to have a farm system; the first to travel by air; and the first to participate in a televised game.

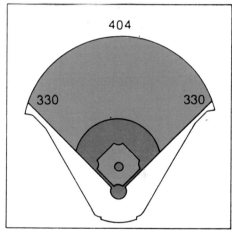

Riverfront Stadium
Seating Capacity: 51,786
First Game: June 30, 1970
Clockwise from left: Pete Rose, Joe Morgan, Gary Nolan, Dave Concepcion

Baseball and the city of Cleveland have had a close and colorful relationship since 1879. Moving from one league to another and back again several times in the early years, Cleveland first gained fame as the National League Spiders in the 1890s. However, when the National League decided to reduce its former twelve-team circuit to eight, Cleveland was one of the cities that was dropped.

The town wasted no time in applying for membership in the infant American League and was officially installed in 1900. The new team was first called the Blues, and later, the Broncos. Napoleon Lajoie came on the scene in June of 1902, and one year later the Cleveland fans, by popular acclaim, changed the club's nickname to the Naps in honor of this great star.

When Lajoie resigned as manager in 1909 he was replaced by Jim McGuire, and the team became the Molly Maguires. Finally, a newspaper contest in 1915 decided the current nickname and the Cleveland team has been called the Indians ever since.

Des. Hitter

3rd Base

Outfield

DH-OF

Under the inspired leadership of Tris Speaker, the Indians won their first championship in 1920, edging out the White Sox and the Yankees in a race for the pennant. The team went on to win the best five-of-nine classic World Series against Brooklyn.

In 1948 another player/manager, Lou Boudreau, piloted the club through a season filled with some of Cleveland's most memorable moments. The Indians waged a long struggle with the Boston Red Sox in September, only to end up in a tie, forcing the first pennant play-off in major-league history.

Rookie left-hander Gene Bearden then proceeded to beat the Sox in Fenway Park, 8–3. Boudreau homered twice and Ken Keltner slammed a three-run homer to send the Indians into the Series against the other Boston team—the Braves. The Indians went on to win the second World Championship in the club's history in six games, drawing 238,491 fans for the three games in Cleveland.

The Indians set an American League record in 1954 by winning 111 games for an impressive percentage of .721. The famous pitching staff of Bob Lemon, Mike Garcia, Early Wynn, Bob Feller, aided by Art Houtteman, Hal Newhouser, Ray Narleski, and Don Mossi, combined to lead the league with a 2.78 ERA.

Today, Tribe General Manager Phil Seghi is counting on another player/manager to tack more years onto the string of 1920, 1948, and 1954. Frank Robinson, a twenty-year veteran player, spent 1975 as "baseball's first black manager." Now he is simply "manager of the Cleveland Indians."

Robinson's experience, together with the talent of people like Rick Manning and Duane Kuiper, the youth of veterans like Buddy Bell, George Hendrick, and Charlie Spikes, and the bats of old pros like Boog Powell and Rico Carty could well make the Indians contenders again. When it happens, that old feeling will be restored and these will be the good old days.

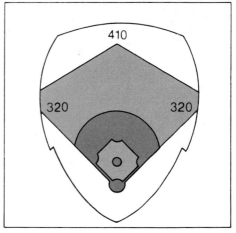

Municipal Stadium
Seating Capacity: 76,713
First Game: July 31, 1932
Clockwise from left: Buddy Bell, Boog Powell, Frank Robinson, George Hendrick

The Detroit team was tagged the Tigers back in 1889 when the city was in the National League. The inspiration came from Manager George Stallings' idea of making striped stockings a part of the players' uniforms. Since that time the Tigers—consistently successful on the field and at the gate—have risen to prestige and power in the American League.

Three great eras stand out in the Detroit ownership and front office management. These are the Frank Navin period, the Walter O. Briggs ownership, and the John E. Fetzer ownership. Each of these men presided over a separate period of triumph.

Navin brought such figures as Ty Cobb, Hughie Jennings and Crawford to the Detroit scene and made possible the first American League championships the Tigers ever enjoyed—in 1907, 1908, and 1909.

Navin was still on hand, with Briggs, his fifty-fifty partner in 1934 and 1935 when the Tigers again crashed through under the leadership of Mickey Cochrane, whose purchase was arranged by Navin and personally financed by Briggs. Those were the days, too, of Charlie Gehringer and Hank Greenberg and the days when Detroit's fandom reached its first frenzied peak, especially when the Tigers of 1935 beat the Cubs to give the city its first World Championship.

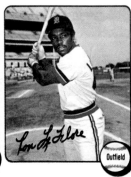

Briggs was in sole command in 1940 when there was another pennant and also in 1945 when a second World Championship, again over the Cubs, came to the Motor City.

In 1968 it all came together again with Denny McLain as king of the hill and Al Kaline, nearing the close of a brilliant career, realizing his one unfulfilled ambition—the chance to play in a World Series. The Tigers took the seven-game Series from the Cardinals, and the city of Detroit blew its top in celebration.

Names like Gates Brown, Bill Freehan, Willie Horton, Mickey Lolich, Mickey Stanley, Norm Cash, Jim Northrup, and Al Kaline constituted a remarkably durable backbone for Detroit over the years.

Today, of course, there are new names; names that the Tigers expect will intrigue fans in the future as others did in the past. Ron LeFlore, Dan Meyer, John Wockenfuss, Tom Veryzer, Vern Ruhle, and Fernando Arroyo received their baptism in 1975. Others are on the futures list, coming up from 1975 championship teams at Montgomery and Evansville, including a duo touted as the best two young right-handers in the minor leagues — Frank MacCormack, and Mark Fidrych.

Numbers, too, mean much to the fans of Detroit, who pride themselves on their fairness and their annually abundant turnouts at Tiger Stadium. In 1975, for instance, the Tigers presented a rookie-laden lineup on its way to a second straight last-place finish in the midst of the worst economic conditions the city of Detroit may have ever experienced.

Despite all of that, season attendance at Tiger Stadium totaled 1,058,836. That marked the eleventh straight season over the million mark. That's real consistency.

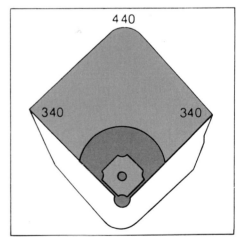

Tiger Stadium
Seating Capacity: 54,226
First Game: April 20, 1912
Clockwise from top: Ron LeFlore, Willie Horton, Bill Freehan, Tom Walker

When Houston was awarded a major-league franchise on October 17, 1960, the baseball world had no idea of the innovations that were to follow: indoor baseball, artificial turf, and exploding scoreboards all became part of the Houston baseball scene.

The Colt 45's played outdoors at Colt Stadium during the 1962–63–64 seasons. But at the start of the 1965 season the team changed its name to the Astros and moved indoors. Indoor baseball, something that once seemed as unreal as walking on the moon, became a reality on April 12, 1965, when the first official major-league baseball game was played under the Houston Astrodome. The Philadelphia Phillies won the contest, 2–0.

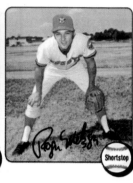
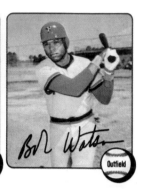

36

When the original grass began to wither under the big dome, another innovation came into being—artificial turf. But that isn't all the Astrodome has to offer. Other outstanding features include a scoreboard with bulls stamping and snorting and rockets streaming when the home team triumphs, a 72° year-round temperature, plush theaterlike seats, and fine restaurants.

Most important of all, though, is major-league baseball, something the city of Houston had never known before 1960. Even though the efforts of such big-name players as Nellie Fox, Jim Gentile, Don Larsen, Eddie Mathews, Joe Pepitone, and Robin Roberts failed to produce a Houston championship, the people of the city have responded well to their team.

In the stadium's first year of operation, over two million fans clicked through the turnstiles to watch baseball and to marvel at the mammoth glass bubble on the Texas prairie. The Astros have drawn over one million fans a year ever since, with the exception of 1975 when attendance fell just short of the mark.

The Astros have yet to win a National League pennant, and the team has been subject to a changing managerial situation as it strives to put together a winning combination. The team's central core of player talent includes Bob Watson, a consistent .300 hitter who has earned the name Mr. Clutch, and Cesar Cedeno, the "guy who can do virtually everything."

There's also Greg Gross, the steady singles hitter, and Larry Dierker, the only twenty-game winner Houston has ever known. With this small but powerful nucleus the Astros and the Astrodome hope to bring a championship to the Bayou City soon.

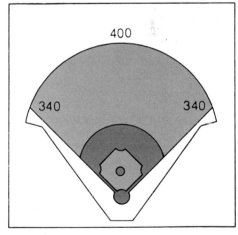

Astrodome
Seating Capacity:
First Game: April 12, 1965
Clockwise from left: Bob Watson, Roger
Metzger, Cesar Cedeno

ROYALS

An expansion club in 1969, the Kansas City Royals chose their name from over seventeen thousand possibilities suggested by fans and supporters. The final selection was announced on March 21, 1968. It derives from the internationally famous American Royal Livestock and Horse Show held yearly in this great town in the country's heartland.

The club wasted little time in becoming one of the most competitive teams in the American League. Building a team through a strong and productive farm system and shrewd trades, the Royals have been able to enjoy more success than any new franchise in a comparable period of time. Three second-place finishes and a victory total that ranks among the top five in the American League since 1971 attest to the fact.

John Mayberry — 1st Base

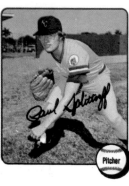

Paul Splittorff — Pitcher

Fred Patek — Shortstop

George Brett — 3rd Base

Royals Stadium, part of the Harry S Truman Sports Complex, was completed for the 1973 season. Designed specifically for baseball, it is a people-oriented stadium with over forty-thousand contoured seats directed toward the action on the diamond. It features the only all-artificial turf field in the American League and boasts a majestic 2-million-dollar-twelve-story scoreboard that provides added entertainment while it keeps Kansas City fans informed. Adjacent to the scoreboard is a unique and colorful water spectacular, complete with falls and fountains, which further enhances the stadium's appearance.

It's baseball, however, that is the center of attention, and the Royals have come a long way under the ownership of Ewing M. Kauffman.

There were highlights in the early years, both on and off the field. Since the initial year in 1969 when a group of Kansas City supporters called the Royal Lancers sold an American League record 6,805 tickets, the club has been the league leader in that department. Attendance has been over the one-million mark every year since 1973.

The Royals made their debut April 8, 1969, by winning a dramatic 12-inning game with Minnesota, 4–3. Outfielder Joe Keough set the stage that day by delivering a game-winning pinch single. That same season another outfielder, Lou Piniella, was chosen A.L. Rookie of the Year. The Royals were on their way to becoming an established team.

The nucleus began to form as second baseman Cookie Rojas, a five-time All-Star, and shortstop Fred Patek developed into the top double-play combination in the league. Amos Otis quickly became recognized as one of the premier outfielders in baseball, while John Mayberry became one of the top power hitters and run producers in the game.

And then there is third baseman George Brett, who, despite his youth, led his league counterparts in virtually every offensive category in 1974. There is also Hal McRae, the first Royal to put together back-to-back .300 seasons (1974 and 1975).

Right-hander Steve Busby heads the Royal's pitching staff with a record twenty-two wins (1974)—the most victories in Kansas City's major-league history.

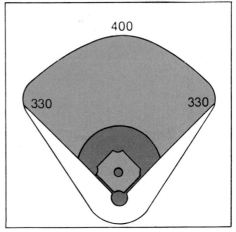

Royals Stadium
Seating Capacity: 40,762
First Game: April 10, 1973
Clockwise from left: Fred Patek, Cookie Rojas, Amos Otis, Hal McRae

Originally in Brooklyn and now in southern California, the team now known as the Los Angeles Dodgers has been a significant presence in baseball for well over eighty-five years. The club's nickname, like the team itself, has gone through many changes.

When the club won pennants in 1889 and 1890, the first in the American Association and the second in the National League, the team became known as the Bridegrooms. This was due to the unusually large number of married players on the roster. Then, when Ned Hanlon took charge in 1889, the nickname was changed to the Superbas. This name stood until 1910. When Wilbert Robinson took over as manager, sportswriters, out of deference to Uncle Robbie, called the team the Robins.

Finally, the Dodgers nickname was applied to the 1911 team. A contraction of Trolley Dodgers, the name presumably referred to the clubs' fans who dodged the new electric trolleys on Washington Avenue on their way to the ballpark.

Los Angeles Dodger history began on October 8, 1957, with Walter O'Malley's announcement of his decision to move the Brooklyn club to the West Coast. The transplant operation proved to be a success, for the Los Angeles Dodgers have consistently averaged more than 2 million fans per season.

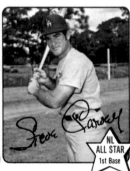
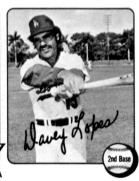

The Dodgers have won fifteen National League pennants and four World Championships since 1900. Winning over the New York Yankees in 1955, the Dodgers ended years of frustration by finally claiming the world title. Eight times since the turn of the century the club had been unsuccessful in Series competition prior to the champagne popping of 1955. And that Series itself was history-making. Never before had a team lost the first two games and then come back to claim the title.

The Dodgers beat the Chicago White Sox in 1959. The team won again in 1963 and in 1965, when the final game victories were pitched by the same man—Hall of Famer Sandy Koufax. Through the years in Los Angeles no Dodger player gained greater admiration than Koufax. He was the Cy Young Award winner in 1963, in 1965, and in 1966, his final season.

The Dodgers, for the first time in their history, retired three uniform numbers in 1972. The numbers belonged to Hall of Famers Roy Campanella (39), Jackie Robinson (42), and Sandy Koufax (32). All three men had spent their entire careers in the major leagues in Dodger uniforms.

The man who managed that first Dodger championship in 1955 is still managing today—Walt Alston. Spanning more than twenty-two years, Alston's career as manager of the Dodgers illustrates the remarkable stability of the team's organization. Vice-presidents Al Campanis (Player Personnel) and Bill Schweppe (Minor League Operations) are both longtime members of the Dodger's front office.

Team operations are directed at the top by Chairman of the Board Walter O'Malley and President Peter O'Malley. The scouting and minor-league systems of the Dodgers have long been recognized as being among the finest in baseball, producing what has become known as the "Dodger Way."

Traditionally, the Dodger Way of winning has been based upon solid fundamentals, good pitching, alert base running, and, on occasion, power. If the first half of the century is any indication, the Dodger Way will continue to have an impact upon baseball for a long time to come.

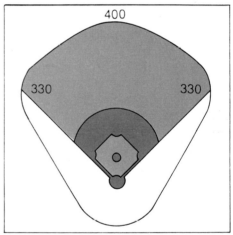

Dodger Stadium
Seating Capacity: 56,000
First Game: April 10, 1962
Clockwise from left: Steve Garvey, Mike Marshall, Bill Buckner, Burt Hooton

Spring is always a time of new life. But for the city of Milwaukee, the spring of 1970 promised far more than the melting snow and fresh flowers could indicate, for it was then that major-league baseball returned to this town the Indians had christened "beautiful land."

Adopting the name "Brewers" from the city's old Triple A League team, the new club was created as the Seattle Pilots were transplanted to Wisconsin. The move created immediate and mixed reactions among the fans and baseball people in Wisconsin. Some thought of how great it would be to have baseball back in town after a four-year absence. Others raised serious questions about how baseball could expect to succeed in a city that could not support a great team like the old Braves.

For the first three years of the franchise, it looked as if the nay-sayers had been right. "Disappointing" was about the mildest adjective one could use to describe the situation. After drawing only 600,000 people in 1972, the Brewer organization decided that something had to happen and soon.

42

The outlook became more optimistic over the winter months when names like Darrell Porter, Pedro Garcia, Don Money, and Jim Colborn were mentioned. Fortunately, those names became very familiar in 1973, helping the Brewers put together a year that not even the most hopeful fans expected.

The turning point came in the spring of that year. Winning ten games in a row in early June, the Brewers vaulted into first place in the American League East. People began to take notice as attendance reached the million mark for the first time. In many cities this might not seem too monumental. But in Milwaukee, with one of the smallest metropolitan populations in the major leagues (just over a million and a half), it was a real milestone. The tide was beginning to turn.

In 1975, home run king Henry Aaron was undoubtedly responsible for a good percentage of the team's success at the gate, but team and individual performances were also a factor. George Scott had his best major-league season ever. Scott broke his own home run record, tying Oakland's Reggie Jackson at 36 for the A.L. lead; for a while his 109 RBIs also led the league. Young Robin Yount also led the league in hitting during the early weeks and dazzled opponents with his defense. Other early season performances by such players as Pete Broberg, Sixto Lezcano, and Gorman Thomas gave fans the feeling that 1975 just might be the year of the Brewers. Unfortunately, because of a disastrous chain of injuries, it was not to be.

Yet, in spite of this turn of events, the fans continued to come out to the park. So much so, in fact, that when the attendance figures were totaled for the 1975 season, Milwaukee placed a solid third in the American League. The Brewers have come a long way since the uncertainty of 1970. There can be no doubt that now, with an All-Star Game under their belts, Henry Aaron planning to finish his career in Milwaukee, and a solid young team, the Brewers have firmly established themselves in the hearts of Milwaukee's fans.

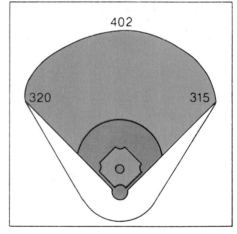

Milwaukee County Stadium
Seating Capacity: 52,198
First Game: April 14, 1953
Clockwise from right: Hank Aaron, Robin Yount, Pete Broberg, George Scott

On October 26, 1960, Calvin Griffith, president of the then Washington Senators, decided to transfer his American League franchise to the fertile territory of the upper Midwest. Rechristening his team the Minnesota Twins —after the Twin Cities of Minneapolis-St. Paul—Griffith set out to surpass the attendance figures run up by the club when it played in the nation's Capital.

In the five seasons Mr. Griffith had operated the club in Washington, his teams drew a total of 2,722,790 fans. The Minnesota Twins drew almost half that number in their very first season. The next year they doubled their attendance and with momentum still building, went on to lead the American League in total attendance for their first decade of operations (1961–70) in Minnesota's Metropolitan Stadium.

That the club has been successful on the field as well as at the gate is demonstrated by the fact that the Twins have represented the American League in one World Series and have taken part in two league championship series over their first fifteen seasons in the great North Country.

Harmon Killebrew is probably the greatest "name" to grace the Twins' roster over those seasons as he took his place among the great home run sluggers of all time. Tony Oliva, however, electrified the baseball world by becoming the first American Leaguer ever to win the batting championship in his rookie season (1964)—and then he repeated the feat the following year! A few years later Tony won another batting championship, but that was after another player had come along to win the first of his five batting crowns in 1969.

That Twin, of course, was Rod Carew, All-Star second baseman in each of his first nine seasons in the league and undoubtedly one of the greatest hitters in the game today. In 1975 Carew won his fourth straight title and in so doing added his name to the company of Ty Cobb, Honus Wagner, and Rogers Hornsby—the only other players ever to win as many as four straight big-league batting championships.

The 1965 season was no doubt the pinnacle for the Twins in Minnesota. After a grueling first half, they pulled away from the pack to win the pennant by seven games.

In the World Series that followed, manager Sam Mele's charges jumped off to a quick two-game lead over the National League's Los Angeles Dodgers in games played in Minnesota. When the two teams shifted to California and Dodger Stadium, however, the tenor of the Series shifted with them. The Dodgers swept all three games played in the West and came back to Minnesota owning a one-game edge, which made it a sudden-death affair for the Twins.

Behind the strong pitching of Mudcat Grant, the Twins bounced back to win game No. 6, 5–1, before Sandy Koufax came on to pitch one of the finest games of his career, nailing down the Series for the Dodgers in a classic 2–0 duel with Jim Kaat.

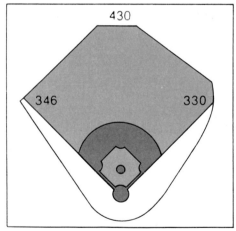

Metropolitan Stadium
Seating Capacity: 45,919
First Game: April 21, 1961
Clockwise from left: Rod Carew, Tony Oliva, Larry Hisle, Bert Blyleven

expos

The Montreal Expos, born out of the 1968 expansion and named after the famous World Exposition hosted by that city in the previous year, quickly succeeded in capturing the fancy of the Gallic-Anglo osmosis that is Montreal.

A culture-rich city so different from any other major-league town, Montreal has added its own touches to traditional baseball with expressions like *un coup sûr* (a base hit), *un circuit* (a home run), and *un championnat* (a championship).

"This is just a helluva city and the fans are just magnificent," veteran broadcaster Bob Prince said during one of his visits to Jarry Park. "The Expos are a lucky team to be playing here."

1B-OF

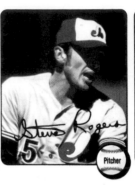
Pitcher

Pitcher

Catcher

Jarry Park, with its 28,000 seating capacity, offers the fans a distinctive ambience. It's something the Expos hope to preserve when they make their expected move to a larger park—the new, multipurpose stadium constructed by the City of Montreal for the 1976 Summer Olympics.

The nucleus of players who will wear Expo uniforms in the new stadium will come from the organization's farm system. There are Gary Carter, a hustling young catcher-outfielder, and Larry Parrish, also in his early twenties, who is playing third base better than the Expos have ever had it played. Both are strong hitters, and both have the makeup to become superstars.

But that's not all. The Expos have additional young talent in pitchers Steve Rogers, Dennis Blair, Dan Warthen, and Dale Murray; catcher Barry Foote; second baseman Pete Mackanin; and outfielder Pepe Mangual.

The Expos of today are a sharp contrast to the Expos of the first few years. When they were first starting out, the team went with veterans. And the veterans almost pulled off a miracle in 1973—the club's fifth season—with the very real prospect of capturing the National League Eastern Division title. Going into the final day of the season, the Expos still had a mathematical chance to tie. But it was not to be. Still, the team's play that year surpassed the fans' wildest dreams and most fantastic odds (150 to 1 before the season began).

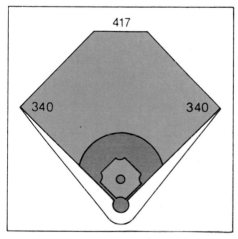

Jarry Park
Seating Capacity: 28,000
First Game: April 14, 1969
Clockwise from top: Pete Mackanin, Barry Foote, Gary Carter, Steve Rogers

47

Nature, it is said, abhors a vacuum. And a vacuum is exactly what the New York Giants and the Brooklyn Dodgers created when they departed the city for points West in 1957. Suddenly there was no team to carry the National League banner in the Big Apple.

Forces were mobilized and various plans set in motion almost immediately. The goal: to bring another National League team to New York City. Three years later, after some very skillful maneuvering that included the preliminary organization of a third major league (the Continental League), the dream became a reality. On October 17, 1960, at a National League meeting in Chicago, New York and Houston were each awarded a franchise.

An effort to choose a name for the as yet playerless team was organized by the franchise's principal owner, the late Mrs. Charles Shipman Payson. A committee was formed to sort through the 1,500 letters and their 468 suggestions with the goal of narrowing the choice to ten possibilities. The results were: Continentals, Burros (originally spelled Boros after New York's five political divisions), Skyliners, Skyscrapers, Mets, Bees, Rebels, NYB's Avengers, and Jets. The public was asked to express its preference, and, happily, it coincided with Mrs. Payson's. Echoing the old Metropolitan ball

Pitcher

Catcher

Pitcher

2nd Base

club of the 1880s, the team became the New York Mets.

The team itself didn't begin to take shape until October 1961, when, permitted to draft players off the rosters of the other eight National League clubs, the Mets bought twenty-two players at a cost of 1.8 million dollars. New York had its wish at last—a bona fide National League club.

Under the colorful managerial reign of the late Casey Stengel, the Mets hardly rose in the baseball standings, but their position in the hearts of the fans was something to behold. The team was a cellar dweller for its first few years, but the fans flocked to its games in droves, beginning to establish what became known as the Met Mystique.

It took until 1969 for the magic to begin, and Met fans and faithful watched spellbound as their team first beat the Cardinals for the Eastern Division title and then the Atlanta Braves in the League Championship Series for the pennant itself. Then, aided by the likes of pitchers Tom Seaver, Tug McGraw, and Jerry Koosman and other talented players including Cleon Jones, Tommie Agee, Donn Clendenon, and Bud Harrelson, Manager Gil Hodges guided his team to the World Championship by beating Baltimore 4–1 in the Series.

Several years of rebuilding followed, and it was a more mature and experienced Met team that again rose to glory under former Manager Yogi Berra in 1973. The team won their second pennant but lost the World Series to the Oakland A's in a suspenseful seven game series.

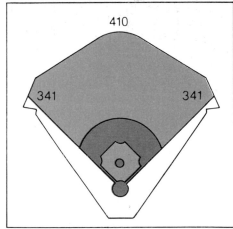

Shea Stadium
Seating Capacity: 55,300
First Game: April 17, 1964
Clockwise from right: Dave Kingman, Del Unser, Ed Kranepool, Jerry Koosman

The New York Yankees are an "expansion" team of sorts. The franchise was originally located in Baltimore at the birth of the American League in 1901. In 1903, however, it was moved to New York where it became known as the Highlanders because it played in Hilltop Park in Washington Heights. That nickname proved to be too long to fit the headlines, and newspaper caption writers objected. So Mark Roth, then a writer with the *New York Globe* and later secretary of the club, gave the team its present nickname of Yankees in 1913. By this time the club was sharing the Polo Grounds with the Giants.

Although New York almost won the pennant in 1905, the franchise waited eighteen years to win its first flag. After that it was news only when the Yankees failed to win. No other team in the history of professional sports has enjoyed a more outstanding record of success than the one established by the New York Yankees during their glory years from 1921 to 1964. During those forty-odd years the team won twenty-nine American League pennants and twenty World Championships.

Coinciding with the incredible string of triumphs and the move to Yankee Stadium in 1923 was the stardom enjoyed by four athletes who are among the most renowned sportsmen in the history of America: Babe Ruth, Lou Gehrig, Joe DiMaggio, and Mickey Mantle. They gave sports fans everywhere some of the most glorious moments and feats in the history of the game.

And, of course, their "supporting cast" included some of the most gifted baseball players the century has known—men like Yogi Berra, Whitey Ford, Lefty Gomez, Red Ruffing, Bill Dickey, Waite Hoyt, Herb Pennock, and Earle Combs—Hall of Famers all. The championship clubs were guided by managers Miller Huggins, Joe McCarthy, Bucky Harris, Casey Stengel, Ralph Houk, and Yogi Berra.

Among the more notable records set by Yankees are Babe Ruth's 60 home runs, Roger Maris' 61 home runs, Joe DiMaggio's 56-game hitting streak, Lou Gehrig's 2,130 consecutive games, Whitey Ford's 32 consecutive scoreless World Series innings, Mickey Mantle's 18 Series home runs, and a record that may never be broken—a perfect game in the 1956 World Series by Don Larsen.

The Yankees' success reached its peak when, under the managerial reins of the late Casey Stengel, the team won five consecutive World Championships between 1949 and 1953—a feat unparalleled in baseball history.

Although the Yankees went more than a decade waiting for their thirtieth pennant, the association with success never seemed to blemish. In the minds of sports fans, the New York Yankees represented excellence. And now, with the complete remodernization of Yankee Stadium, Yankee fans have yet another reason to feel pride in New York and the team that rightfully earned the title "Bronx Bombers."

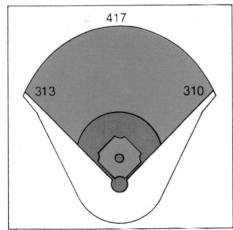

Yankee Stadium
Seating Capacity 54,028
First Game: April 18, 1923
Clockwise from left: Catfish Hunter,
Thurman Munson, Sparky Lyle, Graig
Nettles

The nickname "Athletics" has been synonymous with major-league baseball since the formation of the Philadelphia Athletics as a charter member of the American League in 1901. In fifty years (1901–50) under the leadership of legendary Manager Connie Mack, the Athletics went on to win nine American League titles and five World Championships. Only one team in the American League, the New York Yankees, ever won more pennants.

The modern-day history of the Athletics was launched in 1961 when Charles O. Finley purchased the then Kansas City Athletics, a tenth-place ball club. Finley shortened the name of the team to the A's, organized one of the top talent-producing farm systems in baseball, and seven years later, in 1968, moved the team to Oakland, California.

It was in Oakland that Finley, one of the most innovative men in the history of the sport, added so much of the sparkle that is present in baseball today. His teams were the first to wear white shoes and multicolor uniforms (green, gold, and white). It was at his urging that the American League eventually adopted the "designated hitter" rule and night baseball games for the World Series.

Outfield

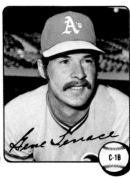
C-1B

Pitcher

OF-1B

And while all of this was taking place, Finley was building one of the most powerful teams in baseball—a team that went on to capture five consecutive division titles (1971–75) and three straight World Championships (1972–73–74). Along the road to baseball's pinnacle of success, the "Swingin' A's" produced some of the most exciting and memorable events in baseball history.

In 1968 Jim "Catfish" Hunter made baseball history against the Minnesota Twins by pitching the first perfect game in a regular season American League contest in forty-six years. Outfielder Reggie Jackson made a run at Babe Ruth's home run record in 1969 by stroking thirty-seven homers in the first half of the season.

A twenty-one-year-old rookie pitcher named Vida Blue was called up from the minor leagues in the final weeks of the 1970 season and in his fourth start pitched a no-hitter against the Minnesota Twins. The next season Blue swept every honor a hurler could win in baseball when his 24 victories, 301 strikeouts, and 1.82 ERA earned him the American League's Most Valuable Player and Cy Young awards.

In 1972, team accomplishments overshadowed individual deeds as the A's won the American League title and went on to stun the heavily favored Cincinnati Reds in the World Series, their first World Championship since Connie Mack's team of 1930.

Boasting never-before-seen long hair and turn-of-the-century moustaches, unconventional looks and behavior became the trademark of the Oakland players as they repeated as World Champions in 1973 and again in 1974, becoming the first team since 1953 to win three consecutive world titles.

Loaded with talent and imagination, the colorful Oakland A's rank as one of the top teams that have ever played the game. It is a team that has fought, shouted, pouted, and played its way into a prominent place in baseball history.

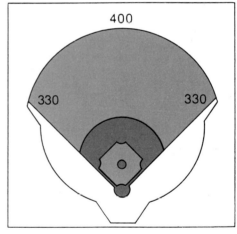

Oakland-Alameda County Coliseum
Seating Capacity: 50,000
First Game: April 17, 1968
Clockwise from right: Vida Blue, Claudell
Washington, Sal Bando, Paul Lindblad

The Philadelphia Phillies were founded by Alfred J. Reach, the first professional baseball player. Philadelphia was a charter member of the National League in 1876 but was expelled after the first year for failing to complete its playing schedule. Seven years later, in 1883, the League realized its mistake and awarded the Worcester, Massachusetts, franchise to Philadelphia. It was Al Reach who purchased the team and moved it to the Quaker City, adopting "Phillies" as the official team name.

During almost one hundred years of activity, the team has enjoyed two seasons of glorious achievement—1915 and 1950.

It was Grover Cleveland Alexander, one of the greatest pitchers of all time, who led the Phils to the pennant in 1915. Alexander won 31 games that season, the first of three consecutive 30-win seasons. His 373 victories is a record for National League pitchers, matched only by Christy Mathewson's total.

Finishing second two years in a row after the 1915 flag, the Phils wallowed near the bottom of the National League until R. R. M. Carpenter, Sr., purchased the club for his son, Bob, in 1943. Seven years later the Phillies celebrated their second league championship as a gang of young players named the "Whiz Kids" rose to glory in capturing the 1950 pennant.

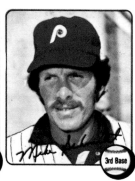

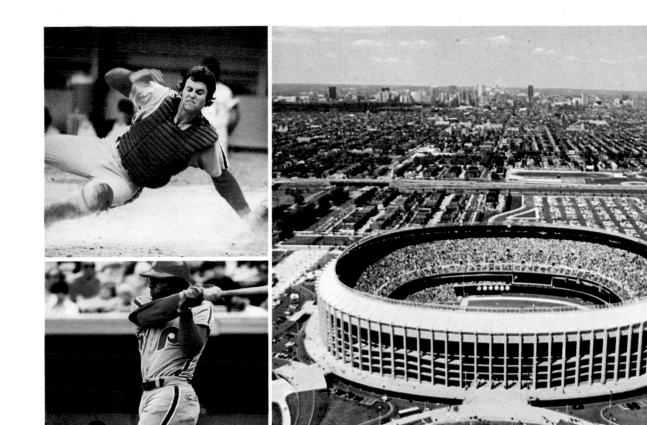

Despite the nucleus of a young club that had promise for the future, the best the Phils could do in the next seven years was a tie for third. John Quinn came on the scene as the general manager in 1959 and hired young, energetic Gene Mauch to manage the club the following season.

Under their guidance the Phillies rose from the bottom of the league again to become a dominant factor from 1963 through 1967. The 1964 club appeared to have won the third N.L. title for the city as they led by $6\frac{1}{2}$ games with just 12 games left to play. However, a 10-game losing streak struck Dick Allen, Johnny Callison, Tony Taylor, Jim Bunning, Chris Short, and company, and the St. Louis Cardinals passed both the Phils and the Reds the last two days of the season to take the title.

In 1971 a brand-new multipurpose sports stadium was opened in South Philadelphia. Veterans Stadium, with a seating capacity for baseball of 56,371, is the largest in the National League. It also has the distinction of being the site of some of the most imaginative fan entertainments in baseball.

A tightrope walker, a helicopter, a kiteman swooping down from the sky, and a man shot from a cannon—all have delighted Philly fans as they delivered the first ball of a season. Dancing waters, the towering Philadelphia Phil and Phyllis and their home run spectacular, and one of the most elaborate electronic scoreboards in baseball all help to attract and entertain over a million fans a year.

Of course, the team itself is the main attraction. And new young Phils like Greg Luzinski, Mike Schmidt, Dave Cash, Larry Bowa, Bob Boone, and Jay Johnstone—as well as people like Dick Allen, Steve Carlton, Gary Maddox, and Tug McGraw—give Phils fans good reason to hope that a pennant will once again fly over their historic city.

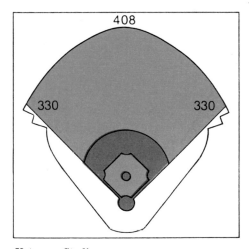

Veterans Stadium
Seating Capacity: 56,371
First Game: April 10, 1971
Clockwise from top: Bob Boone, Dick Allen, Greg Luzinski, Mike Schmidt

PIRATES

The first professional game in Pittsburgh was played on April 15, 1876, in Union Park by the Pittsburgh Alleghenies, of the International Association. Six years later Pittsburgh became a charter member of the original American Association, which then rivaled the National League. The National Agreement of that period permitted any club to resign from its league during the month of November and apply for membership in the rival circuit with no loss of rights. Following an internal association feud, this is precisely what the Alleghenies did. Pittsburgh became a National League city on April 30, 1887, with a 6–2 win over Chicago at Recreation Park.

The Alleghenies became known as the "Pirates" shortly thereafter for allegedly "pirating" second baseman Louis Bierbauer from the Philadelphia club after the disbanding of the Players' (Brotherhood) League in 1890.

The following year the Pirates took over Exposition Park on the north side of the Allegheny River where they remained until Forbes Field opened on June 30, 1909. The colorful history of Forbes Field spanned eight decades. It came to an end on June 28, 1970, when the Pirates opened Three Rivers Stadium on July 16 of that year.

The Pirates have dominated the National League East since the inception of divisional play in 1969, with six divisional titles in the first seven years.

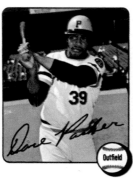  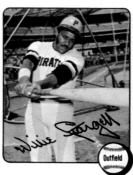 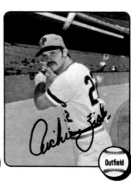

A World Championship in 1971 was, of course, the most recent ultimate success for Pirate supporters, but over the years the team has developed a proud tradition. It has contributed such Hall of Famers as Honus Wagner, Fred Clarke, Pie Traynor, Paul and Lloyd Waner, Max Carey, Bill McKechnie, Branch Rickey, Kiki Cuyler, Roberto Clemente, and Ralph Kiner. These Pirate greats played special roles in six Pirate pennants—1903, 1909, 1925, 1927, 1960, and 1971—as well as four World Series wins—1909, 1925, 1960, and 1971.

Among the many memories cherished by Pirate fans are:

• The first home run over the Forbes Field right field roof by Babe Ruth in 1935 (the 714th and last of Babe's career)
• Willie Stargell's eight subsequent drives over that same roof as well as his four upper-deckers at Three Rivers Stadium
• Roberto Clemente's 500-foot homer in Wrigley Field and his 3,000th hit
• Bill Mazeroski's dramatic ninth-inning homer in the seventh game of the 1960 Series
• Kiki Cuyler's double off Walter Johnson to defeat the Senators in the '25 Series
• The first World Series game ever played (Pirates vs. Red Sox in 1903)
• Dale Long's homers in eight consecutive games; Roy Face's twenty-two consecutive game winning streak; no-hitters by Maddox, Chambers, Haddix, Moose, Ellis, . . .

Umpire Jocko Conlan chasing Frankie Frisch and his umbrella in the rain, Bob Prince's Green Weenie and Babushka Brigade, and Danny Murtaugh's Rocking Chair . . . these are just a few of the thrills and events in the first hundred years of professional baseball in Pittsburgh.

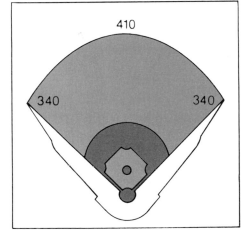

Three Rivers Stadium
Seating Capacity: 50,235
First Game: July 16, 1970
Clockwise from left: Dave Giusti, Richie Hebner, Al Oliver, Rennie Stennett

CARDINALS

When Frank DeHaas Robison bought the old St. Louis Browns back in 1898, he changed the color of the team's uniform from brown to white trimmed with vivid red. A woman spectator, seeing the uniform for the first time, exclaimed: "Oh, what a lovely shade of cardinal." A St. Louis sportswriter named Willie McHale overheard the remark and suggested the nickname "Cardinals" in his story the next day. "What can I lose?" owner Robison figured. The team has been the Cardinals ever since.

The Cards are a team with a past as colorful as their uniforms. This is evidenced by their other nicknames—"The Gas House Gang," "The St. Louis Swifties," and "El Birdos"—which sum up three eras of exciting Cardinal history.

In 1920 the team moved from Robison Field to Sportsman's Park where second baseman Rogers Hornsby won the triple crown in 1922 and 1925 and batted a record .424 in 1924. Hornsby was named manager of the club in May of '25, and he proved as good a manager as he was a hitter. The Rajah piloted the club to its first pennant in 1926 and then turned the town upside down with a World Championship over the Yankees four games to three in the Series.

Shortstop

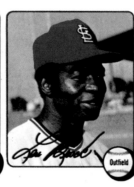

Outfield

Catcher

Pitcher

The 1930s in St. Louis was the decade of the "Gas House Gang," a team that captured the National League pennant on the final day of the 1934 season and went on to defeat the Tigers in a rousing World Series. Such players as Dizzy Dean, Pepper Martin, Joe Medwick, Leo Durocher, and Frankie Frisch not only starred for the "Gang" but also left their marks on the history of baseball.

Cardinal stars also made their presence felt in the 1940s, as the "St. Louis Swifties" won pennants in 1942–43–44 and '46, capturing the World Series in three of the four years. Enos Slaughter, Red Schoendienst, Terry Moore, Harry Walker, and Marty Marion all wore the Cardinal colors with distinction in the years of the early forties, but that era is perhaps best known as the beginning of the career of one of the greatest Cardinals of all time—Stan "The Man" Musial.

Musial made his first appearance in a Cardinal uniform in September 1941 and batted .426 in twelve games. Twenty-two years later, Musial duplicated his September 1941 feat with two hits in his final game against the Reds in 1963.

A year later glory again came to the Cardinals when they roared down the stretch to capture the 1964 pennant on the last day of the season and then went on to defeat the Yankees in the World Series. Two young players quickly established themselves as important parts of the '64 champions and Cardinal leaders in the 1960s: Lou Brock and Bob Gibson, the all-time National League leaders in stolen bases and strikeouts, respectively. These two players typified the spirit of "El Birdos," the colorful teams that drew 2 million people to new Busch Memorial Stadium in each of the pennant-winning years in 1967 and 1968.

The Cardinals look back with pride upon their first hundred years and the colorful teams and players that have been a part of the Cardinal tradition. And the team looks forward to carrying on that tradition for the next hundred years of baseball.

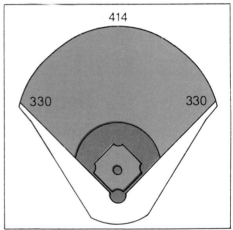

Busch Memorial Stadium
Seating Capacity: 50,126
First Game: May 12, 1966
Clockwise from right: Lou Brock, Bake McBride, Lynn McGlothen, Reggie Smith

SAN DIEGO PADRES

The city of San Diego has the twin distinction of being both the site of the oldest permanent European settlement in California and the home of one of the newest teams in the major leagues—the San Diego Padres. The Padres entered the National League in 1969, but can trace their existence back to the 1930s when, under the same name, they played in the Pacific Coast League. Their name derives from the Franciscan padres who pioneered the area well over four hundred years ago, and it's safe to say that the modern Padres look forward to the day they can share not only the good fathers' name but their hardiness and success as well.

That day has been a long time in coming, and the team's progress, though steady, has been beset with ups and downs. The infant Padres started out their existence rather slowly as the club's first six seasons saw them mired in the depths of last place in the West.

Yet the Padres were not without their share of heroes and national attention. First baseman Nate Colbert made the biggest splash in those early days, tying Stan Musial's record of five home runs in a doubleheader and setting a major-league doubleheader RBI record of thirteen in a 1972 game against Atlanta.

1st Base

Pitcher

Outfield

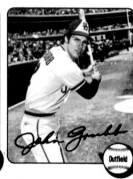

Outfield

The team's low point, however, was still ahead. It came at the end of the 1973 campaign when the club was all but extinct. Financial and attendance problems seemed to dictate a move to Washington, D.C., where the team would continue to carry the National League banner but under a different name.

The script abruptly changed, though, in early 1974, and like the miraculous rescues of fairy tale fame, the franchise was saved for the city by Ray Kroc of the worldwide McDonald's Corporation. Suddenly, the Padres had new life, and they immediately set about creating an entirely new image. Success, obviously, was the goal, but it didn't come right away, at least in the standings.

Under new ownership, the Padres surged to their first-ever million attendance figure in 1974, but, unfortunately, were as yet unable to shake the mantle of cellar dweller in the National League's tough Western Division.

That, however, was half expected. Kroc's own three-year plan for the franchise did not list an immediate escape. Instead, the plan called for a "get-acquainted" first season, a move up in the standings the second year, and then a strong finish in the division after that.

Based on the way things went in 1974 and 1975, the Padres appear to be right on schedule. The club finished out of the cellar in 1975 and drew more than 1 million fans for the second straight season as the final total closed in on 1.3 million.

The team may still be some distance from its ultimate goal. But as those first Franciscan padres knew, a vineyard requires many years of patient growth before it yields its first drop of wine. The San Diego Padres are growing now and, before too long, hope to taste the sweet wine of success.

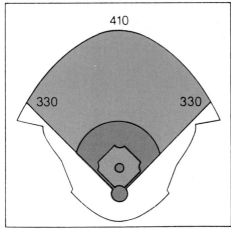

San Diego Stadium
Seating Capacity: 47,634
First Game: April 8, 1969
Clockwise from left: Willie McCovey, Tito Fuentes, Randy Jones, Dave Winfield

Giants

The San Francisco Giants earned their nickname almost a century ago, when they carried the National League banner in New York. The year was 1886, and the name, logically enough, was inspired by the unusual size of a number of players on the team. The name first appeared in a St. Louis paper that year after an exhibition game the team had played in Newark. Joe Pritchard, a St. Louis baseball writer, referred to them as the Gotham Giants, and the name, unlike the city, has been associated with the team ever since.

A new era began for the Giants almost one year to the day after the club's board of directors voted to transfer the franchise from New York to San Francisco. On April 15, 1958, the Giants played their first game in their new home before a capacity crowd in Seals Stadium. Ruben Gomez pitched the Giants to an 8–0 triumph over the Dodgers in the first major-league game ever played on the West Coast.

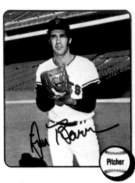

From the very beginning the Giants seemed to thrive in San Francisco. Ignited by a bunch of brash, swaggering youngsters, the team that only two years before had finished sixth in the standings suddenly leapfrogged up the ladder to third place. Led by the spectacular Willie Mays, the team piled up more runs than even the champion Milwaukee Braves and ranked third in N.L. home runs. Only the lack of consistent pitching kept them from winning the pennant.

Unsettled years of victory and defeat followed, though, and it was not until 1962 that the Giants got another crack at the prize. Mays' home run on the last day of the season whipped Houston 2–1 and put the Giants into the play-off against Los Angeles. In a classic drama the Giants pulled out the third game of the series with a four-run ninth-inning rally at Dodger Stadium. The date was October 3, 1962, exactly eleven years since Bobby Thomson's famous homer won the club's last pennant in New York's Polo Grounds.

The World Series against the New York Yankees that year was almost anticlimactic. The Giants lost the tension-filled seventh game to the Yanks in Candlestick Park only when second baseman Bobby Richardson grabbed a vicious liner off Willie McCovey's bat with the winning run on second base. The 1–0 loss stunned San Francisco fans with a heart-wrenching suddenness that left everyone emotionally drained.

The next several years also created their share of excitement as the team put together a string of five consecutive second-place finishes and won a divisional title in 1971. The rebuilding that began with the departure of Willie Mays in 1972 is still under way. The prospects are good, and San Francisco fans look forward to the day their Giants will once again bring home a National League pennant.

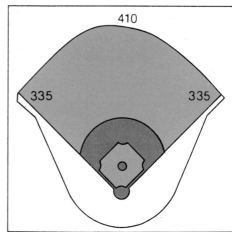

Candlestick Park
Seating Capacity: 58,000
First Game: April 12, 1960
Clockwise from right: Chris Speier, Gary Matthews, John D'Acquisto

TEXAS RangerS

For the early settlers Texas represented many things. It was a land of opportunity, a place to seek one's fortune, and a chance to make a fresh start. Perhaps this is what former owner Robert E. Short had in mind when, in 1972, he moved his Washington Senators to the Lone Star State to become the Texas Rangers.

The team is named after the crack squad of mounted law officers whose famous exploits played a major role in taming this part of the West. Certainly today's Rangers would wish for the same skill in taming opposing ball clubs, but high-caliber success has yet to come for an extended stay.

Located in Arlington, Texas, a north-central town of 100,000 midway between Dallas and Fort Worth, the club has known three managers, two owners, both a winning season and a string of losing ones, both disappointing attendance and two consecutive years over the million mark.

The Rangers made a poor showing their first two seasons. The turning point came in June 1973 when Houstonian David Clyde, just twenty days out of high school, took to the mound against the Minnesota Twins. Clyde, the nation's No. 1 draft choice that year, pitched before the first capacity crowd in Ranger history.

Tension filled the air as Clyde walked the first two batters. But then things came together as, in rapid succession, he fanned Bobby Darwin, George Mitterwald, and Joe Lis. The place exploded with an unforgettable eruption of emotion, as 35,698 people rose to their feet screaming and applauding. When it was over, Clyde had gone five innings, allowed one hit, walked seven, struck out eight, and, with the aid of Bill Gogolewski, won his first major-league game, 4–3.

Jim Bibby added to the momentum later in the season when he pitched the first-ever Rangers no-hitter against the World Champion Oakland A's.

The next season saw Comeback Player of the Year Ferguson Jenkins (25–12) defeat the World Champion A's five straight times. Looking for more hitting strength, the Rangers traded Jenkins to Boston in 1975 for Juan Beniquez. In 1974 Jeff Burroughs hit 25 homers and 118 RBIs to garner the American League's MVP crown at age twenty-three. Mike Hargrove was the league's Rookie of the Year choice after hitting .323, while shortstop Toby Harrah pounded 21 homers and drove in 74 runs. The Rangers, with a record of 84–76, finished second to Oakland in 1974.

There were high hopes for the Rangers in 1975 when the club was sold to a Metroplex group headed by energetic plastic pipe manufacturer Bradford G. Corbett. But despite an attempt to build pitching depth by trading for Gaylord Perry, hopes for a pennant faded early in the season.

Texas is still the land of opportunity. With attendance over the million mark for the second straight season in 1975 and a solid nucleus of young talent, you can bet that when the opportunity comes again, the Rangers will be there to grab it.

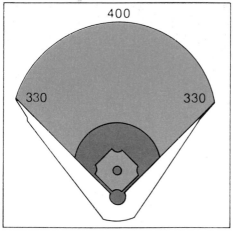

Arlington Stadium
Seating Capacity: 35,698
First Game: April 21, 1972
Clockwise from left: Toby Harrah, Mike Hargrove, Jim Sundberg, Jeff Burroughs

THE DIAMOND

SPARKY ANDERSON: AT THE CONTROLS OF THE BIG RED MACHINE

BY JAMES ENRIGHT

Sparky Anderson is a no-malarkey type guy. His baseball trademark is good players and sound common sense leadership. No con. No frills. No high society. No champagne on a beer budget. He toiled in the minors for ten years. Had his bat been as productive as his good glove, probably half this time would have been spent in the majors. Nevertheless, he made it to the bigs twice before he was named manager of the Cincinnati Reds after the 1969 season. He was a 152-game second baseman for the Philadelphia Phillies in 1959. Then came a season-long coaching stint with the San Diego Padres in 1969.

This was luxury living compared to his farmhand days for the Dodgers. Then he bounced from coast to coast. The bouncing started in the rose capital, Santa Barbara, California. It continued in Yo-Yo manner with stops in Pueblo, Fort Worth, Montreal, Los Angeles (then enrolled in the Pacific Coast League), and finally back to Montreal. After the second stint in Montreal, Sparky was recalled by the Dodgers.

In short order he was on the move again. The Dodgers traded him to the Phillies. His first trade didn't stop the presses in Los Angeles or Philadelphia. Still somebody in the Phillie organization regarded him

highly. They sent the Dodgers three players, pitchers Jim Golden and Gene Snyder and outfielder Rip Repulski, in exchange.

Sparky batted .218 in his only season for the Phillies. With this lowly percentage it was obvious he wouldn't be around for a second season. He wasn't. Now a new Anderson ally surfaced. It was Alvin Dark, a Phillie teammate. Seeking a new landing pad for Sparky, Dark burned up the long distance wires from Florida to the spring training camps in both Arizona and California. Nothing developed. Now it was back to the minors. This time to Toronto in the International League. If Sparky didn't have any thoughts about managing before his introduction to Charlie Dressen (his 1962 manager), he definitely did afterward. "You can manage, kid, and I'm going to help you." Dressen kept his word. He helped him become Toronto's new manager in 1964.

The Maple Leafs finished fifth and proved Sparky still had a lot to learn about managing. What to do? He would start at the bottom and work his way back to the top. His first stop was Rock Hill in the Western Carolina League. In playing a split-season schedule, Rock Hill finished last in the first half. Unhappy but undaunted, Sparky continued to

stick and slug. His reward? Rock Hill won the second half and the pennant play-off.

What followed added up to a See America First junket. Anderson moved from Rock Hill to St. Petersburg, Florida, to Modesto, California, to Asheville, North Carolina. These were happy days. His St. Petersburg team was second-first during the split season in 1966. This finish was repeated in 1967 in Modesto. Asheville won it all in the Southern League in 1968. Now it was on to San Diego to coach for the Padres and Manager Preston Gomez.

This move was designed to put the finishing touches on Anderson's managerial learning in his fifth post-Toronto player year. It did. Nobody knows it better than Buzzie Bavasi, the Padres president. During a discourse on the Amazin' Mets during the 1969 World Series against the Baltimore Orioles, Buzzie was called to the telephone. When he returned, he announced that he would have to find a new coach. Why? "That was Bob Howsam on the phone, and he asked for permission to talk to Sparky Anderson about becoming the new manager of the Reds," Buzzie answered matter-of-factly. Quickly he was besieged with: "Sparky who?" questions.

One year later everybody knew Sparky Anderson. He led the Reds to the first of four Western Division championships in the National League in six seasons. Then, as now, Sparky scoffed at strategy. He believes in the touch-and-luck school with simple signs, and the utmost respect for his players. "Players make managers all the time, and rarely does a manager make a player," the little silver-haired driver of the Big Red Machine claimed.

If the FBI worked with Scotland Yard as a team, it's to be doubted if these super-sleuths could catch or detect one of the Reds' foremost signs. It's a sign catcher Johnny Bench relays to Anderson in the dugout. Decoded, this particular sign means, "Get somebody up and warm in a hurry. This guy [the present pitcher] has lost it."

Anderson's first managing job was in Toronto in 1964.

70

Sparky has such supreme confidence in Bench that he gets the bullpen up on the double. "Whenever I come out of the dugout, it's all over for the pitcher," Anderson said, "but I don't mind saying I follow Bench's judgment."

If time were a factor in Anderson's going for righty hitter versus lefty pitcher situation or vice versa, he could be clocked with an alarm clock just as easily as a stopwatch. "Because I don't fool with percentages," the Reds skipper claimed, "I really don't know all the advantages involved. I feel Joe Morgan can hit a left-hander as well as he hits a right-hander. I don't even think about the percentage when Joe is at the plate.

"I'm getting to think about Ken Griffey in the same way. I think Griffey eventually is going to hit left-handers as well as he hits right-handers. Left-handed hitters really are at a disadvantage against some left-handed pitchers. Especially herky-jerky left-handers like Ramon Hernandez and that [Al] Hrabosky fellow in St. Louis.

"Both are truly unorthodox, and I feel they can give all lefty hitters trouble. Frequently I will switch over against them. By and large I don't think too many natural, normal left-handers are going to bother Morgan or Griffey too much."

With the mention of Morgan, Sparky was asked how he would respond to this situation: The Reds are playing at home. It's a scoreless game going into the bottom half of the third. The lead-off batter singles, bringing the versatile Mr. Morgan to the plate. Would Anderson sacrifice or hit away?

"I'd hit away," Sparky answered, "for two reasons. Morgan is a tough man to double up. Once Joe reaches first, and the lead runner has advanced to third, there's an eighty percent chance he will steal second. Now we have two men in scoring position, and didn't give away an out.

"Also we are moving into our power, and have the makings of a big inning. I won't sacrifice more than once or twice a season with Morgan

The man in red debates a point of baseball law with the man in blue.

71

or Pete Rose, and never with Johnny Bench and Tony Perez. If a close game is on the line and I have fresh men in the bullpen—guys I figure are stronger than the opposing team's relief pitchers—we will sacrifice.

"Especially if we have a hot hand, and somebody like [Rawly] Eastwick is ready. I know he can hold 'em for an extra inning or two.

"I like to compare baseball with boxing when you toss a Billy Conn and a Joe Louis into the same ring. Conn was a jabber, Louis a slugger. That is their style. If one doesn't use his style, he's going to lose. I feel the Reds have to use their style. Maybe failure to sacrifice will cost us a game or two and make some of our fans

angry, but over the 162-game haul we'll beat their brains out if we let our big guys hit. Nobody needs strategy to figure that out."

Anderson favors a five-man pitching rotation, and has the statistics—some of them painful—to prove he's right. "In 1974 we got behind the Dodgers," Sparky started, "after the first two months. During the next three months we shifted to a four-man rotation. We did catch 'em, but when we did, we had nothing left. We were done because our pitchers were dead.

"During the winter we decided we would go with a five-man staff in 1975 unless they forced us out of it. Sure enough we fell five games back.

I told Shep [Coach Larry Shepard] maybe we'll have to trot our four best pitchers out there and let 'em work every fourth day.

"Then we dropped to six and a half back, and I was ready to make the move. He kept urging me to wait just a bit longer. I really feel we would have switched had we gone seven and a half games behind the Dodgers. Larry was right. We started up again. We caught 'em. Then we went ahead, and stayed there.

"I'm still convinced you will have a better and stronger staff working a five-man rotation. Any time a pitcher is working as many as three hundred or more innings a year, you

72

high during the first or second innings, he'd say; 'Don't worry, he will work down and be all right when he adjusts.' Most times he was right. Then he would watch his pitcher like a hawk. If he would start going high in the sixth or seventh innings, he would go get him, saying: 'He's too tired now to adjust and lost his edge. I've gone as far as I can with him.'

"Dressen never permitted his pitcher the opportunity to pitch out of a third jam. He reasoned the pitcher wouldn't have too much left if he pitched in and out of two troublesome situations, and it was too risky to try his luck a third time. I'm with Charlie on that. If my pitcher gets over a couple of rough spots, I'll never know if he did or didn't escape trouble a third time. He's gone."

In the best interests of team unity and spirit, Anderson has his own particular ritual he uses when he moves out of the dugout to change pitchers. "Most times I won't say anything outside of something like 'Today is not the day.' Before the pitcher leaves he is required to put the ball in my right hand. Then I wait for the pitcher coming in from the bullpen," Sparky said. "All the time I make it a point to keep my back to our dugout. That way I won't see how far the pitcher throws his glove after he reaches the dugout, or how many times he kicks the water cooler, a real disaster area in our dugout. As I learned from Walter Alston, I don't have to be concerned about anything I don't see or hear. It has to be different if I do."

Lefty Phillips, longtime Dodger coach, was another of Anderson's benefactors. "Lefty was one of the smartest men in baseball," the Cincy skipper claimed, "and he never operated with any set rules on how to play the game. Being from the old school, Lefty, I'm sure, was convinced there weren't any answers to anything we do in baseball. I never read a baseball book in my life because I feel the things I learned from George Scherger [his first manager], Dressen, and Phillips were more meaningful. They spoke with experience gained by going through the mill.

are headed for trouble. I think Fergie Jenkins was the best pitcher in the game winning twenty or more games for six straight seasons in that park [Chicago's friendly fenced Wrigley Field]. Had Fergie limited himself to two hundred fifty or two hundred sixty innings, I feel he would have been an even greater pitcher."

In his customary frank and free manner Sparky rates Charlie Dressen as the best manager he ever played for, handling pitchers, explaining:

"They always said Charlie's foremost value was stealing signs. He did steal a lot of signs, but frequently he had help. I know, I played for him.

Charlie's way with pitchers really was something special. He always said a manager could wait until the seventh, eighth, and ninth innings to start managing. Frequently that is what he would do. Especially in a close game when he was trying to protect a lead. He always said: 'Now I've got them boxed, watch 'em try to get out of the box.' He could really crisscross pitchers in the late innings because he made it a point to know two things: the moves the opposing manager would try to make to get back in contention, and the players he would use making these moves.

"Charlie practiced another theory which is as sound now as it was then. If his starting pitcher was

Infield strategy, Anderson says, is based on many factors, including the versatility of your personnel.

"When they talk strategy it's a day-to-day thing, based on many factors: the versatility of the personnel at your command, the weather, and the type park you are playing in. All too often I don't think we consider the park where we're playing seriously enough. In Atlanta or Chicago, where all you have to do is hit the ball into the wind and watch it sail out of the park, I feel we can score as many as seven runs a game and win.

"At home in Cincinnati or in Los Angeles, I'll play for three or four runs and try to win with 'em. Our attack will change against certain pitchers. Against guys like Jerry Reuss, Jon Matlack, Tom Seaver, and Andy Messersmith, we'll forget the big inning and start right out hitting and running hard against them. It doesn't always work, but we keep trying."

Voicing his dislike for a drawn-in infield as a defensive weapon, Sparky recalled one of the runaway Reds' road victories, explaining:

"We were losing 4 to 2 in the fourth inning when the opposing team loaded the bases with one out. I had my choice: Pull the infield in, and possibly give 'em two runs, or play the infield at normal depth and maybe give 'em a run while gambling for a double play. We played it normal, and the batter hit sharply to our shortstop. He started a double play, and we were out of the inning.

"Had the infield been in, no way would the shortstop have been able to make the play, and we would have fallen behind two to six. I'll grant a claim that the batter could have topped the ball and beat it out for a run as well as keeping the inning alive.

"It's always been my theory that you are making any batter a fifty percent better hitter the very second you bring the infield in. I'd rather gamble the other way—and go for the double play. Just the other day somebody was recalling Casey Stengel about the time he asked: 'How would you like to have the infield in every time you went to bat?' All I can tell Casey is that I'd love it."

Cincinnati later rallied for a four-run inning to win the game, 6–5, resulting in Anderson observing:

"If we don't get the double play, we could have lost just as easily."

Offensively the free-swinging Reds get a lot of mileage swinging on a 3 and 0 count. "The sign comes from the bench," Sparky said, "but our top six hitters know they are going to get it any time it's 3 and oh. I remember one time when we had Johnny [Bench] taking on that count. Later he asked me why. I told him that he hadn't been hitting too well at the time, and Tony [Perez] had a hot hand—and I figured he was better suited for the situation.

"My guys ask a lot of questions, and that is the way I like it. They know the game, and they like to compare as well as discuss different situations and tactics."

Anderson prides himself upon being a defensive manager because he feels—as Dressen did—that defending a late-inning lead is the manager's most important duty. In winning eleven of twelve games from the Chicago Cubs in 1975, the Reds hit .342 as a team to help lighten the late-inning masterminding. The only Cub Cincy wasn't able to defense properly was third baseman Bill Madlock. In winning the National League batting championship, the

Anderson confers with Rawley Eastwick about the next batter.

"Secretly, I try to manage both teams. . . ."

second-season Cub feasted on Reds' pitching to compile an unbelievable .538 batting average in the year's series between the two clubs.

Stretching from the days of both Connie Mack and John McGraw to the present time, most managers have adopted the age-old theory that you play to win on the road, and play to tie at home to take advantage of the last three outs. With Anderson there is no such division. "We play the same way all the time trying to take full advantage of our power," Sparky claimed. "With me it's a mat-

ter of who the opposing team has in relief compared to my man. Secretly I try to manage both teams, figuring out in my mind who they would like to use in a certain spot. If they pick the man I feel can beat me, he's never going to get that opportunity. It boils down to how you want to eat your poison: your own way in small doses, or permit him to shove it down your throat. If you let him shove it down your throat, you are allowing that man to get what he wants. I'll take it my way—and enjoy a good night's sleep."

Dating back to his days with Dressen in Toronto, Sparky and his coaches have become very astute sign stealers. "We work mainly on the takeoff," Sparky stressed, "because that is the one they are going to mostly. We watch the third-base coach. He's making a lot of signs all the time he's looking into the dugout for the manager. Many times the coach won't spot him immediately, and when he does he will go to one of two signs: the indicator or the takeoff.

"During one four-game series on the road we couldn't pick up the signs in the first two games, but we had 'em for the last two. You just start eliminating them until you get 'em. There aren't two clubs in this league that we don't have their basic signs.

"Once we get 'em, we still don't like to use them too early. Say we call for a pitchout in the second or third inning and catch their man trying to steal. I'd rather wait until the later innings when a stolen sign could help make a big play. Once they realize that you have the signs, they are going to change them immediately. Then the hunt has to start all over, and maybe you won't be as lucky the second time."

What is Sparky's reaction to the emphasis placed on scouting ahead of the two rounds of postseason competition, the championship series in each league before the World Series?

"Mainly the heavy concentration," he answered, "is giving the pitchers an updated book on the hitters. That is fine, but just as important is positioning the defense. Hitters mainly hit to the same zones. As a defensive manager, I always stress defense—hoping to place the right man in the right spot. In Ray Shore, I feel the Reds have one of the very best super-scouts in baseball. Ray is like that story they tell about Paul Brown: When he scouts 'em, he gets everything from shoe sizes to their favorite cereal at breakfast to the numbers on their driver's license. That is really checking out all points."

IT'S A MATTER OF OPINION:

MAJOR LEAGUE MANAGERS DISCUSS STRATEGY.

Baltimore's Earl Weaver is quick off the bench to contest a close call.

Weaver: A Matter of Timing

Fiery Earl Weaver, manager of the Baltimore Orioles, no longer buys the age-old theory that teams play to win on the road and play to tie at home.

"It stands up a bit. but definitely not completely," Weaver opined. "Too many different factors are involved to go all the way with this logic now. What's the inning? What do you have left on your bench?

How early, or how late, do you want to replace a regular?

"I probably play more to tie at home than I do to win on the road. Still it isn't a set rule with me. If I have a .220 batter at the plate who can run some, it's a good guess that I will bunt with him than take a chance with a slower runner who might hit one out. It all depends upon the situation at that particular minute. The manager can't say in advance what he will elect to do."

77

Williams: Asking Personnel Questions

Casey Stengel once said any able hitter would bat at least .400 if the infield was in every time he went to the plate. Dick Williams, manager of the California Angels, agrees with Stengel, and adds: "The hitter probably would be the first in history with two hundred or more runs batted in."

"Bringing in the infield," Williams explained, "strictly is showdown between the situation and personnel—yours as well as the other guy's [opposing manager]. With our offense on the light side, I'll lay back to cut off any run. Even in the first inning. We just can't afford the risk of giving away a single run, and you are apt to do it with the infield in.

"If the two teams are something close to even with the bat, I'll chance it with the infield in. Even then I've got to ask some questions: Who is the batter? Who is the runner or runners? These are the personnel questions a manager has to ask himself before he makes the move in almost every situation. One game it's this situation, and in another it's something else."

Infield tight, hitter's delight.

King: Set 'Em Up

Baseball strategy has been disguised in many different ways. It has been called a game plan, a move to bolster a particular situation, an unexpected maneuver attached to an element of surprise. Clyde King, former manager of the San Francisco Giants and Atlanta Braves, calls strategy "decoying the opposition."

With six hundred players, some one hundred coaches, and twenty-four managers in the major leagues, King admits it's difficult to decoy anybody. He observed two outstanding bits of decoying (nee strategy) first as a manager, and later as a super-scout.

"It was a situation with runners on first and second and nobody out," King recalled, "when I called time. My third batter started to come toward me in the third-base coaching box, when I put up my hand to stop him as I continued toward the plate. When I reached him I said loud enough for the opposing catcher to hear: 'Bear down on this bunt, and make the third baseman field it.'

"In private I said to my man: 'Look for a high fast ball on the first pitch, and hit it hard.' It was obvious the catcher took the bait. He moved his third baseman in before giving the sign to his pitcher. The first pitch was a high fast ball, and our batter hit it out of the park for a three-run homer. Not one fan in the stands realized what happened. They had to think the batter missed the sign. I never did learn the catcher's reaction."

Frequently window dressing is necessary to set the decoy stage as King learned in another game that he scouted.

"The score was tied in the seventh inning, and the home team had runners on second and third with two out. With first base open and the number eight hitter at the plate, I was watching the home manager. He was very busy. After getting his bullpen throwing, he put a left-handed hitter in the on-deck circle and his pitcher ducked out of view. Out comes the other manager to talk to his pitcher. They elect to pitch to the number eight hitter. He hit a two-run single. Quickly the bullpen sits down, the left-handed hitter vacates the on-deck circle, and the pitcher, still in the game, grabs a bat and goes to the plate. If ever I saw the opposition decoyed, it was this time."

Herzog: It Only Takes One

Whitey Herzog, manager of the Kansas City Royals, favors playing an aggressive game hoping to force the other team into a mistake. He claims just one mistake frequently will help produce a win.

"A manager can make all the right moves," Herzog claims, "but just one failure to execute properly can ruin everything. When it works, you call it good strategy. When it fails, there are any number of things you can call it.

Whitey is convinced there aren't any geniuses in baseball.

Marshall: The Suicide Squeeze

When the history of the 1975 Chicago Cubs is written, considerable space will be devoted to the team's use of the suicide squeeze bunt.

Manager Jim Marshall has used the play often trying to get a run without counting on a fly ball. Seeking to compensate for a lack of balanced hitting, Marshall's use of the suicide squeeze was born from necessity. Still the Cubs skipper admits its use is limited due to the difference in playing fields.

"We'll only use the suicide squeeze on natural grass," Marshall explained, "because it's too risky on artificial turf. The safety squeeze, yes, the suicide squeeze, no."

What is Marshall's favorite bit of strategy?

"Give me somebody who can handle the bat, and I'll have him hitting behind the runner at every opportunity. That is the best way I know to advance a runner from first to third—unless somebody hits one out," Jim said.

Alston: **Doing It By the Numbers**

There is no set way to play baseball.

This is the opinion of Walter Alston, the dean of major-league managers who skippers the Los Angeles Dodgers. "When we had pitchers like Sandy Koufax and Don Drysdale to blend with speed and tight defense and only so-so hitting, I would bunt in the first inning shooting for the lead run," Alston recalled, "and frequently that was the only run we'd get.

"Every situation is different, and in most cases it is wise to stay with the percentage. I can't say I always have. At least six times during my career with the Dodgers, I've walked the winning run on base. How many times was I burned? Just once that I can remember, and I like that kind of percentage: five out of six.

"No matter what strategy you use you nevertheless have to have the men on the field who can get the job done. Playing to win on the road and playing to tie at home is pretty much standard, but still doesn't dictate every move."

The Dodgers' Walter Alston is the dean of all big league managers today.

Dark: **Drawing First Blood**

Alvin Dark, a veteran big-league manager, says strategy starts and stops with the handling of the pitching staff because he regards pitching as the name of the game.

"Get one sore arm," Dark explained, "and you are in trouble. Get two sore arms, and you're dead. With solid starters you can frequently win with one run. With dependable people in the bullpen, two runs will get the job done in most cases.

"They can talk about all the other phases, hitting and running, stealing bases, and bunting here and bunting there, but they don't mean a thing without pitching.

"Another thing is to get that first run as quickly as possible.

"Oakland played nine postseason games in 1974, four in the championship series, and five in the World Series. In every case the team which scored first won the game. Pitching and getting that first run on the board is strategy in my book."

Tanner: **My Favorite Play**

Whenever he has runners on first and second with one out and a good contact batter at the plate, the chances are good that the Oakland A's Manager Chuck Tanner will elect to hit and run. "When conditions are right," Tanner says, "the hit and run is my favorite play.

"It's equally tough for the rival team to defense. The third baseman has to cover third, and the shortstop or second baseman, depending whether it's a righty or lefty hitter at the plate, has to cover second. That leaves most of the left side of the infield."

"Once you get the first run home, and the runner on first advances to third, there are many ways you can score the second run. Maybe a steal, maybe a safety squeeze, maybe a sacrifice fly. Also a wild pitch, a balk, or a passed ball will get the job done.

Mauch: **Another Day, Another Play**

Strategy changes from game to game depending upon the rival team's pitcher.

So says Gene Mauch, manager of the Minnesota Twins and a former National League manager. "Strategy is most important to me," Mauch began, "because it's always different every day. I play differently against Tom Seaver than I do some other pitchers. Take the case of Randy Jones. When he's pitching, you better be running or you will be in deep double-play trouble.

"Jones is fast and keeps the ball low. It's not unusual for him to have fifteen to seventeen ground outs a game. If you're not running, he's going to double up on you."

Mauch regards strategy as a manager's knowledge of his individual players, and their reaction to a particular pitcher. "While a lot of teams are running and scratching for a run," Mauch stressed, "big bat teams like the Cincinnati Reds and the Pittsburgh Pirates don't have to worry about this philosophy. They have the power to punch it out, whether they are fighting to come from behind or padding a lead."

IT'S THE SAME GAME

BY JOE GARAGIOLA

A 1-0 thriller between Cincinnati and Oakland during the '72 World Series.

AT BAT	AVG	BALL	STRIKE	OUT	7:45
RUDI	305	1	1	2	

		1 2 3	4 5 6	7 8 9	R	H	E
Ⓐ	CINCINNATI	000	000	!0	1	4	2
	OAKLAND.	000	000	0	.0	3	2

375

One of the things in which baseball takes its greatest pride is the fact that the game changes so little. A favorite phrase that baseball people use to illustrate that thought is: "If a man were shipwrecked and stranded on a desert island for fifty years, then rescued, he would have trouble understanding a lot of things in this world, but he could go to the ball park and understand everything he saw."

I think that the statement is true, as far as it goes. If you hadn't seen a ball game in fifty years, you would still be able to sit back and understand almost everything that happened in the game. You might have to have the "designated hitter" rule explained, but otherwise the game has stayed pretty much the same.

However, that doesn't mean that the fifty-year absentee wouldn't get confused by some of the things he saw. The game itself may be the same, but many things surrounding it are quite different.

Let's start with the ball parks themselves. As that fan of fifty years ago looks around the ball park, he's

going to find a lot of things that are brand-new to him. For one thing, there's the scoreboard. Years ago, the scoreboard was simple. Whether it was the count on the batter, the score of the game, or the player at bat, scoreboards were relatively uncomplicated. The scoreboard man just hung up the proper numbers, tried to do it as quickly as possible, and, in some parks, tried to stay out of the way of the guy with the binoculars who was trying to steal the other team's signals.

Today scoreboards have become electronic extravaganzas. In addition to all the things that they used to tell the customers, these scoreboards can tell them which player is having a birthday, put on a cartoon display, play a trivia game with the fans, and even flash the batting average of the man at the plate. Now, I have to be honest. That might be progress, but it's like everything else. It works to the advantage of the guys who can

Today's scoreboards know how to applaud a big play.

hit. A guy walks up there hitting .360, and he's going to take his time, step out of the box, ask for the signs to be flashed again. And why not?

That .360 is up there in lights for everybody to see. Guys who hit like me are forced into being first-ball hitters.

Cincinnati dries off its field with a sponge disguised as a truck.

Of course one of the biggest changes has been in some of the ball parks themselves. Suppose, for example, our shipwrecked hero was in Houston. He looks out the window and the rain is really coming down. His friends call to invite him to the ball game. He's got to figure they're a little crazy, especially when they say, "Who cares if it's raining. It'll be nice and dry in the ball park."

The Astrodome has been the site of several games on rainy days, including one held during a big storm. There was so much flooding in Houston that the players were unable to get away from the park. Television broadcaster Tony Kubek said, "I've always known about rain-outs, but this is the first time I've heard of a rain-*in*."

The big dome, with its temperature maintained at a constant, comfortable 72°, also eliminates that other climatic problem—heat. When the late Fred Hutchinson was managing in Cincinnati, he got annoyed at hearing his players complain about the heat. Take it from me, that Cincinnati park could get hot, but Hutch got fed up with hearing about it. One day, he called a meeting and told his players that the next guy he heard complaining about the heat was going to be fined.

Later, after about six innings under a real hot sun, Cincinnati pitcher Art Fowler came back to the bench, sprawled out, closed his eyes, and moaned, "Boy, I mean it's really *hot* in this ball park today."

As he opened his eyes, he found himself staring right into the eyes of the manager. Without missing a beat or cracking a smile, Fowler added, "Just the way I like it."

I'd also like to see how our hero would react to going to the Kansas City park, where they have a display of dancing waters. Time was when the only water display at a ball park came when the groundkeeper hosed down the infield grass. Of course, that was in the days when the game was played on grass that needed watering. With artificial turf, you just vacuum and dry-clean.

Can you imagine a dry cleaner

getting a call from a ball club saying, "Would you have your delivery boy stop around tomorrow and pick up some dry cleaning. I've got twenty-nine uniforms, left field, and some foul territory. And could you have it all back by Tuesday?"

Maybe the guy who had been away for fifty years might miss hearing about "bad hops," which went away when artificial turf came in. Most players appreciate that the bounces are truer, but there are still guys who object to the new surfaces. One of those opposed is Dick Allen, who summed up his feelings by saying, "I don't want to play on any grass a horse won't eat."

Grass isn't the only natural element that's going out of style. Our hero probably remembers back to the days when a batter who wanted to get a better grip on the bat would rub his hands with dirt. Today, dirt is becoming obsolete.

In the immortal saga of "Casey at the Bat," we are told that "ten

thousand eyes were on him, as he rubbed his hands in dirt, five thousand tongues applauded, as he wiped them on his shirt." Well, our friend from the desert island might have to wait a long time to see a repeat of that performance. For one thing, dirt has given way to resin and pine tar. Chances are that our hero would remember the resin bag, but he would never have seen a pine tar rag before.

Hitters come up and wipe a rag covered with pine tar all over the handle of the bat, which, incidentally, is usually already pretty well smeared with the stuff. The idea, of course, is to make the bat sticky enough to give the batter a good grip. But some players use so much of it that someday I expect to see a guy get a hit and take off for first only to find that he can't drop the bat.

There is a variation on putting pine tar on your bat. Some guys put it on their batting glove, something

Darrell Thomas knows how to use that pine tar.

else our friend is going to have to learn about. When he was marooned on that island, only the defense wore gloves, the purpose of which was to help catch the ball. Today, batters wear gloves (sometimes on both hands), base runners wear gloves, and fielders wear gloves *under* their regular gloves.

Gloves are only a part of the changes in the items worn by the players. Over the past fifty years the uniform itself has changed radically. It used to be that a ballplayer could smuggle bowling balls in his uniform and nobody would notice. Today, players wear trim double-knit uniforms and seem to compete to see who can wear his the tightest. Uniform shirts, which once had nothing on the back, now carry not only a player's number but in many cases his name as well. For some guys that presents no problem. But I remember Billy Grabarkewitz saying, "I have to pick up both arms, or the people can't see the "G" or the "Z."

Also, fifty years ago the colors of uniforms were very simple. The home team wore white, and the visitors wore gray. Today, clubs wear colors like "robin's egg blue" and "Fort Knox gold." They wear different-colored stockings on different days, and white shoes with various colored stripes on them. It probably won't be too long before we see players wearing sweat shirts with French cuffs.

I guess there would have to be an explanation about batting helmets too, but I don't imagine that would be too tough to understand. Helmets can be summed up best by pointing out that today a batter who is hit in the head with a pitch is given first base. In the old days, he was often given the last rites.

The players aren't the only ones who dress differently these days. When our hero was stranded, it was usual to call umpires "the men in blue." Today a lot of the "men in blue" wear red jackets and gray pants.

And when these men in blue (and red and gray) are asked to summon a relief pitcher, their mission

The height of baseball fashion: double-knits with a v-neck and no-roll waistband.

doesn't take them to the far corners of the ball park anymore, because the bullpens—or at least their locations—have changed. The bullpen guys used to be sort of hidden from the crowd, which permitted some fringe benefits, like hot dogs in the fifth inning, for example. (I once attended a meeting on the mound where the new pitcher swore to the manager that he hadn't been eating in the bullpen. I was standing behind the manager trying to get the pitcher's attention. I wanted him to wipe the mustard off his chin. It was hurting his argument.)

Life in the bullpen was peaceful. When it looked like there was a problem developing, a coach or manager would stand up in front of the dugout and make a sign that would tell the bullpen who should get ready.

If the signal was a hand raised high, that meant to warm up the tall pitcher. Or maybe it would be two hands joined way out in front of the waist, signaling for the pitcher who was fat. Every time I was traded, I'd get a kick out of learning the different signs that were used to deliver messages to the bullpen. Shortly after I joined the Cubs, I saw a coach stand in front of the dugout and make a sign I'd never seen before. He was holding his sides and going through the motions of laughing. I asked the bullpen coach what that meant. He said, "They want you to get ready to catch."

Modern technology has all but done away with the semaphore system of contacting the bullpen. Today's bullpen guys get the word by telephone. The coach or manager dials the number on a dugout phone, and the bullpen answers. That can sometimes present problems. Moe Drabowsky used to amuse himself by picking up the phone in his bullpen, dialing the other bullpen, disguising his voice, and ordering certain pitchers to start warming up.

It's too bad that modern technology doesn't allow the fans to eavesdrop on some of the conversations in the bullpen. It's true that they might sometimes hear a discussion on the hitters in the league, and the best

The black phone is connected to the bullpen. The second one is used if the other is busy.

way to get them out. But more often they'd hear about things completely unrelated to baseball strategy. For example, the bullpen guys might be picking different kinds of all-star teams. Maybe an All-Ugly team, made up of the players considered to be the most homely at their positions. Or an all-star team made up of guys whose last names all began with the same letter. Or guys whose nicknames grouped them into a category, like birds, for example: Birdie Tebbetts, Goose Goslin, Ducky Medwick, etc.

Another new development in bullpen life is the agriculture section. A good example can be found in the Mets' bullpen at Shea Stadium, where coach Joe Pignatano supervises the growing of tomatoes. Who knows, maybe we'll see the day where a club keeps a pitcher on the

roster because his scouting report is: "He doesn't have much of a curve ball, but he does have a green thumb."

Maybe the area where baseball life has changed the most is in the clubhouse. This is the place the public doesn't get to see, which means they miss out on some of the biggest characters in the game—clubhouse men and trainers. Today, youngsters are kind of pampered, perhaps because they represent such big investments to a ball club. In my day, the clubhouse man would treat green kids a little differently.

The first time I ever walked into the St. Louis Cardinals' clubhouse, I said to clubhouse man Butch Yatkeman, "Where's my locker?" He just looked at me for a minute, reached into his pocket, took out a nail, drove it into the wall, then said to me,

"There it is."

It wasn't only the green kids who could be taken down a peg by the clubhouse guys. Yogi Berra was already a star when he sat talking with Charlie Keller in the clubhouse in Yankee Stadium one day. They were talking about the passage of time, and Berra wondered if Keller remembered the first time he'd ever seen him. "I sure do, Yog," Keller said. "You came right through that clubhouse door, and you were wearing a sailor's uniform." Yogi nodded and said, "I'll bet you didn't think I was a ballplayer, did you?" At that point clubhouse man Pete Sheehy spoke up. "I didn't even think you were a sailor," he said.

The role of the trainer has probably changed even more than that of the clubhouse man. Today's trainers work with whirlpool treatments, ultrasonic machines, and the latest in modern medical aids. The Chicago Cubs in the thirties and forties had a trainer named Andy Lotshaw who used to rub down the arms of the pitchers with Coca-Cola.

Lotshaw was a character in a lot of ways. When Pat Malone was one of the Cubs' star pitchers, Andy once told him that he was sick of hearing him talk about how he got this or that hitter out. The conversation finally reached the point where Lotshaw said that even he could get a hit off Malone. So, on the strength of a five-dollar bet, both men went out on the field to settle things.

Malone went to the mound, and Lotshaw stepped into the batter's box. Andy hit the first pitch over the left-field fence. With that he dropped the bat and walked back to the clubhouse. For as long as Pat Malone stayed with the Cubs he kept begging Lotshaw to give him one more chance. Andy kept saying no. To the other players Lotshaw would say, "That big Irishman keeps saying he wants to strike me out, but if he gets another chance he'll throw that ball right down my throat."

If the biggest change in baseball is in the clubhouse, then the biggest change in the clubhouse has to center around the matter of the players' hair.

No longer the man in blue, but he's still the final arbiter.

When I was playing, nobody paid much attention to hair, because we wore caps, and if you were bald, so what. Now, though, that's all changed. Guys who have hair see how long they can let it grow. As a result, standard equipment for a player, right along with his glove and bat, is his hair dryer. As a player I used a combination comb-and-hair dryer myself. It was called a towel. Today guys' lockers are so full of

dryers and hair spray and heated combs that there's hardly any room left for their sweat shirts.

Many aspects of clubhouse life, though, have not changed. There are still certain signs that tell a ballplayer that something is happening. When the clubhouse man gives you a uniform with a high number, for example, he's building you up for a good-bye. Other things give you clues, too. Like when your locker suddenly isn't near the front of the dressing room anymore. Or when you find that the clubhouse man burns your T-shirts in the dryer and doesn't bother to apologize. Or when you get told not to use the star's spot (the area of a baseball where the seams are closest together) when autographing baseballs. These things are signs today just as they've always been.

One thing that *has* changed in the clubhouse is the way teams hold meetings. I guess in John McGraw's day a club would have a meeting before each game and would go over each opposing batter very carefully. A lot of clubs have gotten away from that. Things are simpler now. It's like Yogi Berra said one day at a meeting before an All-Star Game. The American League players were talking about how they should pitch to the National League hitters. When they got to Musial, everybody seemed to have a suggestion or an idea. Finally, Yogi summed it all up as only he can. Yog said, "What a waste of time. You guys are trying to figure out in fifteen minutes what the whole National League hasn't been able to figure out in fifteen years."

Most of the time in team meetings is spent reviewing basics, such as signals between the pitcher and catcher. While there are any number of possible combinations, the fast ball is almost always number one and the curve ball number two. Since this is just about universal, the changes usually come in which signal is to count. For example, a catcher may use only one sign with nobody on base, but switch to a three-sign method when there are runners on. In that case, he will tell the pitcher which sign is the real one, the first, second, or third. One day the St. Louis Browns catcher Clint Courtney went out to the mound after a player had doubled. He told his pitcher, "The middle sign is the one that counts." Courtney then returned to the plate and flashed: "two-two-two."

There are still some guys who believe in long, involved team meetings. Others believe that the pitcher should just run down the way he wants his defense set for each hitter. Some keep it even simpler than that. Like Saul Rogovin, who pitched in the big leagues for about ten years. Saul used to say, "Keep it simple. Throw the ball right down the middle for everybody. That way the high ball hitters will swing over it and the low ball hitters will swing under it."

Another big change in clubhouse life concerns music. Years ago the St. Louis clubhouse used to jump to the sound of the Mudcat Band, featuring guys like Pepper Martin, Bill McGee, Lon Warneke, and Frenchy Bordagaray. Fortunately, their baseball was better than their music. They scared a lot of teams in the National League, but Paul Whiteman slept like a baby.

There were always some guys with an interest in music around some clubs. But today walking into a clubhouse can sound like Carnegie Hall in a slump. In one corner a record player is sending out the latest Latin music. In another corner, Johnny Cash is walking the line. Back near the showers, it's the newest release from Three Dog Night. All of this is turned up as loud as possible. But somehow there are four guys sitting around in different spots who don't hear it—they just go right on playing their guitars.

In the St. Louis clubhouse you might add the sound coming from Reggie Smith as he takes a pregame workout with his drumsticks, which he claims helps his rhythm and timing. Maybe things haven't changed

You still need that good wood to hit the ball.

that much after all—I was on a club
with a guy who used to beat out
rhythm with a pair of coat hangers
because he said it helped loosen his
wrists. His name was Stan Musial.

Another new development
among players has been TM, or tran-
scendental meditation. Followers
have showed up on many clubs, with
players like Ted Simmons talking
about the value of the proper mental
approach to playing baseball.

Years ago, the St. Louis Browns

ownership once tried to improve a
bad ball club by bettering their attitude. The Browns hired a hypnotist,
Dr. David Tracy, and the good doctor set about telling the Browns that
they were as good as the other clubs
in the American League. The problem was that he didn't convince the
other clubs of that fact, and they
kept on beating the poor Brownies.
Before long, the Browns were
deeper in last place and Dr. Tracy
was gone.

I often wonder what would have
happened if the Browns had gotten
hot while Dr. Tracy was there. Other
clubs would have tried it, you can be
sure. In baseball everything gets a
chance. In the first game of a doubleheader one day, Minnie Minoso went
hitless in five trips. Between games
he took a shower, with his uniform
still on. Asked about it, Minnie said
he wanted to wash away the evil
spirits. Everybody laughed. But in
the second game Minoso got three

hits. After that game, eight guys took showers with their uniforms on.

The bench jockeys still jockey today, but maybe not as ferociously as they once did. Umpires are still told to punch holes in their masks, so they can see the ball. When a catcher goes out to advise a pitcher, he might still hear (as I once did): "The only thing you know about pitching is that it's tough to hit." But it somehow never gets to the point it did when pitcher Hi Bithorn threw a knock-

down pitch at Leo Durocher. Which may not sound unusual—but Durocher was sitting on the bench at the time.

I guess what baseball says is true. The uniforms, the hairdos, and the scoreboards change, but the game itself doesn't. It's still ninety feet from base to base. Three strikes is still out. And the game *never is over* until the last man is out. (That last one is true technically. In reality I played on some clubs that lost

games during "The Star-Spangled Banner.")

A man shipwrecked on a desert island for fifty years really would have no trouble watching, remembering, and understanding the game between the lines today. Baseball is proud of that. And it should be.

THE BULLPEN

BY GEORGE PLIMPTON

Just about the best thing in baseball is the bullpen. For me it bears this high esteem largely because of its function—to send out people in moments of considerable crisis to try to put things right : . . to repair an inning that has been damaged. No other sport comes to mind which has such a splendid institution: football, basketball, and hockey have "benches" which people come "off of" to perform great herocis, but usually as substitutes coming in for an injured player; or if a game score is lop-sided, a bench is "cleared" and everybody sitting there gets a chance to play. On the other hand, the bullpen in baseball functions not only at moments of great stress in a highly dramatic way, but does so with plenty of time available for a witness to absorb and relish what is going on.

The first indication of the drama to come (the initial flutter of a curtain about to part) is the appearance of the manager at the top of the dugout steps as he peers out at the troubled pitcher from under the long bill of his cap. If he comes onto the field, a whole procedure begins which is so time-honored that each part of the process, however inconsequential it may seem, adds to the significance of the spectacle. Even the contours of the pitching mound seem to assist in the drama of a pitching change. The manager adjusts his stride to stalk *up* to join the pitcher and his catcher; aloft, he bends forward in consultation; his hand reaches for the ball. If the pitcher has done honorably to that point he stands up there with the manager for a while and he may get a congratulatory, if slightly perfunctory pat on the behind before he half-trots down the incline of the mound and strides across the infield grass for the dugout, as the people begin to applaud. If he has given

Dick Williams of the Angels ponders a pitching change.

up a rash of hits, he is studiously ignored by both the catcher and the manager, and he is likely to stare gloomily at the toes of his baseball shoes until the manager asks for the ball; then he leaves abruptly for the dugout. The distance between the pitcher's mound and the dugout varies considerably—too short for the pitcher who has done a good job as he hears the hand-clapping beyond the dugout roof, and yet an eternity for the failed pitcher who hopes he can cover the distance before a voice like a bugle drifts out of the stands and announces that he's a bum and where did he ever learn to pitch.

Sometimes pitchers have refused to give up the ball. Rather than submit to that sad ritual of resignation, they do something else with it. In the 1975 World Series Jim Willoughby of the Boston Red Sox did a few jig-steps and stiff-armed the ball, as if he were making a hook shot in basketball, to the *umpire*—who caught it, somewhat surprised, and automatically turned it in his palm to look for scuff marks. Perhaps the most legendary such confrontation involved Carl Mays of the Red Sox who not only threw the ball into the stands rather than give it up to his manager, Ed Barrow, but also jumped the club and vowed he would never pitch for Boston again. He was suspended, of course, and eventually ended up with the Yankees—and later his tragic confrontation with Ray Chapman who stood paralyzed at the plate one summer day and was killed by a fast ball off Mays' swift swooping subterranean delivery.

Usually, of course, a pitching change is effected with no more recalcitrance than a sour look. After all, as has been pointed out, with someone coming in from the bullpen on order from the manager, it is going to get very crowded out there on the pitcher's mound if someone doesn't leave.

When the bullpen gates open, just about everyone in the ball park peers over to watch the relief pitcher step out of the enclosure. He used to come to the pitcher's mound by foot, his warm-up jacket hung loosely off his pitching shoulder, walking in the slow stride of a man with a lot on his mind. Sometimes he had a word to say as he passed one of his outfielders, and you could see him look back up at the scoreboard to check what the situation was; he had a long way to come, and there was plenty of time for you to sit there and relish the awful responsibility facing this man—the opposition, sitting on thin haunches on the bases watching him come, would soon enough be poised to caper down the base paths. It was one of those moments when it seemed not much was going on—just a man walking from point A to point B—but it was one of the richest moments in the drama of baseball, a part of the timing and the sense of anticipation. It was dismaying to see those who felt the game had to be "speeded up" begin to tamper with it. Nowadays, the pitcher travels from the bullpen in a mechanical conveyance (back in 1970 all the parks were supplied with electric golf-carts shaped like a baseball cap) and some of his dignity—the sense of being the lone warrior sent to patch things up—is obviously diminished by being driven to the mound in this monstrous toy-like gadget, sitting next to the driver with his glove in his lap like a rather embarrassed guest being delivered up to a fancy-dress party.

Almost all the clubs use the carts. An exception is the Atlanta Braves which uses a 1929 Model A Ford equipped with a modern 283 Chevelle engine with an automatic transmission so that the chances of stalling or breaking down during its short ferrying services to the mound are minimal. For a time its driver was the Braves' mascot, Chief Nok-A-Homa, an Ottowa-Chippewa Indian whose true name is Levi Walker. He spent the game in his Indian regalia sitting in a semilotus position in the doorway of an authentic-looking teepee set in the home bullpen behind a wire fence in deep left field, occasionally getting up to give a war whoop or two, and when the signal came for a relief pitcher to be brought in, he hopped in the Model A, which is kept in an alley next to the bullpen, and started out for the mound with his pitcher. A few years back someone from the Braves bullpen crew put a smoke bomb under the Ford's hood—perhaps a pitcher taking umbrage at the mechanical age's encroachment on baseball—and the device went off just as the car approached the infield, enveloping it in such a thick cloud of smoke that Nok-A-Homa lost his bearings and revolved a number of times in a tight circle before he could get himself straightened out. Some pitchers refuse to use the cart. Mike Marshall of the Dodgers trots for the mound. So did Bob Veale when he pitched out of the Red Sox bullpen. Clay Carroll of the White Sox comes out of the bullpen at a slow amble, then he strides off with increasing speed, breaking into a trot, and finally into a run—a habit he has cultivated over the years to get his adrenalin going so that when he reaches the pitcher's mound he feels revved up to full pitch. His former Cincinnati teammates have speculated that a long approach, such as the great distance between the bullpen and the pitcher's mound in Milwaukee, would get Carroll moving at such a clip that unable to stop he would bowl over his manager and catcher standing on the pitcher's mound and finally fetch up in a tumble in the dugout beyond.

Whatever his method of reaching the pitcher's mound, the relief pitcher has only the momentary comfort of the presence of the manager and the catcher as they offer him last words of advice and encouragement before they step off the mound to leave him (in Thomas Wolfe's grand phrase) ". . . alone, calm, desperate, and forsaken in his isolation." He has one small consolation however hard he tries to dismiss such pessimistic thoughts—that out behind him in some distant recess of the ball park someone is getting ready in the bullpen to come in and take over if things get too bad . . .

No one, much less the pitcher out there, knows quite how the bull-pen got its name. One of the accepted theories is that the term is derived from the many Bull Durham tobacco signboards erected out beyond the outfield fences at the turn of the century. In 1909 the tobacco company put up 150 of these signs in baseball parks, the advertisements dominated by a large peaceful-looking domestic bull. Local merchants would pay up to $50 if a batter could hit the bull on the fly. Relief pitchers warmed up under or behind the sign, and many authorities believe the area began to be called the "bull-pen".

Others suspected it is lifted from the prison terminology for the detention area—the "bullpen"—where people waited around until they stood trial . . . an accurate enough mini-description of the life-cycle of a relief pitcher.

Yet another theory suggests that the bullpen was originally where fans were herded behind ropes when games were standing-room only, or where they had to wait until an inning was over before being seated, which, like the theatre, was the practice before the turn of the century.

It is appropriate that the geographical and physical proportions of the bullpens around the major leagues have remained as varied as the notions of their beginnings. Some are set such a distance from home plate that one wonders if the architect had those Bull Durham signs in mind when he designed the ball park. Milwaukee's are 360 feet from home plate. Detroit's are not only a long home run shot away from the infield but they are sunk into the ground so that the players peer out through a wire fence at ground level like a row of prairie dogs . . . an odd sight that once prompted Hubert Humphrey to say that he felt the premises out there were "inhuman." The players would agree. They speak of Detroit's bullpens being sunk into a type of "bog"—invariably damp, and infested with so many mosquitoes in the warm summer nights that an essential piece of equipment along with the ballbag is an aerosol can of bug-spray. Sometimes the players take

rubber bands along with them and compete to see who can knock off the most insects, mosquitoes, and flies, but in the night games they let the moths go, the pale-wing variety that settle on the damp wood of the bullpen bench, their wings moving like the lift of a lung breathing: "too easy."

Pittsburgh's are not popular either—alcoves in the corner of the outfield where only four players at a time, perched up on the top plank of the bench, can see what is happening. Minnesota's are difficult: three sets of wire fencing to look through. Shea Stadium in New York has a clear sheet of plastic set in the outfield fence for the players to watch the game, but it is scraped with grafitti, and spike marks from players tilting back and putting their feet up. Squinting through the maze of marks has been compared to the view someone would get who is troubled with cataracts. San Francisco is blamed for *causing* eye problems—the wind currents picking up the dust from the sliding pits and the pitcher's mound and depositing it in violent eye-smarting gusts in the bullpen areas so that often the players shield their faces with their gloves, peeking out between the leather fingers to keep track of what is going on.

The players' favorite seems to be the bullpen arrangement in Chicago's Wrigley Field—quite close both to the dugouts, which means that the relief corps has an excellent view of the field, and also to the grandstand fence so that the fans are right there and the girls can pass over notes and cakes and open up conversations with the relievers.

Just before the opening game of the 1975 World Series between the Red Sox and the Cincinnati Reds I went out and took a look at the bullpens in Boston's Fenway Park to get a sense of what such premises are like. The bullpens, which are considered to be about average are situated beyond left and left-center field, behind a fence painted pale municipal green and padded to keep the outfielders from damaging themselves against it. The fence is just the right

The name bullpen may have derived from the many Bull Durham tobacco signboards erected out beyond the fences in the early 1900s. Relief pitchers would warm up behind the signs.

height for the relievers on the other side to lean against, their arms crossed at shoulder-height, and to look out on the field of play like passengers at a ship's rail. The two bullpens, which are identical in proportions and facilities and decor (except for a *We're Number One* sticker on the back of the Boston bench) are separated by a wire fence that the management had blocked in and raised a few years back so that the opposing teams would not get to fraternizing over it like housewives. Behind the bullpens are the bleachers, and the crowd leans over the fence and calls down when the players come out, establishing the type of contact, even if it is good-natured acrimony, that the players seem to miss if they do not have at hand. One of the most unpopular visitors' bullpens is the one in Atlanta—which is in a huge park with a severe attendance problem. The only souls out near the visitors' bullpen are a disgruntled and cynical clutch of police who are on the premises to direct crowds which are non-existent. They

are well-known for their active support of the visiting team—apparently in the hope that in the wake of a long losing streak the crowds will dwindle to such a degree that their detail will be terminated and they will be assigned to do something else. What could they prefer? A squad car out on the turnpike? Could there be a better assignment than a summer afternoon spent watching a ball game from a left-field corner aisle? Even if one stood alone among hundreds of seats painted baby-blue, the dominant color in that ball park, swinging a night stick and hunching forward off one's heels from time to time. One might even be able to keep a scorecard.

The Boston bleachers are raucous and lively, permeated with such a spirit of carnival that spectators often opt to sit there and get battered with sensations rather than bask in the more sedate surroundings of the grandstand. The bullpens being directly in front of the bleachers, a great deal of attention is paid its personnel. Former Red Sox

pitcher Roger Moret, a spindly Puerto Rican who looks like an elongated street waif, on one occasion a few years ago, took off his cap in such a manner that it hung from his fingers like a beggar's cup (whether by chance or design no one is quite sure) and almost $15 in coins was immediately flung down at him from the bleachers.

For those ballplayers who shun the public attention of the Boston bleacherites, they can sit up out of sight under the roof of the shed that runs the length of the bullpen bench. But there is a small slot-like space between the back edge of the roof and the bleacher wall through which the fans stick programs they hope the ballplayers will sign, or birthday cards, or tokens of their esteem, or packages of food, or whispered requests for so-and-so to step out from under the shelter to be photographed, so that as the players sit on the bench there is a constant scrabbling around just behind their heads, like jackdaws busy in the thatch of a roof.

Each bullpen at Fenway has two pitching lanes so close to each other that when a right-hander and a left-hander warm up at the same time they take the lane that keeps their hurling arms to the outside to keep from being entangled down the middle. I looked for the resin bag. There was none. Apparently it comes out with the bullpen crew in the ballbag; the back-up catcher will toss it down between the two rubbers for the pitchers' use. There is not much else that comes out to the bullpen in the way of equipment—only the red plastic squares that the catchers kneel on to keep the knees of their uniforms from getting soiled. In Atlanta the bullpen catchers use clubhouse towels that they fold twice and set down in the dirt. Invariably the first activity organized when a crew arrives in the bullpen (usually at the same time the managers are meeting at home plate) is a scouting contest to pick out the prettiest girl in the stands, and also (to utilize that careful research completely) the ugliest . . . an eye-straining practice not only universal with major-league teams, but one which remains in practice throughout the game, taking precedence over whatever else may be going on ("For Chris*sakes*, look over *there.*").

Word games are also a universal pastime in the bullpens. The Yankees play Password. The Red Sox, usually under the direction of their irrepressible pitcher Bill Lee play charades. During the World Series he gave them the name of Jack Billingham of the Reds to guess; in front of the bench he capered about, pantomiming like a gigantic puppet, offering them first the bill of a baseball cap as a clue, the adjectival ending of a familiar cussword as the "ing," and for the "ham" he rushed forward and pointed at his teammate, Reggie Cleveland's thigh—which was the heftiest one he could find along the bench.

There are bullpen games which require physical dexterity. The iron tent pegs that pin down the canvas tarpaulins that shield the pitching lanes are used in a number of ways:

for mumblety-peg, darts (the outside of the visitors' outhouse in Fenway is scarred raw by gouges from tent pegs), and a game called "Stretch" which involves flipping a tent peg into the earth as close as possible to an outstretched leg. The Yankees organized a handball game one summer day until the management noticed the activity from the dugout and got on the bullpen phone to stop it. "The guys were really pissed," said their great reliever Sparky Lyle, who was involved. "When the bullpen phone rang, the score in our little game was tied."

The oddest physical activity I heard of was Bill Lee's pastime in Fenway's bullpen—molding lumps of Bazooka bubble gum into baseball-sized balls which in simulated field-goal attempts he would try to punt between the upright arms of a friend up in the first row of the bleachers. The distance was substantial, but Lee became accurate with practice, the pink bubble gum soaring true off his foot. The fans would crowd down to the bleacher fence to cheer him on when he was getting ready to try, raising their arms aloft in the referee's signal for a successful field goal when he accomplished it.

Lee, who keeps himself busy when he finds himself in the bullpen, also distinguished himself with the bleacher crowd with his large pieces of sculpture—what he calls "constructions"—made from objects tossed into the bullpen. Quite a lot gets thrown in: Shoes, umbrellas, a pistol, bottles and cans by the thousand, a Bible, firecrackers, eight thousand miles of toilet paper, a live duck, a mimeographed volume of unpublished verse, a wig, paper gliders by the thousand; this and much else has been recorded. There is always a particularly heavy barrage on Kid's Day promotions when just about anything that fits nicely in the palm of a throwing hand, such as an orange, becomes a projectile. Lee had the bill of his cap turned around by an apple on one such day, but rather than retreat to the shelter of the bullpen shed, he busied himself with the first of his fruit "construc-

tions," topping it off with a lofty arrangement of bananas.

For all the artistic temperament of a Lee, and despite the considerable amount of time that a bullpen crew spends in its quarters, little is done to fix the place up. Bullpens are as unhomely and uninviting as a buzzard's perch. True, the Los Angeles Dodgers have a room off their bullpen inside the wall which is called The Brewery—not because beer is made or even consumed there, but to honor the name of Jim Brewer, a relief pitcher who spent ten years with the Dodgers. It has a radio and a heater and a glass window through which to watch the game. Chief Nok-A-Homa's teepee in Atlanta was probably the fanciest bullpen facility. He had a carpet in there, a portable radio, a folding chair, and occasionally he would invite bullpen players to visit. But then in 1969 the teepee caught fire during a game against the St. Louis Cardinals—ignited, Nok-A-Homa has always suspected, by a Cardinal taking umbrage at the opulence out there. The fire was a brisk one, and it burned up about a third of the teepee despite Nok-A-Homa's desperate attempt to stamp it out, first with a horsehide shield, which caught fire itself, and then a broom, which also went up; the fans did what they could to help . . . with a downpour of Cokes and beer from the parapet of the stands directly above.

Perhaps the most unexpected bit of home decor is the small garden plot of tomatoes traditionally grown in Shea Stadium's home bullpen. No one is quite sure who plants it every year, or who is supposed to enjoy the crop, but the bullpen crew respects the patch: no one would think of directing a stream of tobacco juice in that direction.

These small concessions to the comforts of home are rare, however, and perhaps it is in the nature of the bullpen that it should exist as a somewhat stark place apart—it always has been: a wood bench just at the edge of the uncut meadow grass, a lane worn smooth in a corner of a sand-lot, a tin-roof shelter with the needles of the loblolly pines on the dirt floor.

But the future of the major-league bullpen, this sacrosanct area, is by no means assured. Some of the architects of modern ball parks have done away with the geographical location out beyond the fences and have simply extended the dugouts and settled the bullpen crew down at the far end. When the manager wants a relief pitcher to get ready he walks a few feet down the length of the dugout and shouts: the pitcher comes up the dugout steps and warms up in foul territory next to the outfield lines; his catcher has his back to home plate, which requires a third man from the quasi-bullpen to stand with a glove to protect him from low foul drives.

Cincinnati's is a park which uses this system . . . a model stadium for the baseball of the future, many think—artificial-surfaced field, a vast carpet with the seams showing, and the only evidences of earth at home plate, the pitcher's mound, and the sliding pits near the bases; an outfield fence that curves in perfect symmetry (with the distances marked up on the fence in meters); a press box that is glass-enclosed and sound-proofed so that what goes on down on the field is as soundless and distant as the movements of underwater life seen through the sides of a glass-bottom boat. I can never quite rid myself of the mental picture that when the season is over in Cincinnati, or the field is being prepared for football or some other event, a machine comes out and plucks the entire pitcher's mound out of the ground—a monstrous sort of "corn plaster," in the words of a visiting ballplayer hearing about it—and carries the mound out through the center-field runway and deposits it under the stands for safekeeping. ("What's that under the canvas over there in the corner?" "Oh, that's a pitcher's mound.")

No surprise, then, that the bullpen has disappeared in such an environment. The relief corps huddles at the far end of the dugout. They seem to miss the freedom of exercise they had in their bullpen enclosure. Sometimes they loosen up by reaching overhead and clinging to the edge of the dugout roof with their fingertips, their legs lifted up, so that they swing, four or five at a time, like a row of gibbons.

Some pitchers, to be sure, approve of this system, the opportunity to be more involved with the game through the proximity of the dugout to the field. Mike Marshall of the Los Angeles Dodgers likes to be close to a game so that he can see what the batters are doing: what he learns about them from close range can be of great help subsequently if he is called.

Al Hrabosky of the St. Louis Cardinals has mixed emotions. He would like to start off a game sitting in the dugout where he can root for his teammates, "rev them up" as he says. But then toward the end of a game when his services might be needed (he is a "short reliever," meaning that he makes his appearance in the late innings, usually in crucial situations), he likes the notion of an area apart where he can "get into myself."

Sparky Lyle of the Yankees prefers the traditional bullpen. He has a curious reason for wanting to stay out of the dugout during a game. He says that he cannot help laughing when a ballplayer, even a teammate, strikes out. It just doubles him up with merriment, especially when the victim puts on a great show of disgust and begins stomping around the dugout and cussing— "They're *very* funny to watch when they go bananas," Lyle says, and being aware that team spirit can be undercut by hand-muffled guffawing at such times, he prefers to sit in a bullpen where he is too far away to be titillated into laughter by a teammate's misfortune.

Speaking as a fan I hope bullpens stay as they were. One of the joys of baseball is the great *variety* of areas where there is activity—the pitcher's mound, home plate, the coaching boxes, a corner of the outfield, the base paths, the recesses of the dugouts, the bullpens . . . so that during the course of a game a spectator cranes this way and that, coming half out of his seat to gawk at something down the line: indeed, if a panoramic photograph were taken of a section of the grandstand it would almost certainly catch everybody looking in a different direction, yet each of the spectators would be absorbing an integral element of the game. Marianne Moore, the great Brooklyn Dodger poet laureate, and noted Yankee fan, was fond of concentrating on the pigeons at the ball park: for her they were an intimate part of the spectacle, especially when they dropped off the girders in the Old Yankee Stadium and banked swiftly on dihedral wings through the tumultuous uproar caused by a great play on the field below.

The bullpen is not only a unique place, but it has a special breed of people who occupy it. Larry Shepard, the Cincinnati coach, once told me, "Aw, anyone can start a ball game. But relievers are different. We don't allow starters out there in the bullpen. That's the reliever's territory and we don't let anyone impinge on it. We're very special people."

One of Shepard's charges was the veteran Clay Carroll who has been a relief pitcher for eleven years. At a party in his home town of Clanton, Alabama—a very small community, known for its homecoming and to which Carroll returns as a prodigal son—his hostess asked him curiously, "Clay, do you *like* what you're doing, that relief pitchin'; or would you rather be doing the Real Thing?"

Carroll stared at her for an instant. Then he announced "Ma'am, I *am* the Real Thing!" and after wandering around the party for a while he became so upset by her impertinence, however innocent, that he turned on his heels and left.

It is fitting that a person like Clay Carroll have a place he can think of as a home.

THE DYNASTIES

The Cincinnati Red Stockings of 1869 won 65 games in a row.

INTRODUCTION

by JOE REICHLER

Connie Mack once said that no team could be called a true champion until it had won not one, or even two, but three pennants in a row. Connie Mack had in mind, of course, his own Philadelphia Athletics, which finally achieved the feat of winning three pennants in succession from 1929 through 1931, after knocking on the door without success on two previous occasions.

Nine franchises have succeeded in finishing on top three or more seasons in a row since the turn of the century, the period commonly known in baseball as the modern era. One of these franchises, that of the New York Yankees, won three or more titles in succession seven times, including five in a row twice. Only one other team, the 1921-24 New York Giants, was able to win more than three straight years.

Selecting the most dominating of these dynasties is bound to be provocative, although hardly anyone will contest the selection of the Yankees as the most powerful aggregation of teams over a long period of time. From 1921 through 1964, the Yankees won 29 times in 44 years, a phenomenal feat light years away from the hopes and dreams of other clubs. After winning seven pennants in eight years from 1936 through 1943, the Yankees rested for a while and then roared back with 14 flags in 16 years.

Next to the Yankees, the team with the most successes in the American League was Connie Mack's Phila-

delphia Athletics. Mr. Mack's first great team won in 1910 and 1911, missed in 1912 and won again in 1913 and 1914. After a long famine, the Athletics became a challenger again in the late twenties. After two straight second place finishes, they won three titles in a row and just missed a fourth with a second place finish in 1932. The St. Louis Cardinals did not win their first championship until 1926 but once they tasted the wine of victory, they continued to drink from the championship cup with regularity, winning eight more times in the next 20 years, including three straight in 1942-43-44. The Oakland A's, offshoots of the parent Athletics, had a small dynasty of their own, winning three straight in 1972-73-74.

John McGraw's Giants won ten National League pennants from 1903 through 1924, including four in a row in the last of those 22 years. Including 1925, McGraw's team finished in the runner-up role nine times, giving them 19 first or second place finishes in 23 years. The Giants' most persistent rivals in those years, particularly in the earlier ones, were the Chicago Cubs, a dynasty of sorts in their own right, winning pennants in 1906, 1907, 1908 and 1910. The Cubs won 100 or more games in each of those years except 1908, when they reached 99. Over an 11-year period, from 1903 through 1913, they did not finish lower than third. The 1906 team won 116 games, which still stands as the most victories by any team in baseball history.

The Baltimore Orioles of an earlier vintage ". . . one of the smartest clubs baseball has ever seen . . ."

THE BALTIMORE ORIOLES 1894-1898

BY JOE REICHLER

The Baltimore Orioles of Ned Hanlon, the prim, precise, and peerless manager they called Foxy Ned, is one of the legendary teams of baseball. It is not simply a case of distance lending enchantment. The Old Orioles of 1894–98 vintage were not a group of individual stars, but a team in every sense of the word. Except for Willie Keeler, who "hit 'em where they ain't," and Big Dan Brouthers, who hit 'em a mile, they did not boast of the individual hitting, base-running, pitching, and fielding stalwarts that played on the more famous teams of comparatively recent times.

It has been said of Hanlon's Orioles that the team played as one man. It isn't so. It played as one brain cell, so coordinated was its functioning. It was one of the smartest clubs baseball has ever seen—

the club that made a science of inside baseball, with hit-and-run tactics, the squeeze play, elaborate signals for moving infield and outfield. Frank Selee's Bostons may have been ahead of them in some of their methods, but the Orioles were trail blazers who went beyond the Beaneaters. No club since has achieved their mastery of inside baseball. Certainly no other club had their genius for making scattered hits pay off in runs. Any time the Orioles left a runner stranded, he had a personal grievance and a bone to pick with his mates for abandonment.

The process was a single or base on balls followed by a steal or a sacrifice, then a timely single. And these scoring singles were, it seemed, in anyone's bat. The number of Orioles left on base was astonishingly low. They would go hitless for three or four innings at a time. But when one of them got on base, in whatever way, it was always a fair bet that he'd get around.

The revolution that the Orioles started with their inside baseball is revealed in the outraged wrath of John Montgomery Ward when his New York Giants met Baltimore in the opening series of the 1894 season. The Giants were picked to win the pennant while the Orioles were consigned to the cellar. Baltimore took all four games in the series and in the process executed thirteen hit-and-run plays, stole fourteen bases, and either sacrificed or bunted safely twenty-one times.

Ward was so incensed at the Orioles' tactics that he demanded to know what kind of game Hanlon's team was playing. It wasn't baseball, he protested. Verily, the game may

have been brought up somewhere else, but it was in Baltimore that it put on its long pants and began to walk like a man.

After more than three quarters of a century the appellation "Old Orioles" is still uttered in awe and admiration. Consequently, it is difficult to believe that this team, under the guidance of Foxy Ned Hanlon, achieved almost overnight success. But it's true. Last in a twelve-team league in 1892 and eighth in 1893, the Orioles not only won the championship just a year later, but maintained its dominance over the National League until Hanlon, partly because of the team's monotonous success, moved to Brooklyn. Hanlon took many of his stars with him, and the fact that Brooklyn proceeded to win two straight pennants after his arrival was more than mere coincidence.

Hanlon, a player of some renown in the 1880s, went to Baltimore from Pittsburgh in 1892 at the request of Harry Von der Horst, the beer-baron president of the Orioles.

Ned was determined to have not only a pennant contender but also a club that would make the baseball world sit up and take notice. In the spring of 1894, after the club had finished eighth, he took it south to Macon, Georgia, a practically unheard-of expedition. It was in Macon that Hanlon worked out the system. Every morning he had his men on the field, perfecting them in the hit-and-run technique, in laying down bunts and hitting to right, center, or left field. For defense, he had his men study and perfect an elaborate signal system for moving the infield and outfield in response to opposing batters. How well this stratagem worked is best illustrated by the team's won/lost records in the succeeding five years. From a 60–70 record in 1893, the Orioles improved to 89–39 in 1894, to 87–43 in 1895, to 90–39 in 1896, and to 96–53 in 1898.

The improvement in the players was instant and phenomenal. The 1894 Orioles team batted .343 as a team. Willie Keeler, who was to develop into one of the game's great hitters, batted .371. His outfield mates, Joe Kelley and Steve Brodie, batted .393 and .366 respectively. Dan Brouthers, the first baseman, hit .347. John McGraw, at third, hit .340. Hughey Jennings improved his average from .182 to .335. The team stole 343 bases and led in fielding with .944. The pitching staff, a fair one at best, was led by John "Sadie" McMahon (25–8).

Ned Hanlon's genius for developing players and winning teams was aided by his uncanny ability to judge players and to impart to them his remarkable warehouse of knowledge as well as a desire to rise to the heights.

But the one thing the Old Orioles, collectively, learned from Hanlon was what they could do better than any other team. They learned how to get runs—one at a time—and to make them stand the test over nine innings.

Foxy Ned Hanlon was the genius behind the Orioles' success.

CHICAGO CUBS 1906-1910

by JOE REICHLER

The colorful Cubs of Chicago, who can trace their existence in the National League back to 1876, have known in that remarkable span both good days and bad. Some of their best were in that long, long ago, when they won a half dozen pennants in the 11 seasons between 1876 and 1886. In the more recent past, they have had some very good teams, such as the championship teams of 1932, '35, '38 and '45. But easily the most glorious years in Chicago's National League history were 1906-1910 when the Cubs under the leadership of Frank Chance, captured three pennants and narrowly missed a fourth. In that period, the Cubs had perhaps their most magnetic heroes —Mordecai (Three-Fingered) Brown, Johnny Kling, Johnny Evers, Joe Tinker, Wildfire Frank Schulte, Ed Reulbach and others.

Nine championships belong to the Cubs since the turn of the century and one third of them were manufactured by Chance's teams between 1906 and 1910. But no mere accounting of championships or statistics can tell the story of a ball club that has had such an emotional hold on the great American midwest. Chicago loves its White Sox, to be sure, but there is also a fierce and proud loyalty to the Cubs that has been handed down from father to son and from father to son and daughter. Despite the docile name, the Cubs, under Frank Chance in the first decade of the 20th century, were the original "Gashouse Gang." Led by the snarling Johnny Evers, the taunting Joe Tinker and the challenging Frank Chance, the Cubs engaged in almost daily bitter warfare with John McGraw's Giants and Fred Clarke's Pirates.

With due and proper respect to the White Sox, who had their loyal following, especially on the South Side, it was those early Cubs who commanded the fiercest allegiance of the baseball fans in Chicago. Still repeated today is Franklin P. Adams' immortal bit of doggerel:

"These are the saddest of baseball words,
Tinker to Evers to Chance.

Trio of bear cubs and fleeter than birds,
Tinker to Evers to Chance.

The legendary 1906 Chicago Cubs.

Frank Chance: One-third of the Tinker-to-Evers-to-Chance double-play combo.

Thoughtfully pricking our gonfolon bubble,
Turning a Giant hit into a double,
Words that are weighty with nothing but trouble,
Tinker to Evers to Chance."

The move that transformed the Cubs from an also-ran to the team to beat for the pennant was the appointment of Frank Chance as manager in 1905. Starting in 1906, Chance's Cubs won three straight pennants, finished second, then won another first over a five year span.

The 1906 team won 116 games, a mark that has yet to be approached. This was the team of the famous Tinker-to-Evers-to-Chance double play combination; the outfield of Jimmy Sheckard, Artie Hofman and Jimmy Slagle, the superb Johnny Kling catching, the pitching staff that included Mordecai Brown, Ed Reulbach, Orvie Overall, Carl Lundgren and Jack Pfeister. Breathing fire from the first pitch to the last, meeting every challenge both on and off the field with a furious fighting instinct, Chance's gang steamrolled its way to the pennant. There never was before, nor has there been since, such a runaway race in major league baseball. The inflamed Cubs careened through the league like a hopped-up hippopotamus, winning 116 games and losing only 36. They left the second-place Giants 20 games behind. Three-Fingered Brown won 26 games and lost only six. Harry Steinfeldt, the steady third baseman, led the hitters with a .327 average.

Beating the White Sox in an all-Chicago World Series, the Cubs bounced back to win again in 1907. This time they won by 17$\frac{1}{2}$ games, finishing with 107 victories and 45 losses, and went on to whip the Detroit Tigers in the World Series. The

Cubs made it three in a row in 1908 but this time it took one of the most sensational finishes in one of the most dramatic of all pennant races to pull it off.

The Cubs-Giants rivalry reached a peak that year. No two managers ever went at each other's throats as did Chance, the Peerless Leader, and McGraw, the Little Napoleon. The feud reached a fever pitch on September 23, in a never-to-be forgotten game between the Giants and Cubs. In the last of the ninth, the score tied at 1-1, Moose McCormick of the Giants was on third and Fred Merkle on first. Two men were out. Al Bridwell, the Giants' shortstop, lashed a clean single to center-field and McCormick trotted gleefully home. While the fans poured out onto the field, Johnny Evers stood at second base screaming for the ball and at the same time shouting at umpire Hank O'Day. Evers finally got the ball, stepped on second and claimed a forceout because Merkle had headed for the clubhouse without bothering to touch second.

O'Day ruled the game a 1-1 tie. The season ended a week later with the Cubs and Giants tied for first place. The tie game was replayed after the regular season. Chicago won, 4-2, with Three-Fingered Brown, in relief of Jack Pfeister, beating the great Christy Mathewson, winner of 37 games that year. It was the third straight pennant for the Cubs. Once again the Tigers were the opponent in the World Series and once again the Cubs emerged victorious. The Cubs made a gallant bid for four straight in 1909 and although they won 104 games, they finished second to the Pittsburgh Pirates. But they clawed their way back in 1910, putting 13 games of daylight between themselves and the second-place Giants. Even though they lost the World Series to Connie Mack's Athletics, Frank Chance's men had established themselves as one of the great dynasties of all time. Over a five-year stretch, they won 540 games, an average of 108 games a season. No club has ever been able to match that.

THE PHILADELPHIA ATHLETICS

1910-1914
1929-1931

BY JOE REICHLER

The World Champion Philadelphia Athletics of 1913.

The story of the Philadelphia Athletics and Cornelius McGillicuddy, better know as Connie Mack, is virtually one and the same. The two are inseparably intertwined. For fifty years, from the very beginning to the day he turned the reins over to Jimmy Dykes, the A's were Connie Mack and Connie Mack was the A's.

Only one baseball club has been under the domination and management of one individual for a half century. Under Connie Mack, who managed and shared ownership of the team without interruption from 1901 through 1950, the A's for extensive periods overpowered the American League with marvelous teams only to strip these teams of their talent to the point of becoming doormats for the rest of the league.

But when the A's were good, well, they were simply unbeatable. Take, for example, Philadelphia's two greatest representatives, the 1910–14 and the 1929–31 dynasties. Between them, they won seven of Connie Mack's nine pennants and all five of his World Championships. His good teams were so strongly constructed that once they gathered full momentum, it took years to halt them.

The list of famous players man-

aged by Connie Mack would make a respectable Hall of Fame by itself. In addition to Rube Waddell, generally considered to be one of the most colorful characters in baseball, as well as one of the most brilliant of all left-handers, Mack had two of the most famous pitching triumverates in Chief Bender, Eddie Plank, and Jack Coombs, and the latter trio of Lefty Grove, George Earnshaw, and Rube Walberg. Two won over 30 games in a season, two won 300 or more lifetime victories, and four earned places in the Hall of Fame. Mack's catchers were Wally Schang and Mickey Cochrane, the latter generally regarded as the best backstop of all time. The A's 1910–14 "hundred-thousand-dollar" infield of Stuffy McInnis, Eddie Collins, Jack Barry, and Home Run Baker, which, by today's standards, would be equal to a five-million-dollar infield, may be the best of all time. Not far behind was the A's 1929–32 infield of Jimmie Foxx, Max Bishop, Joe Boley, and Jimmy Dykes. Outfielders? Mack was blessed with the best. Amos Strunk, Rube Oldring, Danny Murphy, Socks Seybold—they patrolled the outer garden for Mack's champions in 1910–14. They were so good that Connie could afford the luxury of disposing of Shoeless Joe Jackson, one of baseball's greatest natural hitters. In later years there were Al Simmons, Bing Miller, Mule Haas—stars and superstars, all of them.

Perhaps the most renowned of all of Connie Mack's stars did not play for either of his greatest machines. Connie lured Napoleon Lajoie away from the Phillies at the turn of the century when the fledgling American League decided on a war with the National. With the Fabulous Frenchman hitting .422, the A's won the pennant in 1902. They finished second in 1903, fell to fourth in 1904, came back to win in 1905 only to lose four out of five to the New York Giants in the World Series. That was the Series in which Christy Mathewson hurled three shutouts.

Mack immediately set out building a new dynasty. In 1906 he picked up a young New York semipro outfielder, Rube Oldring. Later in the season, he came up with a youngster who appeared in several games under the name of "Sullivan." This was the peerless Eddie Collins, a great athlete at Columbia University, who wanted to retain his amateur standing. From Colby College came Jack Coombs. He already had plucked Eddie Plank from Gettysburg College and Albert "Chief" Bender from the Indian school of Carlisle. In 1908 he acquired the former Holy Cross shortstop Jack Barry. And from the Reading Tri-State League he brought up Frank Baker. In 1909 John "Stuffy" McInnis, along with Amos Strunk, joined the club. Connie Mack's great machine had taken shape, and by 1910 it was fully formed and ready to steamroll.

Although the 1910 Philadelphia Athletics were considered too young to win a pennant, they ran away with it anyway. Jack Coombs won 31 games, losing only 9. Chief Bender won 23, losing only 5. Eddie Collins led the league in stolen bases with 81. Five A's batted .300 or better. The A's went on to overwhelm the National League champion Chicago Cubs in five games. The one game they lost was a 4–3 decision in ten innings. The A's repeated in 1911. Collins hit .365; Baker led the league with 11 home runs and 115 runs batted in. Coombs won 28 games, Plank won 22. This time their opponents were the New York Giants, who had humbled them in 1905. The A's proceeded to cop the championship in six games, winning the finale 13–2. "We had everything that season," Mack once recalled. "Pitching, hitting, defense, speed, and brains."

Nevertheless, the Athletics dropped to third place in 1912. Mack added three pitchers that year. Herb Pennock, who was destined to become a Hall of Famer, Bullet Joe Bush, and Bob Shawkey. The A's rebounded in 1913 to win the pennant and again met the Giants. Connie's team mangled its old rivals, winning the five games to become the first team to win three world titles. The only New York victory was a 3–0

ten-inning shutout by the redoubtable Christy Mathewson.

Philadelphia won its fourth pennant in five years in 1914. The Federal League had opened in opposition to the established majors, and throughout the year stars were being enticed to the outlaw circuit with juicy offers. The A's players were eager listeners. With their minds on other things, they fell easy prey to the Boston Braves, who had captured the imagination of the country with the most fantastic comeback baseball had ever witnessed. In last place in mid-July, the Braves, behind the pitching of Dickie Rudolph, Lefty Tyler, and Bill James, swept past the other seven teams to win the pennant. As a climax, they drubbed the star-studded A's in four straight.

Saddened and disgruntled by the humiliating defeat, disturbed by the inroads of the Federal League which grabbed Bender, Plank, and Murphy among others, and in need of financial help, Mack dismantled his world beaters before the snow had set in that year. First, he sold Eddie Collins to the White Sox for $50,000, a staggering price in those days. Then, in rapid succession, he disposed of

Coombs, Pennock, Shawkey, and Barry. The A's finished last in 1915. Connie was not through selling. Schang, Strunk, Bush, and McInnis were next to go. The following decade found the A's flirting with the cellar. Nevertheless, Mack uncovered some fine players during those lean years. Among them were George Burns, Eddie Rommel, Charlie Jamieson, Joe Dugan, Tillie Walker, Jimmy Dykes, Whitey Witt. Lefty Grove was purchased from Baltimore for $106,000. The A's also acquired Max Bishop and Mickey Cochrane. Frank Baker tipped Mack off to a kid down in Easton, Maryland, who would knock the ball out of sight. He was Jimmie Foxx, who eventually hit 527 home runs. Al Simmons also joined the club.

The A's were ready to win again in 1927 but ran into one of the mightiest aggregations of all time, the 1927 Yankees of Murderers' Row fame. The A's won 91 games that year, but the Yankees set the league record of 110 victories. The Yankees were still powerful in 1928 but so were the A's. Trailing the Yankees by 12½ games on July 4, they caught fire and dissolved the lead in two months. They actually took the lead on September

Here are five key figures of the awesome A's: First baseman Stuffy McInnis, outfielder Danny Murphy, third baseman Frank "Home Run" Baker, shortstop Jack Barry and second baseman Eddie Collins. McInnis, Baker, Barry and Collins comprised the famed $100,000 infield.

The 1931 Athletics chalked up 107 victories.

8, but the Yankees fought back to win their third straight flag. The '28 A's surge was an indication of things to come. In 1929 Philadelphia won 104 games to make a cakewalk out of the race, defeating the Yankees by 18 games. They allowed the National League champion Chicago Cubs to win but one of the five games in the World Series. And these were the Cubs of Hornsby, Cuyler, Wilson, Hartnett, Stephenson, and Grimm.

Philadelphia won the 1930 pennant almost as easily as the year before but met sterner opposition in the St. Louis Cardinals, just becoming known as the "Gashouse Gang." It took them six games to win this time. Philadelphia was led by the pitching of Grove and Earnshaw and the hitting of Simmons, Foxx, and Cochrane.

Mack had often said: "A champion is not great until he repeats." Now he said: "To be truly great, a champion must win three times in succession." His players took the hint. They rolled to another runaway victory in 1931, chalking up 107 victories for a .704 percentage, highest ever made by a team. Grove had the astonishing record of 31 victories and 4 defeats. Simmons retained his batting crown with .390. And again the Cardinals were champions, and it was a chance for Mack to be the first manager ever to win three World Championships in succession. But the Cardinals, led by the fiery Pepper Martin, defeated the A's in seven games. The A's were still a magnificent club in 1932, but the Yankees were better so they had to be content with second place. Their era had come to an end, and like the 1914 champions, this great aggregation was soon to be scattered to the winds. First to go were Simmons, Haas, and Dykes. They brought $150,00 from the White Sox. The A's slipped to third in 1933, and Mack sent Mickey Cochrane to Detroit for $100,000. Grove, Walberg, and Bishop went to Boston for $125,000. The following year Foxx was shipped to the Red Sox for $150,000. Sale by sale, the last of the wondrous A's of 1929–32 had vanished. So had the last of the Philadelphia A's dynasties.

THE 1927 NEW YORK YANKEES – THE GREATEST OF THEM ALL!

BY JOE REICHLER

It was in the middle 1950s and the Yankees were engaged in still another World Series, this time with the Brooklyn Dodgers as the opponent. The hospitality room, where food and drink were plentiful, was jammed with baseball people of all description—club officials, managers, coaches, scouts, former big-leaguers looking for a job, and of course, sportswriters, broadcasters, and photographers covering the Series. Someone volunteered that this was as good a Yankee team that ever represented New York.

Joe Devine, a stoutish, balding man in his sixties, and a scout for over thirty years, spoke up.

"There never was and never will be a team as great as the Yankees of 1927," he stated somewhat defiantly. "They were so good they had most of the clubs licked even before the game started.

"I'll never forget the 1927 World Series as long as I live," Devine continued when nobody bothered to challenge his assertions. "The Yankees played the Pittsburgh Pirates for the World Championship. I was scouting for the Pirates then, and they had a good team with the Waner brothers and Pie Traynor. You know what happened, don't you? The Yankees chewed them up in four straight. If they had played a hundred games, I honestly believe the Yankees would have won all one hundred. That's how scared the Pittsburgh club was.

"I know. I was in the Pittsburgh clubhouse before the opening game. I'll never forget the player meeting called by Donie Bush, the manager. He gathered all the players around him and said, 'Boys, we'll now go over the Yankee lineup and check the weaknesses of each batter.' Dan Howley, then manager of the St. Louis Browns, and Billy Hinchman,

Often called "The Greatest of Them All", here are the 1927 Yankees:
First row: (Left to Right) Dutch Reuther, Joe Dugan, Ben Paschal, Benny Bengough, Myles Thomas, Mike Gazella, Ray Morehart, Ed Bennett (mascot).
Second row: Bob Shawkey, Joe Giard, Johnny Grabowski, Charley O'Leary, Miller Huggins (manager), Art Fletcher, Herb Pennock, Julie Wera, Pat Collins.
Third row: Lou Gehrig, Bob Meusel, Babe Ruth, Wilcy Moore, George Pipgras, Earle Combs, Otto Miller, Waite Hoyt, Tony Lazzeri, Mark Koenig, Urban Shocker, Cedric Durst, Doc Wood (trainer).

106

a veteran baseball man who had scouted the Yankees during the season, and I, had been asked to attend.

" 'Let's see, now,' Donie began, 'lead-off man—Earle Combs. Now, what's his weakness, Hinchman?'

" 'Nothing,' Billy answered. 'Combs has no weakness. He can hit anything you throw, and he hits to all fields, so it doesn't matter where you pitch to him.'

" 'Okay, we'll skip Combs and trust to luck,' Bush said. 'Now, Mark Koenig, what about him?'

" 'Well,' replied Howley, 'for a while we had fair success with him pitching low and inside, but not for long. We switched to high and outside, but soon that, too, was not so good. He'd wait for a walk and you know who came up next—Babe Ruth. Toward the end of the season, we just threw the ball down the middle to Koenig because we didn't want to walk him.'

" 'Okay,' Bush sighed. 'I guess there's no use to go over the weaknesses of the next four hitters— Ruth, Gehrig, Meusel, and Lazzeri. From what I've been told they don't have any. That brings us to Joe Dugan.'

" 'Well,' began Howley.

" 'Say, Donie,' interrupted Pie Traynor, captain and third baseman of the Pirates, 'you don't really expect Howley to tell us how to beat the Yankees, do you? Why, his Browns dropped twenty-one straight to the Yanks last year before they finally eked out a 3–2 victory.'

" 'Oh, well,' Bush said resignedly. 'What's the use. Let's go out on the ball field and hope we all don't get killed.'

"The Yankees are already practicing when the Pirates sneak out on the ball field,' recounted Devine, "and I do mean sneak. It looked like they were trying to get to the bench without being seen by the Yankees.

"Well, the Babe is taking his batting practice cuts. The stands are nearly full. Jack Russell, a veteran American League pitcher, is on the mound. Wham! goes his first pitch into the right-field stands. Bang! Ruth cracks Russell's second pitch

into the center-field stands. Another goes into left field. A fourth clears the park altogether.

"The Pittsburgh players, by this time, have all made their appearance. Not one has sat down yet. They all remained standing, appalled by the tremendous power being displayed by the Babe.

"Babe, always a great showman who never failed to take advantage of any situation, stepped back out of the box, looked over at the Pirates, and pointing to the bleachers, said: 'Okay, sonnies, if any of you want my autograph, go out and collect those balls in the bleachers. I'll sign 'em for you.'

"Gehrig follows Ruth and I'll be roped and tied if Lou doesn't almost duplicate Babe's feats. He sprayed those balls into the stands like buckshots. Then came Meusel and Lazzeri. It was the greatest power display of home run hitting I have ever

seen or ever hope to see again.

" 'My g-gosh,' sputtered Glenn Wright, Pittsburgh's shortstop. 'I've never seen anything like this before. Do they do that all the time?'

"Soon it was the Pirates' turn to hit," Devine went on. "That was the year the Waner boys—Paul, Big Poison; and Lloyd, Little Poison—were the big guns of the Pirates. When Paul stepped up to hit, the Babe leisurely strolled over from the Yankee dugout, looked him up and down, then said out loud so that all could hear: 'Hey, what goes on here? Who are we playing? High school kids?' With that he uncorks that big, good-natured grin at Paul, winks, pats him affectionately on the head (the Babe was a full head taller than Paul), and says, 'Don't mind me, kid. I'm all for you.'

"Well, you know what happened. The Yankees flattened the Pirates like an old carpet. I never did wait

Babe Ruth: The heart and soul of the '27 Yankees.

around for the end. I knew what was going to happen after the second game and packed up for home in a hurry. After the fourth game, I got a letter from Remy Kremer, Pittsburgh's best pitcher, and one of my best friends.

" 'Well, Joe,' the letter began, 'that Ruth ain't so tough. I held him down—to four line drives and a single off my shins. I hope I can resume walking by the time the 1928 season opens.'

"Bush was the happiest man in the United States when the Series was over," Devine concluded. 'Am I glad it's over,' he said. 'Nobody was killed and we're all safe and sound.'"

A year before, the Yankees had been defeated by the Cardinals, four games to three, in the 1926 World Series. In 1927 the Pirates beat out the Cardinals for the National League pennant by one and a half games. After the clean sweep over the Pirates in 1927, the Yankees gave the same treatment to the Cardinals in the World Series of 1928. In the ensuing half century, in poll after poll of the nation's top sportswriters and sportscasters, the team voted the greatest of all time more often than any other club in the annals of baseball has been the New York Yankees of 1927.

"We had a great team, a really great team," said Al Simmons, the mighty mauler of the world champion Philadelphia Athletics of 1929–30. "But when you compare us with the really great Yankee world champions who preceded us, we simply weren't in their class. I'm not trying to kid myself, nor anyone else. I fought those Yankees as hard as anyone in the American League, but when they got us into a tough series, they just batted our brains out."

They had terrific power, with Babe Ruth setting the home run record of 60 and Lou Gehrig driving in 175 runs, a major-league record at the time, along with superb pitching and stout defense. They defeated the second place Athletics by 19 games, winning 110 games, a figure exceeded only once in the big leagues before—by the 116 victories of the 1906 Chicago White Sox—and once since—by the 111 victories of the 1954 Cleveland Indians.

The 1927 Yankees swept the series with every club. Oddly, the sixth-place Cleveland Indians made the best showing against the Yankees, winning ten of the twenty-two games between them. It was a different story against the seventh-place Browns. The Yankees licked Dan Howley's entry twenty-one straight times before the Missourians got away with the twenty-second.

The 1927 Yankees batted .307 as a team, scored the high total of 975 runs, and hit 158 home runs. Earle Combs, the impeccable center fielder, had a superb season, hitting .356, scoring 137 runs, and cracking out a league-leading 231 hits. Bob Meusel, with the greatest arm in the game, was in left field and batted a vigorous .337. Push-'Em-Up Tony Lazzeri, the clutch-hitting second baseman, batted .309. Ruth batted .356, and Gehrig was the team batting leader with .373.

Never was the term "Murderers' Row" more applicable than when it was bestowed on Ruth, Gehrig, Meusel, and Lazzeri, who comprised the center of the 1927 Yankees' batting array. Not only did each of the quartet bat in over 100 runs during the season but their grand total of runs batted in was 544!

There was more to the Yankees than just slugging. They had a great pitching staff, perfectly rounded and complemented by the addition of Wilcy Moore, a bald-headed Oklahoman who was about to quit the season before when apparently nobody noticed him after he had won thirty games and lost only four for Greenville in the Sally League. The Yankees noticed him, however, and purchased the twenty-year-old sinkerball pitcher for $4,500.

Moore was in fifty games for the Yankees in 1927 and was equally effective as a starter or in relief. He won nineteen and lost seven and led the American League with a 2.28 earned run average. Waite Hoyt was the leader of the staff with twenty-two victories, seven defeats, and a 2.64 ERA. Herb Pennock, the great left-hander, won nineteen and lost eight. Urban Shocker, the spitball ace, won eighteen ad lost six. George Pipgras, who became a starter in the second half of the season, was ten and three. Other pitchers were Dutch Reuther (13–6), Myles Thomas (7–4), and Bob Shawkey (2–3).

Another important factor was the coming of age of the club's keystone pair, Tony Lazzeri and Mark Koenig. Together with Gehrig at first and Jumping Joe Dugan, one of the finest defensive players in the game, at third, the Yankees boasted a star-studded infield. Ruth, Combs, and Meusel formed what many still regard as the greatest outfield of all time.

The '27 Yankees' infield extraordinaire of first baseman Lou Gehrig, second baseman Tony Lazzeri, shortstop Mark Koenig and third baseman Joe Dugan.

ST. LOUIS DYNASTY 1926-1934 1942-1946

BY BOB BROEG

After St. Louis won its first National League pennant ever in 1926, the Cardinals won nine pennants and six World Championships over a twenty-year period. And six other times they finished second.

The Redbirds finished first in 1926, 1928, 1930, 1931, and 1934, five times over a nine-year period, then prevailed again in 1942–43–44 and 1946 and, ultimately, in 1964, 1967, and 1968, adding eight World Championships to go with their twelve pennants.

Branch Rickey could see the dynasty coming. His farm system had sprouted a bumper crop, including a smiling, swaggering Ladies Day favorite at first base, Sunny Jim Bottomley (who had been so green that when he first reported to spring training, looked down the bat rack, and saw a long, lean bat, he asked politely, "I'd sure like to meet this Mr. Fungo.")

The Cardinals won their first pennant in 1926, and then defeated the powerful New York Yankees in the World Series. They finished second to the Pirates in 1927, won the pennant again in 1928, but were trounced, four games to none, by the Yankees in the World Series.

In 1930, under manager Charles E. "Gabby" Street (a World War I sergeant best known as Walter Johnson's batterymate, and as the man who had caught a ball dropped from the Washington Monument), the Cardinals languished around .500 well past mid-season, before spurting to their third pennant in five years.

The last day of the 1930 season, with the flag theirs, they unfurled a sunken-cheeked, lanky fellow named Dizzy Dean, who pitched a three-hitter to beat Pittsburgh, 3–1, and talked so loud and long the next spring that when the Cardinals optioned him out, relief pitcher Jim

The 1930 version of the St. Louis Cardinals won the National League pennant.

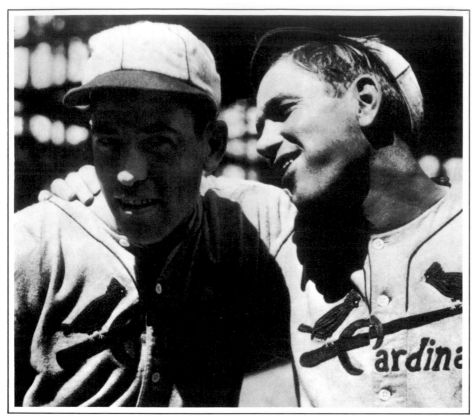

The Deans—Daffy (left) and Dizzy.

Lindsey said sarcastically, "Gosh, there's the first time a ball club ever lost thirty games in one day."

The Cardinals didn't need Ol' Diz, as the young pitcher called himself, because they had another rookie phenom, Paul Derringer; and a wide-shouldered, hawk-nosed rookie retread named Pepper Martin.

The 1931 Cardinals won 101 games, breezing to the pennant, and upsetting a truly fine team, Connie Mack's Philadelphia Athletics, who were seeking a third straight World Championship.

The Redbrids wouldn't have been in it at all if it hadn't been for Martin, Wild Horse of the Osage.

The plain, open-shirted Oklahoman caught the fancy of the hard-put country. In the first five games he had twelve hits, stole five bases, drove in five runs, and scored five. Afterward, Judge Landis hugged him and said: "I'd sooner trade places with you than any man in America."

"Fine, Judge, just as long as we can trade salaries, too," said a grinning Martin, who was making $5,000 to Landis' $60,000 then.

The club that Manager Frankie

Frisch fielded in 1934 bore almost no resemblance to the team that had won four times in six seasons through 1931. Oh, Jesse Haines, now called Pop, was still there at forty, and Pepper Martin, who had played center field in '31, was the third baseman, courageous but scatter-armed, and Frisch, nearing thirty-seven was still the second baseman.

Rickey gave up Derringer and acquired Lippy Leo Durocher for shortstop. Rip Collins had taken over for Bottomley at first base and Ducky Medwick was in left field.

The big star, a thirty-game winner, was Dizzy Dean. Seven games behind on Labor Day, the Cardinals caught the Giants the next-to-last day of the season, and Ol' Diz polished off Cincinnati to nail it down on the final afternoon, 9–0.

The 1934 World Series in which the Gashouse Gang outroughed the Detroit Tigers was a seven-game classic.

Martin's Mississippi Mudcats, a homemade band of musical depreciation, kept the club almost as loose as Pepper's tricky sideline pepper game amused fans everywhere. It was

nothing on Ladies Day, 100° in the shade, for Pepper and his sidekick in hijinks, Dizzy Dean, to sit cross-legged in front of the dugout like Indians wearing blankets, and start a bonfire. Enough psychological impact to wear down the heat-stricken foe.

Ah, but how that Gang could give it to the other guys. And when Medwick lashed out with his spikes at third baseman Marv Owen in the anticlimactic seventh game of the 1934 Series, at which time the Tigers trailed a pussy-cat 10–0, the angry, disappointed Detroit crowd vented its displeasure by throwing everything at Medwick except a fit. Judge Landis was late taking command of the issue. He'd just gone back a few rows to tell a friend, excitedly, that watching Pepper Martin, he'd finally learned how to spit tobacco through his teeth.

Finally, getting down to cases, the Judge exchanged profanities with Medwick and Frisch, then threw out the Cardinals' slugger for his own protection, and Dizzy Dean coasted to an 11–0 shutout and his second Series victory, matching brother Paul's pair.

For once, Ol' Diz had been a shy piker. Before the season, he had predicted, "Me 'n' Paul will win forty-five games." They won forty-nine, not including the four in the World Series.

Arm injuries soon licked the brothers Dean, and the Gashouse Gang ran out of gas. St. Louis, so accustomed to pennants, didn't win again until 1942, the year Branch Rickey was a lame-duck general manager (informed by Breadon that the big boss no longer cared to renew the contract that, with B.R.'s percentage of sale profits, gave Rickey $80,000 a year).

The 1942 Cardinals, called the St. Louis Swifties by New York sports cartoonist Willard Mullin, were perhaps the fastest ball club ever, with a brilliant defense highlighted by tall Marty Marion at shortstop and master center fielder Terry Moore.

Terry Moore was the oldest regular and the inspiration, the man who railed at younger players in bitter memories of second-place finishes of 1935, '36, '39, and '41. The only player not developed by the productive farm system was relief pitcher Harry Gumbert.

Moore was the middleman for one of the greatest all-round outfields ever. Enos Slaughter played right, and that slim, line-driving hitting rookie, Stan Musial, was in left.

The Coopers, Mort and Walker, were a standout brother battery. Johnny Beazley came up from the minors and won twenty-one games as a rookie.

Still, defending champion Brooklyn was so hot that by mid-August the Dodgers led by 12 games. In September the Cardinals finally caught the Dodgers at Ebbets Field.

After tying at Brooklyn with fourteen games to play, the Cardinals could do no better than divide a doubleheader at Philadelphia, but they nosed in front because Brooklyn lost a doubleheader to Cincinnati.

Here's where both clubs showed their mettle. The Cardinals won four in a row. Brooklyn lost one, and Breadon cheerfully announced the Cardinals would accept World Series reservations.

The 1942 Dodgers didn't fold, either, winning nine of their last ten, but St. Louis, after losing a game at Chicago, won seven straight.

Losing just forty-eight games, St. Louis had 106 victories, the most by a National League team since 1909.

How did the Cardinals do it? Not by knocking the ball over or against fences. They hit only 60 homers, 49 behind New York, and their only .300 hitters were Slaughter (.318) and Musial (.315). But that speed, stretching singles into doubles, pressuring the foe into errors, also cut off enemy hits and bids for extra-base hits. And the pitching was so great that it limited the other side to an average of just 3.1 runs a game.

Mort Cooper and Beazley were

1–2 in the league in victories and earned-run average. Cooper, 22–7 with 10 shutouts and a 1.77 ERA, won the Most Valuable Player Award. Beazley, 21–6 with a 2.13 ERA, beat Musial for Rookie of the Year recognition.

Although 9 to 20 underdogs, the Cardinals ran away in the World Series from the Yankees, who had won eight straight Series games and, in fact, lost just four games since their upset by the Cardinals in 1926.

The dynasty of the 1940s ended when Enos Slaughter dashed from home on a king-sized single in 1946 for a seventh-game victory, 4–3, over the Boston Red Sox, who had been 7 to 20 favorites. It would be eighteen years until the Cardinals won again, typically, when far back in 1964 with a 40–41 record at the All-Star break, they caught slumping Philadelphia at the finish, thanks largely to the arrival of Bob Gibson and Lou Brock as the newest St. Louis superstars.

The 1946 World Champion Cardinals:
First row: (left to right) Marty Marion, George Kurowski, Stan Musial, Al Brazle, Clyde Wares (coach), Eddie Dyer (manager), Mike Gonzalez (coach), Buster Adams, Terry Moore, Enos Slaughter, Murry Dickson.
Second row: Fred Schmidt, Walter Sessi, John Beazley, Red Schoendienst, Harry Walker, Bill Endicott, Howard Pollet, Ervin Dusak, Ken O'Dea, John Grodzicki, Charles Barrett, Leo Ward (traveling secretary).
Third row: Vernal Jones, Dick Sisler, Clyde Kluttz, Howard Krist, Del Rice, Ken Burkhart, Dr. Harrison J. Weaver (trainer), Ted Wilks, Joe Garagiola, Blix Donnelly, Harry Brecheen, Joff Cross   Seated on grass: Bob Scanlon (batboy) and Eddie Dyer, Jr.

The World Champion Yankees of 1950.
First row (left to right): Whitey Ford, Phil Rizzuto, Billy Martin, Eddie Lopat, Jim Turner, Frank Crosetti, Casey Stengel (manager), Bill Dickey, Jackie Jensen, Billy Johnson, Gene Woodling, Charlie Silvera, Johnny Mize.
Second row: Gus Mauch, Bob Porterfield, Wally Hood, Dave Madison, Gerry Coleman, Bobby Brown, Tommy Henrich, Hank Bauer, Joe Collins, Lew Burdette, Joe Ostrowski, Ernie Nevel, Johnny Hopp.
Third Row: Tommy Byrne, Cliff Mapes, Hank Wookman, Fred Sanford, Tom Ferrick, Yogi Berra, Joe Page, Ralph Houk, Joe DiMaggio, Allie Reynolds.
Sitting: B. Padell and J. Carrierri. Missing: Vic Raschi

THE 1949-1953 YANKEES

BY PETER GOLENBOCK

It was clutch time for the New York Yankees, the late innings. New York led three games to two in the 1953 World Series. The sixth game was tied, 3–3, in the bottom of the ninth. Hank Bauer, who was once described as having a face that looked like a clenched fist, was leading off second. Baby-faced Mickey Mantle was a few steps off first. With one man out, Billy Martin, Manager Casey Stengel's street fighter, was up. From the mound Brooklyn's Clem Labine wheeled in a fast ball that Martin stroked on a blur over the bag at second. Bauer was running immediately, and he rounded third and scored the winner.

The Series' victory was the Yankees fifth straight, their sixteenth Series win in twenty tries. Between 1949 and 1953 the Casey Stengel-led Bronx Bombers monopolized baseball, the only time a team has won a Series so many years in a row. This feat is even more remarkable in that during this period the Yankee roster

was in a state of flux. General Manager George Weiss and Manager Stengel were constantly reorganizing their cast, replacing aging prewar stars with young farm prospects.

Charles Dillon "Casey" Stengel had never managed his Dodger and Braves teams into a first division in nine years of trying. His reputation was one of a clown, not an astute handler of men. Thus there was consternation among the press and Yankee fans when Weiss announced that personable Bucky Harris was fired and beginning in 1949 the manager would be this old man. At the news conference announcing his appointment Stengel stood before the press, lines crisscrossing his pliable face, and on his cheeks, pronounced creases flowing toward a jutting jaw. He had palm leaf ears and a broad nose, and his legs angled oddly. When he talked he waved his arms and made exaggerated gestures. He looked comical, like an elderly gnome. What he said, though, was not amusing. "I didn't get this job," he said in a low, gravelly voice, "through friendship. The Yankees represent an investment of millions of dollars. They don't hand out jobs like this because they like your company. I got the job because the people here think I can produce for them."

George Weiss especially felt that way. He trusted Stengel, knew he could work closely with him, understood that he had the rare ability to instruct youngsters. Equally important Stengel would be the perfect buffer to keep the nosy press from the shy and private general manager.

In early 1949, despite the loss of Joe DiMaggio to his painful heel injury, the Yankees were winning. Three rookies, gentleman Jerry Coleman at second and in the outfield Hank Bauer and Gene Woodling, contributed heavily. Stengel moved Tommy Henrich, Old Reliable, from the outfield to first base where he anchored the infield. Henrich led the team, a playing-coach, and very often drove in the winning run. Yogi Berra, after an intense training period during which Bill Dickey "learned him all his experience," quickly developed into an all-star. And when Joe returned late in June, he hit close to .400.

Only at the end, as Boston closed with a rush, did the Yankees relinquish the lead. With two games in the season remaining—both against the Yankees—the Red Sox led New York by one game. But then the Yankees overcame a 4–0 lead on a home run by little-used Johnny Lindell to win for Joe Page, and in the finale somber Vic Raschi pitched a 1–0 game into the eighth, the Yankees finally winning, 5–3, for the pennant. The Yankees then mangled the Dodgers in a five-game series.

It was a little easier in 1950. They won in the final week by three full games over the pesky Detroit Tigers. Shortstop Phil Rizzuto hit .324 and was named the Most Valuable Player in the league. Joe DiMaggio drove in 122 runs, and the first of Weiss' newcomers, Whitey Ford, a lithe lefty, was 9–1 after arriving

in mid-season. Then they swept the Philadelphia Phillies Whiz Kids in four straight.

In 1951 it was the Feller-Wynn-Garcia Cleveland Indians who made the strongest challenge, but the Yankees held them off to win by five games. Yogi Berra, the original Ugly Duckling, was now a shin-guarded swan. Leading the Yankee attack, he was voted the American League MVP. Berra was a dead-pull left-handed hitter whose skills were perfectly suited to the cozy right-field dimensions of Yankee Stadium. His lifetime average was .285, but with men on base in critical situations he was a terror. "When it gets around the seventh inning," said White Sox Manager Paul Richards, "Berra is the most dangerous hitter in baseball." In the Series the Yankees whipped the New York Giants in six games.

After the Series, Joe DiMaggio,

the Yankee Clipper, since voted the Greatest Living Ballplayer, retired. DiMaggio was a lifetime .325 hitter with 361 home runs, but his deteriorating physical condition made it impossible for him to continue. His retirement was a transitional point from Stengel's dependence upon the Joe McCarthy-trained veterans to his own, self-trained youngsters, among them Mickey Mantle, a rawboned, switch-hitting bolt of greased lightning from the mine fields of Commerce, Oklahoma. He was only nineteen, a painfully introverted youngster who was so green that in one exhibition game he was hit in the head with a fly ball because he didn't know how to flip down his sunglasses. Stengel loved the kid and his unlimited potential. Immediately the Yankee manager switched him from shortstop to the outfield to take advantage of his blinding speed and strong arm.

After smashing one of his 536 lifetime homers, Mickey Mantle is greeted by Yogi Berra (8).

Another rookie Stengel switched was Gil McDougald, a second baseman in the minors. Stengel asked him if he would play third. "I've never played there before," McDougald said fearlessly, "but I'll try. They can't do more than knock my teeth out." In 1951 McDougald played second and third, batted .306, and was named the Rookie of the Year. For ten unheralded seasons McDougald starred at second, short, and third, one of the most versatile athletes the Yankees ever boasted.

Billy Martin, another Stengel favorite, took over at second when Coleman went into the service after the 1951 season. Martin was a heady player, one who scratched and gouged for every advantage because he never felt he had the natural talent of some of the others.

"There has been a tendency to underrate Martin," Stengel once said. "Because he is scrawny, is no beauty with that big schnozz of his, and looks like he was underfed and weighs only 135 pounds. But he has been a strong factor in every club for which he has played. I defy anyone to knock Martin down as a great ballplayer. Can he make double plays? Will he fight, especially against big

odds? Will he come through when coming through means the most? You have to say yes to all three questions. They say I have been biased in favor of Martin because I gave him his first chance and nursed him along to be sold to the Yankees. Well, if liking a kid who will never let you down in the clutch is favoritism, then I plead guilty."

With Mantle, McDougald, and Martin playing important roles, the 1952 Yankees again won the pennant —finishing two games ahead of the Indians. They defeated the Dodgers in the Series when in the final game Martin made a spectacular running catch of a dangerous high pop-up with the bases loaded and two outs. The catch choked a last-gasp Dodger rally.

It was the superb Yankee pitching staff that helped make the difference. Whitey Ford was in the army, and it was again the trio of Raschi, Reynolds, and Lopat who led the young team to the flag.

Vic Raschi, the Springfield Rifle, was an earnest, intelligent, nononsense individual. A cold, humorless quality kept him at arm's length from strangers and reporters. On the mound his latent hostility ac-

tively simmered. He was grim and ornery, a frightening man to face. For seven years he was the most dependable man on the Yankee staff, between 1949 and 1953 compiling records of 21–10, 21–8, 21–10, 16–6, and 13–6.

Allie Reynolds, the Superchief, wasn't as mean as Raschi, but because he could throw a baseball as fast as Bob Feller, hitters were reluctant to dig in on him. Between 1949 and 1953 Reynolds, too, compiled a solid record of success: 17–6, 16–12, 17–8 with two no-hitters, 20–8 with a 2.06 ERA, and in 1953 13–7 with 13 saves in relief.

The third starter, Eddie Lopat, was one of the smartest pitchers to ever play the game. Lopat was bereft of a fast ball. The press called him "the Junkman," but he was combative, intelligent, and had exact control over his varied assortment of breaking pitches. His record during this period was 15–10, 18–8, 21–9, 10–5 with a 2.53 ERA, and 16–4 with a 2.42 ERA to lead the league.

After four years of close pennant races, the Yankees romped to the fifth one as the team of youngsters jelled. Ford returned from the army and won 18 games to augment the Big Three. Relief specialist Johnny Sain was 14–7 with 9 saves.

In May the Yankees won their last four games, and in June they won fourteen in a row more. After that it was a runaway, a tribute to the teaching and leadership of Manager Stengel, whose philosophies were reflected in the excellence on the field. Like Stengel, this team was multifaceted and imaginative. Stengel always preached that "ball games are lost, not won," and rarely did the Yankees make the mental mistakes that lose ball games.

After the final game victory against the Dodgers in the 1953 Series, reporters surrounded Martin, whose twelve hits, including the Series winner, earned him the Babe Ruth Award as the outstanding Series performer. "The Dodgers are the Dodgers," said bellicose Billy. "If they had had eight Babe Ruths, they couldn't have beaten us."

Vic Raschi

BROOKLYN DODGERS 1951-1956

BY LEONARD KOPPETT

Frustration, when fully satisfied at last, generates the most intense joy, which is why the Brooklyn Dodgers of the 1950s were the most beloved of all great baseball teams. They weren't the best in the history of baseball, or the most successful, or the most talented—although they ranked among the highest in those qualities too—but they were the most passionately appreciated by the largest number of people, far beyond the geographic confines of Brooklyn itself. Beloved is the right word.

The underlying reason for this was the team's unique ability to maintain an apparent contradiction: The Dodgers managed to remain underdogs while winning. To see how this was possible, we must recall the social climate, the baseball history, and the special circumstances of that time.

The racial question was a major part of the social atmosphere immediately after World War II. And it was fundamental to the Dodgers' popularity because it gave the team universality. The war years were perceived as the successful struggle against Hitler and his theories of Master Race. American society was openly acknowledging and repudiating its own antiblack racism for the first time. Jackie Robinson was a worldwide symbol of progress toward integration, and his presence on the Dodgers stirred the allegiance and interest of millions of people who otherwise might have taken the fortunes of any baseball team more casually.

But the Jackie Robinson story, in itself, belonged to the second half of the 1940s. It was no longer an issue, in those terms, for the 1950s.

The 1955 Dodgers bring first world title to Brooklyn:
First row (left to right): George Shuba, Don Zimmer, Joe Becker (coach), Jake Pitler (coach), Walter Alston (manager), Billy Herman (coach), Pee Wee Reese, Dixie Howell, Sandy Amoros, Roy Campanella.
Second row: John Griffen (clubhouse man), Carl Erskine, Sandy Koufax, Lee Scott, Roger Craig, Don Newcombe, Karl Spooner, Don Hoak, Carl Furillo, Frank Kellert, Doc Wendler.
Third row: Russ Meyer, Jim Gilliam, Billy Loes, Clem Labine, Gil Hodges, Ed Roebuck, Don Bessent, Duke Snider, Johnny Podres, Rube Walker, Jackie Robinson. Seated: Charlie DiGiovanna (batboy).

By that time the door he had opened had brought Roy Campanella, Don Newcombe, Joe Black, Jim Gilliam, and other black players to the Dodger uniform. The significance of the lowered racial barrier for the Dodgers then was that it was giving them championship players.

Dodger history leading up to these glorious years could be summed up in one word: frustration.

In 1941 a Dodger team under Leo Durocher had won a pennant for the first time in twenty-one years—only to be quashed by the Yankees in the World Series. The Dodgers finished in a tie for first—the first pennant tie in baseball history—in 1946, but lost the play-off two straight to the St. Louis Cardinals. Robinson played with the team for the first time in 1947, and the Dodgers won the pennant—only to lose the World Series again, to the Yankees, in seven eventful games.

The next year, in mid-season, Durocher—the ultimate Brooklyn Bum in the beloved sense—suddenly switched to the most hated rival, the New York Giants. The Dodgers finished a fairly strong third and began bringing together the players who would dominate the 1950s.

In 1949 they won another pennant, on the very last day of the season—only to be beaten again by the Yankees, in five games. And in 1950, with a chance to tie for first place on the final day of the season, they lost to Philadelphia in the tenth inning after missing golden opportunities to score in the ninth.

That was the heritage of near-miss, victory-short-of-the-ultimate, excellence-but-not-top-excellence, the Dodgers brought into 1951—when the greatest frustration of all would take place while, in an appropriately contradictory manner, the foundations for the final achievement were being laid.

By the time Walter O'Malley replaced Branch Rickey as chief officer and principal owner of the club following the 1950 season, the Dodgers had already fashioned an absolutely solid team at eight positions. Gil Hodges, huge, quiet, remarkably graceful, was at first base; Robinson was at second; Pee Wee Reese, who had been anchoring the infield since that first pennant of 1941, was at short; Billy Cox, a fantastic fielder, was at third; Duke Snider had become a star center fielder, and Carl Furillo was pure gold in right field, with an exceptional arm.

Few doubted that Roy Campanella was the best catcher in baseball. And the pitching staff was gilt-edged: Newcombe, Preacher Roe, Ralph Branca, and Carl Erskine to start, Clyde King to relieve. The one hole—left field, the only position not yet manned by an established star—was filled by Andy Pafko, an outstanding right-handed hitter, through a last-minute trade with the Chicago Cubs.

With all the pieces in place, the Dodgers really began to move. It wasn't long before cries of "break up the Dodgers" echoed through the National League.

The next four months, of course, became the most-told story of all baseball lore: the $13\frac{1}{2}$-game lead of mid-August of 1951 that disappeared in late September, the three-game play-off with the Giants and Bobby Thomson's ninth-inning home run off Branca (which sailed, by the way, over the head of the helpless Pafko).

But that most dramatic of all defeats also forged the greatness that followed. This truly outstanding collection of players responded by vowing never to let it happen again.

So the same team, in 1952, won the pennant by $4\frac{1}{2}$ games, and in 1953 by 13, winning 105 games that season. But each of those seasons ended with another World Series lost to the Yankees, the first in seven games and then in six. By now the whole world knew the sad statistic: No Brooklyn team had ever won the World Series.

But in 1955 the Dodgers ran away from the league and won by $13\frac{1}{2}$ games—and in a 2–0 seventh game pitched by Johnny Podres, defeated the Yankees in the World Series. The peak, at long last, had been attained. Walter Alston, who had been promoted to manager from

116

Brooklyn catcher Roy Campanella (kneeling) with four ace Dodger hurlers. They are (left to right): Ralph Branca, Carl Erskine, Preacher Roe and Clem Labine.

citizens of Brooklyn in their private lives.

Brooklyn fans *knew* their players and their personalities to an unprecedented degree. Reese, a slightly built man whose eyes crinkled when he smiled, was the elder statesman. He was the Kentuckian who made evident his acceptance of Robinson when such gestures were still a matter of significance. Snider, whose earliest records were set by striking out, had grown into the richest of baseball arguments: Did you prefer Snider or Willie Mays or Mickey Mantle?

Campanella, squat and garrulous, full of stories about the Negro Leagues, an implacable competitor beneath a jolly exterior; Furillo, often angry, not jovial at all, with the traditional Italian strong emotions; Newcombe, dominant and swaggering some years, struggling in others; Roe and Cox, "country boys," slicker than city slickers expected; Pafko, most simply summarized by the word "gentleman"; Erskine, the college-boy collar-ad type in appearance; Branca, never able to escape his identification but enormously successful as a person; it was not so much their individual qualities, but the depth to which their followers knew these qualities, that set the Dodgers apart.

Of course, performance was also a factor. The four pennants in five years (1952–56) the team won has only one parallel in National League history: the New York Giants, who won four straight in 1921–24. In those five Dodger years, the team won 484 games, exactly 200 more than they lost.

When you consider the team as a whole, it's no surprise that the Brooklyn Dodgers have inspired more literature than any baseball team other than—in a quite different context—the Black Sox of 1919. Other baseball teams, though very few of them, did compile better records than the Dodgers of the fifties; but none generated a richer collection of memories, more closely held by so many people.

the team's farm system in 1954, was no longer unknown.

The magic worked again in 1956 when the Dodgers, their stars aging, beat back the Milwaukee Braves and the Cincinnati Reds for a next-to-last-day victory. The World Series went to seven games again, against the Yankees again, and the Dodgers lost. But it didn't matter so much

then, not after the triumph of 1955.

The third and perhaps most important factor that made the Dodgers unique was the special relationship the team had with its fans. The players were very much a part of the community life of Brooklyn, in intimate daily contact with the fans because of the cozy structure of Ebbets Field, but also highly visible

The World Champion Bronx Bombers of 1962:
First Row (left to right): Whitey Ford, Bill Skowron, Roger Maris, Tom Tresh, Jim Hegan (coach), Frank Crosetti (coach), Ralph Houk (manager), Johnny Sain (coach), Wally Moses (coach), Clete Boyer, Mickey Mantle, Bobby Richardson, Yogi Berra.
Second row: Joe Soares (trainer), Bud Daley, Dale Long, Tony Kubek, Jim Bouton, Elston Howard, Bill Stafford, Tex Clevenger, Phil Linz, Don Seger (trainer), Bruce Henry (traveling secretary).
Third row: Luis Arroyo, Hector Lopez, Jack Reed, Bob Turley, John Blanchard, Marshall Bridges, Rollie Sheldon, Ralph Terry, Jim Coates, Spud Murray (batting practice pitcher)   Batboys (front): Fred Bengis and Frank Cammerata.

THE 1960-1964 YANKEES

BY PETER GOLENBOCK

For Yankee officials there followed a bitter winter of discontent after a dismal 1959 season during which the team had finished a distant third to the Chicago White Sox. Who to blame? Owners Topping and Webb considered firing Manager Casey Stengel despite his nine pennants in eleven tries. Stengel was seventy now, no longer patient with the youngsters, no longer as sharp as once he had been. General Manager George Weiss, personally humiliated by the sorry season, considered retirement.

Through that winter Weiss sought another power hitter. In December he landed one: Kansas City Athletics' right fielder Roger Maris.

Roger Maris. There was a star quality sound to it. And despite Maris' imperfect public image as a churlish villain, between the years 1960 and 1964, another five-year string of Yankee pennants, it was Maris, the American League's Most Valuable Player in 1960 and 1961, who was the catalyst.

During the spring of 1960 Maris hit with authority, leading the league in homers. "He has more power than Staleen," said Stengel.

With Maris, a lefty pull hitter sandwiched between sluggers Mantle and Moose Skowron, the Yankees were developing a Murderers' Row to challenge the legendary Yankee cast of the 1920s: Babe Ruth, Lou Gehrig, Lazzeri, and company. With some of the offensive responsibility lifted from the Mick's shoulders, he was more relaxed and was hitting better. By June the old Yankee enthusiasm, missing during the dismal 79–75 1959, had returned. "We're hungry again," exulted Moose Skowron. "We want to prove we're not a third-place club. Also, we sure missed that World Series check."

The pitching, so poor in '59, also improved markedly. Ford struggled with arm miseries, but underrated and little-noticed Art Ditmar buoyed it with fifteen wins. Bullet Bob Turley, Cy Young winner in '58 but a bust in '59, rebounded with a 9–3

Bobby Richardson, Bill Skowron and Tony Kubek.

record. It was three kids, though, the hope of the future, who were making the difference this year: Ralph Terry, a young strong-armed Yankee prospect shuttled to K. C. and then summoned back by Weiss, won ten games. Jim Coates was 13–3. A lean, hard-throwing good ole boy from the backwaters of Virginia, Coates was a mean headhunter on the mound. The third pitcher was Bill Stafford, tall, military-straight, and cocky, 6–1 after coming up in August. Stafford looked to be the

best rookie pitcher on the Yankees since Ford in 1950. For the bullpen in June Weiss added a potbellied, cigar-smoking minor-league screwball artist, Luis Arroyo. Arroyo won five games and saved seven more after coming to the Yankees from the Cincy Reds' Jersey City farm club. "Who'd ever think a guy like that would be lying around dead somewhere?" said Stengel.

The rejuvenated Yankees led the Baltimore Baby Birds by .002 percentage points with fifteen games left in the 1960 season. Then in one of the most stunning pennant drives on record, the Yankees won every last game, sprinting to the title.

Overlooked, the team's inner defense had become impregnable with the development of Bobby Richardson at second, Tony Kubek at shortstop, and youngster Clete Boyer at third. Richardson, the Quiet Man, was a devoutly religious athlete, a complete player who was admired for both his ability and his ethics. Between 1961 and 1966 he averaged over 175 hits a year, finishing second to Mantle in the MVP balloting in

1962. Between 1961 and 1965 he won the Gold Glove Award for second basemen. Equally tight-lipped, Tony Kubek was a boyish, awkward-looking string bean with a flattop crew cut who toiled efficiently in relative anonymity. Years after Stengel had left the Yankees he said of Kubek, "Who could be more valuable in fifty years of my life?" Boyer, starting his first year as a regular, was a magician, a vacuum cleaner who threw runners out from his knees with his cannon arm. Behind the plate Yogi Berra and Elston Howard were the best in baseball, and in the outfield Maris, Mantle, and Hector Lopez, a dependable clutch hitter, carried unmatched authority at the plate. Mantle's forty home runs led the league. Maris finished second with thirty-nine.

After winning the pennant, the Yankees drubbed the Pittsburgh Pirates in three games of the series, 16–3, 10–0, and 12–0 but were unable to win a fourth game, losing when Bill Mazeroski hit a ninth-inning home run over the ivy in left off Ralph Terry.

Mickey Mantle at bat—a frightening sight to opposing pitchers.

Two days after the Series ended, Topping held a press conference. Casey Stengel was being "retired." Quickly Casey made it clear he had been fired. "I'll never make the mistake of being seventy again," he said bitterly. Said Topping, "We were ridiculed when we hired him. Today when he is leaving, we are ridiculed again." One reporter called Stengel's dismissal "two millionaires' inhumanity to a fellow millionaire."

Two weeks later Weiss "retired." George Martin Weiss had been the Frank Lloyd Wright of the Yankee dynasty since 1932. He was humorless, impersonal, and dictatorial, but the short, paunchy, somber aristocrat had one of the great minds in the history of baseball management. When Weiss learned that his services with the Yankees were no longer required, he told reporters, "The Yankees have five more years at most." He was deadly accurate.

Though Weiss was gone, between 1961 and 1964 his backlog of talent assured the Yankees of four more seasons of pennant prosperity.

To manage the team Topping and Webb selected Yankee coach Ralph Houk. Stengel in his latter years had been caustic and harsh on his men. Houk chose to praise and encourage them. Under Houk the players were able to relax, and because he didn't believe in platooning, his starters felt more secure in their roles.

In late May of 1961 the team exploded into headlines. In one game against Boston Maris, Mantle, and Skowron each hit two home runs, and Berra hit another for a total of seven in one game! All season long the slugging continued, and attendance records were set wherever the Yankees played.

The Yankees ripped through challenging Detroit in early September to assure themselves of the 1961 pennant.

Never had there been a team with more power throughout the entire lineup as the 1961 Yankees. Richardson and Kubek were the advance men, runners to be driven in by the others: Maris (61 home runs, 142 RBIs), Mantle (54 home runs, 128 RBIs), Skowron (28 home runs,

89 RBIs), Berra (22 home runs), Elston Howard (21 home runs), John Blanchard (21 home runs including 4 in a row), and Clete Boyer (11 home runs). During 1961 the Yankees hit 240 round-trippers, breaking the old record of 221 set by the 1947 Giants and the 1956 Reds.

From the tenuous pitching staff held together by rookies in 1960, the 1961 staff was strong and deep. Houk did not believe in spotting his starters, so for the first time since he began pitching in 1950, Whitey Ford pitched every fourth or fifth day regardless of opponent or park. Ford finished 25–4, the Cy Young Award winner. Ralph Terry finished 16–3. Stafford was 14–9. Both Rollie Sheldon, a rookie promoted directly from Class D in the spring, and Coates were 11–5. In relief Arroyo finished 15–5 with 29 saves, most of them for Ford. Slugging, defense, pitching, this team had it all. The 1961 club was the apex of the modern Yankee dynasty.

Afterward it was downhill toward oblivion. The Yankees kept winning through 1964, but each year the hitting slackened, and the team's ability to win depended more and more on stout pitching and the defense of Joe Pepitone, Richardson, Kubek, Boyer, and Howard. In 1964 the Yankees won in a rush under rookie Manager Yogi Berra only with a late season addition of Mel Stottlemyre (9–3 with a 2.06 ERA since August) and because of the collapse of Baltimore and Chicago.

After 1964 the impregnable fortress crumbled. Maris, Howard, and Jim Bouton were seriously impaired. Kubek retired at age twenty-nine. Then Richardson quit at age thirty-two. Finally the deluge. Maris, Boyer, and Howard were traded for players who produced little. Whitey Ford suffered from circulation blockage in his pitching arm and had to quit. Only a heroic, one-legged Mantle remained as a regal reminder of the Glory Days. Like the fall of Rome, the Yankee collapse had been swift and complete. The Yankees have not won a pennant since.

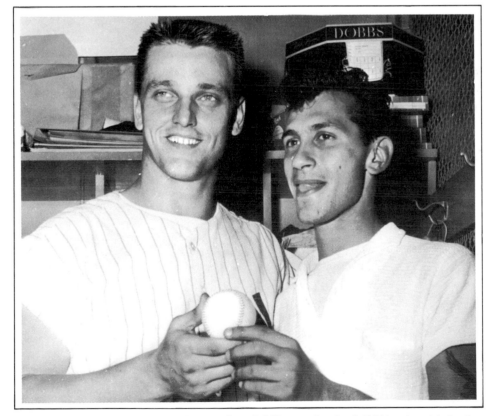

Roger Maris poses with Sal Durante, the man who etched his name into baseball history by retrieving the ball Maris hit for his record-breaking 61st home run in 1961.

THE BALTIMORE ORIOLES 1969-1971

BY JOE REICHLER

When the Baltimore Orioles won their first World Series in 1966, Personnel Director Harry Dalton deftly sidestepped the talk of a possible dynasty which shadows every winner. "You can't anticipate dynasties," Dalton said. "You can only recognize them after they happen. We have a chance for a dynasty if we can put together consecutive championships, or be in a race strongly every year and win more than our share of league championships."

Well, with the Orioles playing in four World Series in six years, with them winning five titles in the American League Eastern Division (including three straight in 1969–70–71), who can deny them their place as one of the great teams?

The Orioles' so-called dynasty had its roots in the late 1950s with the proliferation of its farm system. It began to come of age on American League playing fields with two near misses in 1960 and 1964. But it took a major deal to "put it all together," and that, of course, was the trade in which Baltimore acquired Cincinnati's Frank Robinson in return for Milt Pappas, the Orioles' biggest winner, and two off-season acquisitions—Jack Baldschun and Dick Simpson.

In his first season with Baltimore, Frank Robinson won the Triple Crown, the first player to do so since Mickey Mantle ten years earlier. Frank also garnered the American League and World Series MVP awards. He hit 49 homers and drove in 122 runs with a .316 average. Frank had lots of help from Boog Powell, the powerful first baseman (34 homers and 109 RBIs), and Brooks Robinson, the impeccable third baseman, who despite a second-half slump, hit 23 home runs and had

A World Championship for Baltimore—the 1970 Orioles:
First row: (left to right) Tom Phoebus, Don Buford, Jim Frey, Bill Hunter (coach), Earl Weaver (manager), George Bamberger (coach), George Staller (coach), Dave McNally, Chico Salmon.
Second row: Clay Reid (equipment manager), Andy Etchebarren, Boog Powell, Pete Richert, Mark Belanger, Dave Leonhard, Brooks Robinson, Elrod Hendricks, Merv Rettenmund, Dave Johnson, Eddie Watt, Ralph Salvon (trainer).
Third row: Marcelino Lopez, Jim Palmer, Moe Drabowsky, Frank Robinson, Mike Cuellar, Dick Hall, Bobby Grich, Curt Motton, Terry Crowley, Paul Blair. Seated in front: Jay Mazzone (Batboy).

100 RBIs.

Tight defense, long a Baltimore trademark, was tighter than ever in 1966 with an infield composed of Powell, rookie Dave Johnson at second, Luis Aparicio at short, and Brooks Robinson, the best in the league.

The Orioles had four young starters and four veterans on their pitching staff. The rotation included Steve Barber (age: 27), Dave McNally, (23), Wally Bunker (21), and Jim Palmer (20), while the bullpen was comprised of Stu Miller, Eddie Fisher, Moe Drabowsky, and Dick Hall. Barber and Bunker developed sore arms toward the latter part of the season, making the Orioles' four-game sweep of the Dodgers in that year's World Series all the more remarkable. After relief ace Drabowsky was credited with a victory in the first game, Jim Palmer, Wally Bunker, and Dave McNally hurled successive shutouts to stun the Dodger supporters.

The next two years were hardly illustrious as the Birds slipped to sixth in 1967 and finished second in 1968. After the '68 season, the Orioles added veteran pitcher Mike Cuellar to the staff—acquiring him from Houston for Curt Blefary—and things immediately began to improve. Both Cuellar and McNally became 20-game winners. Palmer registered 16–4, despite forty-two days on the disabled list in mid-season.

Boog Powell drove in 121 runs and Frank Robinson had an even 100. Paul Blair helped the cause with 102 runs and 76 RBIs while lead-off man Don Buford drove in 64 and scored 99 times.

The magic was back as the Birds won 109 times and then swept the American League Championship Series (the first ever played) three games straight over the Minnesota Twins. The season ended on the downbeat, however, when the team lost the five-game World Series to the New York Mets.

In 1970 the Orioles roared back to win 108 games, swept the Twins again in the ALCS, then beat the Reds four out of five to win their second World Championship. Palmer joined McNally and Cuellar as a 20-game winner, and Boog Powell, with 114 RBIs and 35 homers, won the American League's Most Valuable Player Award.

The O's took longer to get to the top in 1971. It wasn't until June 5 that they overtook the Boston Red Sox, and there was a bit of a scare late in the season when the Detroit Tigers pulled within five games on September 18. But then the Birds took off on another end-of-the-season

The unmatched glove-work of Brooks Robinson.

123

All-Star righthander Jim Palmer.

eleven-game winning streak (as they had done in 1971). This time the streak was extended to sixteen straight by virtue of yet another three-game sweep of the ALCS— at Oakland's expense—and victories in the first two games of the World Series against Pittsburgh.

By winning 101 games in 1971 the Orioles became only the third team in history to crack the 100 mark three years in a row. The others were the 1929–30–31 A's and the 1942–43–44 Cardinals.

That year, for the second time in baseball history, one pitching staff produced four 20-game winners: Dave McNally, Mike Cuellar, Jim Palmer, and Pat Dobson. Only the White Sox quartet of 1920 (fifty-one years earlier) composed of Red Faber, Claude Williams, Dickie Kerr, and Ed Cicotte had ever accomplished that feat before.

After winning the first two games of the Series against the Pirates, the Birds dropped three in a row at Three Rivers Stadium. They returned to win the sixth game in one of the most exciting finishes in club history, then lost to Steve Blass in the seventh game, 2–1.

Frank Robinson won the Triple Crown as an Oriole in 1966.

124

OAKLAND A's 1972-1974

BY LEONARD KOPPETT

Only three times in baseball history has a team been able to win as many as three World Series in a row. The New York Yankees of 1936–39 won four straight, and the Yankees of 1949–53 won five straight.

Then, in 1972, 1973, and 1974, the Oakland A's did it.

Their creator, of course, was Charles Oscar Finley, who took pride eventually in serving as his own general manager and who acquired the team—in Kansas City, in 1961—

when it was a perennial tailender. By hiring an unending stream of first-class baseball brains as scouts and managers and farm directors, Finley started building. He succeeded in signing some outstanding college players (when the free-agent draft was just starting) and subsequently maintained a high level of new young talent. At the same time, he proved to be especially astute in making good trades.

The very force of Finley's per-

sonality and his constant presence in the limelight through conflicts with his players, his managers, other clubs, and the public helped obscure, at first, the achievements of his team.

And the A's faced conditions that earlier legendary teams did not. To win a pennant, the A's had to win a three-of-five play-off no matter how well they did during the regular 162-game schedule. No other "dynasty" faced that hazard. And, in fact, the

The mod A's of 1973, champions of baseball.
First row: (left to right) Reggie Jackson, Catfish Hunter, Pat Bourque, Ron Pieraldi (batboy), Dick Green, Vic Davalillo and Bill North.
Second row: Bert Campaneris, Vida Blue, Paul Lindblad, Jerry Adair (coach), Vern Hoscheit (coach), Dick Williams (manager), Irv Noren (coach), Wes Stock (coach), Sal Bando and Gene Tenace.
Third row: Trainer Joe Romo, Traveling Secretary Jim Bank, Angel Mangual, Jesus Alou, Joe Rudi, John Odom, Mike Andrews, Ted Kubiak and equipment manager Frank Ciensczyk.
Fourth row: Horacio Pina, Ken Holtzman, Deron Johnson, Rollie Fingers, Billy Conigliaro, Ray Fosse, Darold Knowles, and Allan Lewis.

A's did finish in first place five years in a row; but in 1971 they lost a play-off to Baltimore and in 1975 to Boston, ending their reign.

They had two managers: Dick Williams, who took over in 1971 after Finley had used about a manager a year for a decade, and who won the first two championships with them; and Alvin Dark, who moved in after Williams resigned and won the 1974 championship. That in itself is a rarity in "dynasties."

Six every-day players were the backbone of their lineup through the three championship years:

Reggie Jackson, right fielder, home run hitter, fine base runner, and the charismatic spokesman for "the Swingin' A's."

Sal Bando, third baseman, power hitter, team captain.

Joe Rudi, left fielder with exceptional defensive skill and a power hitter.

Dagoberto "Campy" Campaneris, shortstop, who shone as a base-stealer and consistent hitter as well as defensively.

Dick Green, second baseman, who sealed the infield so well that his offensive weakness was easily carried.

Gene Tenace, catcher and first baseman, another home run hitter.

That meant that there was change at only two positions: center field and either first base or catcher.

In 1972 Jackson played center sometimes, Angel Mangual at others, with Matty Alou winding up in right field. Mike Epstein played first, Dave Duncan caught, and at the end Tenace, who had been platooning at first, took over behind the plate.

In 1973 and 1974 Billy North, acquired from the Chicago Cubs, became the regular center fielder, and Jackson settled back in right. Tenace played first base all of 1973, with Ray Fosse, acquired from Cleveland, the regular catcher. But in 1974, when Fosse was injured for a long time, Tenace went back to catching, Rudi moved to first base, and another brilliant newcomer, Claudell Washington, moved into the outfield.

In those two years, the designa-

Homerun slugger Reggie Jackson typified the A's spirit in the early 1970's.

126

ted hitter had entered the American League, too. In 1973, it was mostly Deron Johnson, another powerful right-handed hitter; in 1974 Johnson was traded away early in the season, and Mangual or Washington usually filled that slot.

Here was a team with terrific home run power, great speed on the bases, outstanding defense and versatility. But its true strength was pitching.

There were three superb starters: Jim "Catfish" Hunter, Ken Holtzman, and Vida Blue. Hunter, starting in 1971, won 21 games three years in a row and upped that to 25 in 1974. Holtzman, a left-hander already established with the Cubs before Finley traded Rick Monday for him after the 1971 season, won 19, 21, and 19 the next three years. And Blue, the sensation of baseball as a rookie in 1971, was a holdout for half of 1972, but won 20 games in 1973 and 17 in 1974.

Behind them, even better, were relief pitchers of quality and depth. Right-handed Rollie Fingers was the key. In the three seasons, he appeared in 203 regular-season games, getting 27 victories and 61 saves. Left-handed relieving was done by Darold Knowles and Paul Lindblad, while Bob Locker was Fingers' partner in 1972.

Both Williams and Dark were masters of manipulating pitching staffs, and used relief pitchers early and often.

In 1971 the A's won 101 games and finished far ahead in the Western Division, but the more experienced Orioles beat them in three straight in the play-off. In 1972 the divisional race involved a challenge from the Chicago White Sox, and the A's had to go five games to get past the Detroit Tigers. They were underdogs in the World Series, but beat Cincinnati in seven games (as Tenace equaled a Series record by hitting four home runs).

In 1973 Kansas City was the team that had to be beaten off in the regular season, and the play-off with Baltimore also went the limit of five games. So did the World Series,

Vida Blue was both the American League's Most Valuable Player and Cy Young Award winner in 1971.

127

Rollie Fingers, one of baseball's great relief pitchers and the owner of the game's most celebrated moustache.

against the surprising New York Mets, and the A's had to win the last two games at home to make it.

In 1974, under Dark, the team sputtered much of the season, but rose to late challenges by Kansas City and Texas, and polished off Baltimore in four games. It reached its peak in the World Series, beating the Los Angeles Dodgers in five.

And all through 1975, the goal was a fourth straight World Championship. The A's finished first again easily enough, but were snuffed out by the Red Sox in the play-off, abruptly ending that dream.

While all this was happening in actual games, the A's habitually made more news off the field. Finley never hesitated to use plain language, in public or in private (and his

phone calls were legend). His salary disputes with players, detailed instructions to managers, conflicts with the commissioner, and suggested innovations constantly made news. His players, picking up the cue, were just as outspoken about their disagreements with him—and about everything else.

An argument between Williams and Epstein, on the eve of the 1972 Series, led to Epstein's departure. Blue's bitterness toward Finley never diminished. During the 1973 Series, there was a storm when Finley tried to have Mike Andrews, whose errors had just led to a defeat, placed on the injured list.

By that time, Williams had already decided to leave, although his contract still had two years to run.

He announced his "retirement" as soon as the Series was over, but when he then tried to join the Yankees, Finley took legal action to block him. And it wasn't until spring training was about to start that Finley hired Dark, who had managed the A's in Kansas City under him and had been fired in 1967.

The A's seemed to thrive on such controversy, but one proved destructive. Hunter, finding that Finley was not observing the letter of his contract about deferred income, took his case to arbitration and was declared a free agent at the end of the 1974 season. He accepted an offer from the Yankees, and the A's had nothing to show for his departure. They finished first anyhow, but his absence from the play-off certainly made Boston's task easier and probably hastened the end of the dynasty.

But it was a remarkable collection of players that Finley brought together. Jackson, Bando, and Monday (for whom Holtzman was obtained) were products of Coach Bobby Winkles at Arizona State at Tempe (and Winkles, after being replaced by Williams as manager of the California Angels halfway through 1974, wound up as a coach with the A's). Campaneris, Rudi, Tenace, Duncan, Green, Hunter, Blue, Fingers, and Lindblad were "home-grown" in the farm system Finley developed. They formed a group with few inhibitions, awareness of the outside world, and enormous confidence in their talent under pressure. They won big games, rather than compile big statistics. And they led the way into the hirsute era by growing moustaches in connection with one of Finley's promotions, and keeping them long afterward.

Among the things that did not get recognized about them was their lineage, that they were direct descendants of the Athletics of Philadelphia, who had been so prominent in so many baseball eras. But these A's—the name Finley preferred—had a balance of skills and competitiveness the equal of any, and belong on any list of "great teams."

UNFORGETTABLE MOMENTS

**Introduction By
JOE REICHLER**

Of all our sports, Baseball is the most distinguished by the number of its remarkable happenings that our memories preserve. They could be simple, sudden, instant incidents or continuous innings of suspenseful action or a series of game-gripping gatherings of diamond history. These memories accumulate over the years, yielding a full feast of recollection for the Baseball lover's memory bank.

The author has not enjoyed the privilege of witnessing first hand all the "Most Memorable Moments" recounted in this book but their visions as well as memories are worth recapturing for the pleasure of the young and the old who make up this remarkable being called the Baseball Fan.

These "Most Memorable Moments" are not merely great Baseball stories; they are the greatness of Baseball, the legends that have made the players the best remembered of all athletes and the game of Baseball the national pastime.

Merkle's Boner
September 23, 1908

Opinions differ on just who was to blame for what happened on September 23, 1908, and the principal characters involved never did agree on who did what, when, and where. But this much is clear: The New York Giants lost the National League pennant to the Chicago Cubs on a technicality that year, and a nineteen-year-old player named Fred Merkle acquired a nickname that clung to him for the rest of his life—Bonehead! To this day whenever a player commits a mental error on the base paths, it is referred to as a "Merkle."

Johnny Evers, the Cubs brainy little second baseman, may or may not have engineered the affair. But it is a fact that, intentionally or not, he laid the groundwork for it earlier that month when the Cubs faced the Pirates on September 4.

It was the last of the tenth. The score was 0–0 with two out. The Pirates had the bases loaded when Chief Wilson came to bat and singled to center field, scoring the winning run. But Pirate rookie Warren Gill failed to run to second base. As was the custom of the day whenever one runner scored the winning run, the other men on base would simply head for the clubhouse. And that's exactly what Gill did.

Second baseman Evers, however, had other plans. Quickly he called for the ball from outfielder Artie Hofman, touched second, and asked umpire Hank O'Day to rule it a force play. That would give Chicago the third out and nullify the Pirate's run. O'Day refused. And when the Cubs lodged an official protest the next day, the umpire testified that he was so preoccupied with the runner crossing home plate that he didn't see whether or not Gill touched second.

O'Day added that if the play should ever occur again, he would watch for it and call it. The Cubs lost the game, but the stage had been set.

The three-way race for the flag between the Pirates, Giants, and Cubs was still neck and neck when New York and Chicago met in the Polo Grounds on September 23. And as luck would have it, umpire Hank O'Day was behind the plate again with umpire Bob Emslie on the bases.

The bottom of the ninth found the Giants at bat with the score knotted at 1–1. There were two out, with Moose McCormick on second, when Fred Merkle came up to bat. Merkle, playing only because the Giants regular first baseman, Fred Tenney, awoke that morning with a backache, singled to send McCormick to third. Al Bridwell, the next hitter, singled to center, driving in McCormick for the winning run. Or so it appeared to the joyful fans who, believing the game was over, mobbed the field.

Merkle, heading for second, suddenly veered off course and sprinted for the clubhouse as soon as he saw McCormick touch the plate. And that was just what Johnny Evers was waiting for. He called for the ball.

From that point on no two persons had the same version of what actually happened. Evers claimed that the ball came in over his head and ended up in the hands of Giants Coach Joe McGinnity, who, realizing what Evers had in mind, tossed it into the crowd. Chicago pitcher Floyd Kroh grabbed it and tossed it to Tinker who flipped it to Evers. "I stepped on the bag and made sure that O'Day saw me," Evers said. "'The run does not count,' O'Day announced and walked away. Base umpire Bob Emslie refused to take a stand."

John McGraw, the Giants manager, gave an entirely different story that had the ball being thrown into the left-field bleachers and Evers grabbing one of the spare balls from O'Day's pocket to make the play.

In his official report to National League President Harry Pulliam, umpire O'Day agreed with Evers' version.

The next day the game was officially ruled a tie. Giants President John T. Brush appealed to the N.L. Board of Directors. He even presented a notarized affidavit from Merkle claiming that he had indeed touched second. But the ruling stood.

Should the season end in a tie between the two teams, a play-off was ordered to be held on October 8, the day after the regular season ended. The 1908 season did end in a Giants-Cubs deadlock. With 35,000 on hand, the Cubs, with Mordecai Brown pitching brilliantly in relief of Jack Pfeister, outpitched a weary Christy Mathewson, 4–2, giving the Cubs their third successive National League pennant.

Walter Johnson's Most Gratifying Victory — The World Series That Was Lost By a Pebble, October 10, 1924

For eighteen years Walter Johnson waited to get into the World Series. The pitcher generally recognized as the greatest of them all finally got his chance when the Washington Senators, of whom it had been said "First in war, first in peace, but last in the American League," captured their first pennant in 1924.

Walter was in the evening of his career, thirty-seven years old, and getting so he'd tire in the late innings. His fast one was a shade slower than in other years, and he needed more rest between starts. So perhaps it wasn't surprising that Johnson lost the first game to John McGraw's New York Giants, 4–3 in twelve innings. He tried again in the fifth game and lost that one, 6–2. That was it. There would be no more chances. His hopes of ever pitching a World Series victory appeared ended even though the Senators fought back valiantly to deadlock the Series at three games each.

The Senators knew that if they were to win the seventh game, they'd have to find a way to neutralize Bill Terry, the Giants' leading hitter in the Series (.429). Fortunately, Washington player-manager Bucky Harris had a plan. He knew that Terry hit right-handed pitching best. So he started the game with right-hander Curly Ogden, only to switch to southpaw George Mogridge after two batters. The end result was Terry's removal from the lineup in the sixth inning.

There was still rough water ahead, though, and the eighth inning saw the Senators trailing the Giants, 3–1. Then Bucky Harris singled to drive in two runs knotting the score at 3–3.

Harris got a big ovation, but it was nothing compared to what happened a few minutes later when the delirious fans saw Walter Johnson come in to pitch in the ninth. Over 31,000 fans, President Calvin Coolidge among them, stood up and cheered and cheered. Utter strangers were hugging each other in the stands because Walter, the "Big Train," was getting one more chance in the Series. It was his ball game now.

"I didn't have much confidence in myself," Johnson recalled later. "I was pretty far gone after pitching and losing two games. Bucky must have noticed the look on my face when he handed me the ball. 'You're the best we've got, Walter,' he said. 'We've got to win or lose with you.' "

Johnson was in trouble from the start. Frankie Frisch tripled with one out and Ross Youngs walked.

But Walter bore down and struck out George Kelly and then retired Irish Meusel on a fly. The Giants put at least one man on base in each of the tenth, eleventh, and twelfth innings, but Walter was able to call upon his reserve to hold them in check. The only trouble was that the Senators couldn't seem to score.

It was still 3–3 when New York's Jack Bentley took the mound in the bottom of the twelfth. He retired the first batter and looked as if he had the second one, too, when Muddy Ruel lifted a pop in back of the plate. Hank Gowdy, the Giant catcher, reached for it but stepped on his mask, stumbled, and dropped the ball.

Given a reprieve, Ruel doubled to left. Harris allowed Johnson to hit for himself, and the veteran pitcher was safe when Travis Jackson fumbled his grounder to short. That brought up Earl McNeely. The rookie outfielder bounced one sharply but right towards the waiting glove of third baseman Freddy Lindstrom—almost. Fate intervened, for just as Lindstrom was setting himself to field the ball, it hit a pebble and bounced over his head.

"I turned and saw Ruel crossing the plate," Johnson remembered. "Tears were in my eyes. We'd won. I'd won. I felt so happy that it didn't seem real. They told me later that President Coolidge kept watching me all the way into the clubhouse.

"Later Mrs. Johnson and I slipped away to a quiet little restaurant where I used to eat on Vermont Avenue, and you know that before we were through with our dinner, two hundred telegrams had been delivered there."

Grover Cleveland Alexander Fans Tony Lazzeri
October 10, 1926

It was the seventh inning of the seventh game of the 1926 World Series. Grover Cleveland Alexander, better known as Pete or Alex or, in light of his nearly forty years, the Old Man, came out of the bullpen and approached the pitcher's mound by way of the circle route. He veered, sort of walking sideways, as though he might be going over to take a seat in the left-field box. Then he oriented himself and came on, walking slowly, as if strolling along a country lane, toward the center of the diamond. His Cardinal-billed cap rode high on top of his head, too small and looking somewhat as if he might have borrowed it from a kid in a corner lot.

It has been said that the Old Man *was* feeling the effects of a previous evening's celebration on that fateful Sunday afternoon, October 10, 1926, at Yankee Stadium. It has also been denied by the main people involved: the Old Man and Rogers Hornsby, his manager. Be that as it may, Alex himself did admit that after having gained his second victory of the Series over the Yankees the day before, he had visited a midtown tavern and stayed there quite late into the night. And it *is* true that the Old Man was catching up on his sleep in the bullpen the next day.

Jesse "Pop" Haines had pitched the Cards to a 3–1 lead going into the seventh, but then his knuckles started to bleed from the constant use of the knuckle ball. When Haines allowed one run and then walked Lou Gehrig, Hornsby signaled to the bullpen. Art Reinhart, the left-hander, started in, but Hornsby sent him back, signaling for a right-hander. Herman Bell, the right-hander, pushed open the gate and was coming in, but the Rajah waved him back, too.

That left only the Old Man, who hadn't warmed up at all. But Hornsby knew that in a spot like that he needed the very best and that meant only one thing: Grover Cleveland Alexander.

When Alex arrived at the mound, Hornsby handed him the ball and said, "Pete, there are three men on base." Alex looked toward first. He looked toward second. He looked toward third. "I'll be damned if you're not right," he drawled. Then, gesturing toward the batter, "There's no place to put this fellow. I guess I'd better strike him out."

It was the last of the seventh. The bases were loaded. There were two out. The score was St. Louis 3, New York 2. And that "fellow" at bat happened to be "Push-'Em-Up" Tony Lazzeri, one of the most feared sluggers in baseball.

Lazzeri was a high-ball hitter, and all during the Series Alex had pitched him low. But this time Tony went into an unnatural crouch and Alex pitched him high. Lazzeri was so surprised that he let it go for a strike. Then Alex wheeled in another high one and the crowd let out a roar. Tony had gotten hold of it and sent a screamer into the left-field seats. But the ball curved foul at the last instant and missed being a grand-slam homer by several feet.

Alex then threw a wicked curve on the outside. Umpire George Hildebrand called it a ball. Alex walked slowly to the plate. "What was the matter with that?" he asked quietly. "It was a quarter of an inch outside," said the umpire. "Okay," Alex replied, "I'll make sure the next one isn't." True to his word, Alex fanned Lazzeri on the next pitch.

St. Louis went on to win the Series when, with Alexander pitching three up and three down in the eighth and striking out two in the ninth, Babe Ruth tried to steal second, only to be easily put out by Rogers Hornsby.

Babe Ruth
Calls His Shot
October 1, 1932

Old-timers are still arguing whether or not Babe Ruth really "called his shot" when he hit that dramatic home run off Chicago Cub pitcher Charlie Root in the third game of the New York Yankees' four-game sweep of the 1932 World Series. Ruth always insisted that he did. Root, on the other hand, was equally adamant that he didn't. So bitter was he that he refused to play himself in the Hollywood film about the Babe, claiming that it was not a premeditated home run.

Historians estimate that Ruth hit over 1,000 home runs, if you include the 15 in World Series competition and some 300 in various exhibition games. But the one that gave the Babe the biggest kick was that home run off Root, the last one he ever hit in World Series play.

The Babe was talking about it shortly before he died in August 1948. "Nobody but a blankety-blank fool would have done what I did that day," he said. "I could have struck out just as well as not because I was mad and made up my mind to swing at the next pitch if I could reach it with a bat. Boy, when I think of the good breaks in my life, this was one of 'em."

There was a bitter feeling in this World Series because Mark Koenig, whom the Yankees had traded to the Cubs, was voted only half a share by the Chicago players. The Yankee bench jockeys were really on the Cubs for being "cheap" and the Cubs retaliated by putting the needle to Ruth.

The Series didn't last long, but it was a honey. Pat Malone and Burleigh Grimes, who didn't talk like Sunday school graduates, outdid themselves in thinking up insults to shout at Ruth. But they didn't help because the Yankees won both the games played in New York and moved to Chicago for the next two. By this time, the Cubs were fit to be tied. Ruth had never played in Wrigley Field before, but in batting practice he hit nine balls into the bleachers. Observing several Cubs standing around with their mouths open, he yelled derisively: "I'd play for half my salary if I could hit in this dump all my life."

When the Babe came up for the first time, Andy Lotshaw, the Cubs trainer, waved a towel at him and yelled: "If I had you on my team, I'd hitch you to a wagon, you big balloon belly." Ruth responded by getting hold of one with two men on and parking it into the stands for a three-run lead. But the Cubs had come back when the Babe came up again in the fifth, with the score tied at 4–4. Again came the cries of "Big Belly" and "Balloon Head" from the Cubs bench. Ruth

got them even madder by giving them the choke sign—the thumb and finger at the windpipe. That's when the the Babe decided to go for broke.

As Root got ready to pitch, Ruth turned to Gabby Hartnett, the catcher, and said, "If that bum throws one in here, I'll hit it over the fence again."

Root's first two pitches were called strikes by umpire Roy Van Graflan. After the first strike Ruth held up one finger. After the second one he held up two fingers. And then he pointed dramatically toward the bleachers in right center.

"I want to set one thing straight," Ruth said. "I didn't exactly point to any spot, I just sorta waved at the whole fence, but that was foolish enough. As long as I'd called the first two strikes on myself, I had to go through with it. I felt pretty sure Root would put one close enough for me to cut at. All I wanted was to give that thing a ride—outa the park—anywhere. It was silly but I got away with it."

Root wound up and let go a fast one. Ruth swung. The ball disappeared precisely where he had pointed. "I knew it was gone when I hit it," Ruth remembered. "You can feel it in your hands when you've laid good wood on one. How the mob howled. Me? I was just laughing to myself and thinking what a lucky bum I was. I called a homer and got away with it."

Root saw it differently, of course. "Sure, the Babe gestured me," he acknowledged. "He challenged me to lay the ball in. After I had gotten the first strike over, Babe pointed to me and yelled: 'That's only one strike.' Maybe I had a smug look on my face after he took the second strike. Babe stepped out of the box again, pointed his finger in my direction, and yelled: 'You still need one more, kid.'

"I guess I should have wasted the next pitch and I thought Ruth figured I would, too. I decided to try to cross him up. The ball was gone as soon as Ruth swung. It occurred to me then that the people in the stands would think he had been pointing to the bleachers. But that's the way it was."

The people in the bleachers could not hear Babe's laughter as he rounded the bases. But they couldn't help seeing him stop on third, turn to the Cubs bench, and extend an exaggerated low bow. The Cubs had run out of taunts. There wasn't a single response.

Carl Hubbell
Fans Five
Immortals
In Succession
July 10, 1934

Carl Hubbell, the slender southpaw who pitched the New York Giants to three pennants in five years, performed a feat on July 10, 1934, no other pitcher can boast of: He struck out, in rapid succession, five of the most feared hitters who ever lived and missed adding a sixth by a single pitch. The five were Babe Ruth, Lou Gehrig, Jimmie Foxx, Al Simmons, and Joe Cronin—Hall of Famers all.

The event took place at the All-Star Game before nearly 50,000 fans at New York's Polo Grounds. As Hubbell took the mound for the National League, both he and everyone else knew that the American League, which had won the inaugural All-Star Game the year before, was a heavy favorite to win.

Charlie Gehringer was first up. He singled on the first pitch and took second on Wally Berger's error. Hubbell had made only one pitch and already the American League had a man on second base. Pitching carefully to Heinie Manush, Hub walked him on a 3–2 count.

Catching for the National League was Gabby Hartnett. He halted the game, removed his mask, and walked toward the pitcher's box. "Look, Hub," admonished the Cub catcher, "never mind all that junk about being careful and pitching this way or that way. Just throw that thing. It'll get 'em out. It always got me out!"

"That thing," of course, was Hubbell's screwball, an unnatural delivery in which he twisted his arm backward and let the ball go from the side of his hand.

Ruth strode to the plate. Hubbell threw him four screwballs. Strike one called. Ball one. Strike two swinging. Strike three called. Ruth couldn't believe it. He said something indistinguishable to umpire Cy Pfirman, who just repeated "Strike Three." The Babe then turned to say something to Hartnett, who just laughed and tossed the ball back to Hubbell.

Gehrig was next. It took Hub six pitches to strike him out, but Gehrig got his money's worth, swinging at all three strikes. On the third strike, Gehringer and Manush worked a double steal, but Hubbell appeared unconcerned.

As Gehrig passed Foxx in the batting circle he whispered: "You might as well get your cuts. It won't get any higher." It was true, but Foxx at least got a foul before returning to the bench.

The crowd, which had been roaring on every strike, gave King Carl a standing ovation as he strode off the mound. In the National League half, Frankie Frisch, leading off, hit a home run and Hubbell was ahead.

Simmons was first up in the second inning. Hubbell fanned him on four pitches. Next came Cronin. He, too, was whiffed on four. Then Bill Dickey came to bat. Strike one; ball one; strike two; the third pitch—*bingo!*—Dickey singled to left.

"I got a little inside," explained Hubbell, "but it was a legitimate hit."

Lefty Gomez went down swinging on three pitches.

It was a demonstration of pitching never equaled before or since. Five straight strikeouts is unusual at any time, but the man they called the Meal Ticket had mowed down the flower and power of the American League—Ruth, Gehrig, Foxx, Simmons, and Cronin—with only one, Foxx, able to even hit a foul off him. In all five instances Carl Hubbell's screwball was the pitch that did them in.

Johnny Vander Meer's Back-to-Back No-Hitters
June 11-15, 1938

Perhaps the greatest pitching feat in all baseball history was the two successive no-hit, no-run games hurled by Johnny Vander Meer of the Cincinnati Reds in 1938. This fantastic display took place within a period of five days and involved a twenty-three-year-old pitcher who, at the start of that season, was not sure he would be permitted to wear a big-league uniform.

A poor 3–5 record in 1937 did not deter Manager Bill McKechnie from seeing his potential and from working with him to change his motion from part side-arm to overhand. Never a master of control, Johnny became even wilder. Fortunately, Lefty Grove, the great left-hander, watched him during an exhibition game, took an interest in him, and gave him some pointers. With the faith of McKechnie and the help of Grove, Vander Meer improved.

The first of the two famous games took place on Saturday June 11, when Vander Meer pitched his way into the Hall of Fame by handcuffing the Boston Bees 3–0 without a hit. Only three men reached first, all on walks, and not one advanced to second. Two of the base runners were picked off base by the unerring arm of catcher Ernie Lombardi. In his first full season in the majors, Vander Meer had pitched the first no-hit game in the National League since Paul Dean did it for the St. Louis Cardinals in 1934.

Four days later, the Reds met the Brooklyn Dodgers at Ebbets Field for the first night game in Brooklyn's major-league history. The park was filled to capacity, and, while nobody expected the left-hander to pitch a second no-hitter, there was a healthy curiosity as to how long he could continue the string of hitless innings.

The crowd gave Vander Meer a warm cheer when he walked to the mound for his last warm-up pitches. Then, when the game began, they gave him the traditional Brooklyn razzing reserved for opposing pitchers. No-hitter or not, this guy was trying to beat their beloved Bums and he had to be given the full treatment.

When Vander Meer mowed down the Dodger hitters with a blazing fast ball, the atmosphere of carefree excitement turned to one of tense, tingling anticipation. Vandy pitched the Reds through six perfect innings and a 5–0 lead before walking Cookie Lavagetto and Dolph Camilli in the seventh. By then, even the Dodger fans were rooting for him. Vander Meer succeeded in pitching out of the hole caused by the two walks and set down three more Brooklyn hitters in the eighth.

The air was charged with electricity as Vandy walked to the mound in the bottom of the ninth. He got Buddy Hassett on a grounder for the first out. But his terrific speed veered out of control and he walked Babe Phelps, Lavagetto, and Camilli, filling the bases.

All nerves were taut as he faced Ernie Koy, a right-handed slugger. With a 1–1 count, Koy grounded to third base and the putout was made at home plate for a force play. A single out remained as Leo Durocher came to bat. The crowd groaned when Leo sent a screeching liner past first base. It was barely foul. Vander Meer shuddered, the perspiration pouring off him as he stood out there on the mound. Johnny took a deep breath and fired another fast ball. Leo swung and the ball arched lazily toward short center field where Harry Craft camped under it for the putout, which brought a 6–0 victory to the Reds and lasting fame to Johnny Vander Meer.

Gabby Hartnett's "Home Run In The Dark" September 28, 1938

On September 28, 1938 a home run was hit that very few people saw. It didn't only win a game. It won a pennant. It was hit in Wrigley Field and it pushed the Chicago Cubs past Pittsburgh to the National League pennant and broke the hearts of the Pirates.

It was an afternoon that beggared description, an afternoon of glory in the life of a stouthearted Irishman who, as darkness almost hid him from sight of nearly 35,000 quaking fans, changed the map of baseball with one devastating blow. Only the day before, the Cubs, with Dizzy Dean on the mound, had defeated the Pirates to climb within a half game of the league leading Bucs. Now, as the ball disappeared into the darkness after having been hit by Gabby Hartnett, the catcher, the manager, the team inspiration, Billy Herman, the Cubs' second baseman, stared almost unbelievingly and whispered hoarsely: "Lord God Almighty."

It was a game that climaxed a stirring comeback by the Cubs. Only ten days before, the Pirates had held what seemed to be a comfortable three-and-a-half game lead.

Now, the Pirates' lead was a slim half game. Nine pitchers trudged to the mound that day as first one team then the other took the lead. The tide of battle surged bitterly through breaks, good and bad. The Pirates, smarting and in a vengeful mood, finally went ahead 5-3, with two runs in the top of the eighth. The Cubs roared back in there to tie the score at 5-5.

It had been a dark, dreary afternoon. Now it was getting difficult to see. The umpires conferred. They decided to let the teams play one more inning. Charlie Root got through the first half of the ninth without a score. Two went out in the Cub half. The next hitter was Gabby Hartnett, Old Tomato Face. He had succeeded Charlie Grimm as manager in the middle of the season. It had become extremely difficult to see and it was clear to all that after Gabby's turn at bat, the game would be called because of darkness.

Mace Brown, the Pirates' relief ace, wound up and threw. Gabby swung. Everybody in the park heard the crack as bat met ball. And it seemed as though everybody in the left field bleachers was reaching for it the next instant.

Harnett once recalled his great moment this way: "I knew it was gone the minute I hit it. I got the kind of feeling you get when the blood rushes out of your head and you get dizzy. A lot of people have told me they didn't know the ball was in the bleachers. Well, I did—maybe I was the only one in the park who did. I knew it the minute I hit it. When I got to second base I couldn't see third because of all the people there. I don't think I walked a step to the plate—I was carried in."

The Cubs were in first place. They won again the next day—10-1. The heart had gone out of Pittsburgh. The Cubs clinched the flag the following day. Hartnett's home run in the darkness had blacked out the Bucs.

Lou Gehrig's Farewell
July 4, 1939

It was Lou Gehrig's worst and greatest moment. On July 4, 1939, when all the world already knew that Lou Gehrig had contracted a fatal disease, there took place the most tragic and most touching scene ever enacted on a baseball diamond. It was Lou Gehrig Appreciation Day. It occurred in Yankee Stadium, when baseball and the entire world let Lou know how much they loved him.

As tears rolled unashamedly down his cheeks, an already weary and haggard Gehrig stood uneasily before the vast audience that included his old teammates, the powerful Yankees of 1927, the famous Murderers' Row, and spoke into the microphone. Even Babe Ruth had ended the period of aloofness between them by throwing his arms around Gehrig and hugging his former teammate.

"I may have been given a bad break," Lou said, "but with all this I have a lot to live for. I consider myself the luckiest man on the face of this earth."

Twenty-three months later, Lou Gehrig was dead.

The first indication that something was wrong surfaced in 1938, which ended with Gehrig's average falling below .300 for the first time since his very first season with the Yankees. When he came to spring training in 1939 the deterioration was obvious. His fielding was uncertain. He could get no power in his swing. Still, no one suspected a serious physical disability. Lou played the first eight games of the 1939 season, hitting .143 with just four singles to his credit. Sunday, April 30, was the eighth game. He failed to get a hit that day. In the field, he barely managed to make the putout on an easy grounder and muffed a routine toss from the pitcher.

Monday was an off day. Gehrig spent the day at home in Larchmont, New York. He stayed to himself and did a lot of thinking. He had to make the toughest decision of his life, and he had to make it alone. Tuesday, May 2, the team met in New York to open a series against the Tigers. That morning Lou went to see Joe McCarthy, the Yankee manager. "Joe, I always said that when I felt I couldn't help the team anymore I would take myself out of the lineup," he said. "I guess that time has come."

"Think it over, Lou," McCarthy said, "before you make any final decision."

"I've thought it over. I'm no good to the club, to myself, to the fans, to you."

McCarthy nodded. "When do you want to quit?"

"Today," Gehrig said. "Put Babe Dahlgren in."

Early that afternoon, as team captain, Lou Gehrig walked out to home plate at Briggs Stadium and handed the home-plate umpire the Yankee lineup. For the first time in fifteen years the name of Lou Gehrig did not appear. He never played another ball game. But from June 1, 1925, until May 2, 1939, Lou Gehrig had played in 2,130 consecutive games. It is a record that will stand unsurpassed.

Joe DiMaggio's 56-Game Hitting Streak
May 15–July 16, 1941

The longest hitting streak ever recorded in the major leagues began on May 15, 1941, when Joe DiMaggio of the New York Yankees rapped out a single, in four tries, against Edgar Smith, the stocky Chicago White Sox left-hander.

The next day DiMaggio broke loose with a triple and a home run off the White Sox's Thorton Lee. After Chicago came St. Louis, Boston, Detroit, and Washington with such pitchers as Hal Newhouser, Lefty Grove, Bobo Newsom, Schoolboy Rowe, Dizzy Trout, and Sid Hudson numbering among his victims. But it was not until the streak had reached twenty that people began taking notice, and sportswriters started to mention it with a note in the bottom of their game accounts.

As the streak climbed to thirty, Joe's daily doings became feature material. The entire baseball world was becoming excited now, as the tension rose on the field and in the press boxes all over the league. DiMaggio became the target of enemy pitchers who wanted to be the one to stop the streak.

One such pitcher was ex-Yankee Johnny Babich. Babich had beaten his former teammates five times in 1940, and when the Athletics met the Yankees again in the spring of 1941, he was determined not to allow DiMaggio to hit him safely. He deliberately walked Joe the first two times up. The third time Babich threw three wide pitches. The fourth was wide, too, but Di-Maggio reached out and hit a vicious drive between the pitcher's legs for a single.

"I remember that well," DiMaggio recalled. "Babich always felt the Yankees let him go without giving him a chance and he had no love for them or anybody connected with the club. Normally, I would never think of hitting that pitch, but I knew that it would be the best I was going to get all afternoon. I'll never forget the look on his face. In his haste to get out of the way of the ball, he fell flat on his behind. He was as white as a sheet when he got up."

The Yankee Clipper set a new modern record when he skipped by George Sisler's major-league record of forty-one straight games with a hit on June 29. That left only one record to overhaul: the forty-four-straight by Wee Willie Keeler of the 1897 Baltimore Orioles. The pressure on DiMaggio was tremendous. In a doubleheader against the Red Sox on July 2, DiMaggio knocked a long drive off pitcher Heber Newsome in the first inning . . . only to have it snagged by Stan Spence. In the fourth, he stroked a sure hit to left center, but a fellow named Dom DiMaggio made a spectacular catch to rob his brother. Joe made sure the next one would not be caught by smashing it into the left-field stands for a home run and a new record.

Setting records now instead of breaking them, the question of the day was: How long will the streak last? Joe ran the string to forty-five, to fifty, to fifty-five. On July 16 he rapped three hits off Cleveland pitchers Al Milnar and Joe Krakauskas to make it fifty-six in a row.

Then, on the night of July 17, Joe faced lefty Al Smith in Cleveland Stadium. He smashed two wicked drives inside the third-base line, but each time Cleveland third baseman Ken Keltner came up with the ball and threw him out. He walked once. In his last time at bat, he faced Jim Bagby, a right-hander. It was the eighth inning. The crowd, realizing it was his last chance, pleaded with Joe for a base hit. The count was one ball and one strike when he hit a sharp grounder toward the hole between second and third. Lou Boudreau, the shortstop, raced over, scooped up the ball, and whipped it to second, starting a double play. The string had been snapped. Al Smith and Jim Bagby were the stoppers.

The tension was over. The next day DiMaggio started another streak. This one lasted through sixteen games. Just a foot or two and Joe could just have easily had seventy-three straight.

Ted Williams Reaches .406 on Final Day
September 28, 1941

Ted "the Kid" Williams, the tall, handsome, sometimes wonderful, always controversial Boston Red Sox outfielder, was the greatest hitter of his time—and perhaps of all time. The last to achieve a .400 batting season, his lifetime average of just under .350 is the highest in a generation.

The greatest of all Williams' batting accomplishments, of course, is the .406 average he achieved in 1941. Williams was hitting over .400 when the schedule had a week to go and Joe Cronin, the Red Sox manager, told Ted he could take the rest of the season off and protect his average if he wished. Ted refused on the grounds that if he was to be a .400 hitter, he'd be a legitimate one. (The Yankees had already clinched the pennant and the remaining games were meaningless, but Williams insisted on playing out the string.)

On the final day of the season, Williams' batting average had slipped a few points and his average stood at exactly .400. The newspapers speculated that Williams would sit out the last day so as to be assured of becoming the first American Leaguer to hit .400 since Harry Heilmann hit .403 for the Detroit Tigers in 1923.

The Red Sox were scheduled for a Sunday doubleheader in Philadelphia. Cronin approached Ted again before the first game. "What do you say, Ted?" Cronin asked him. "It's up to you. Do you want to play or sit it out?"

"To hell with that," Williams said, "I'll play. I don't want anyone saying I got in through the back door."

It was a cold damp afternoon. Only 10,000 fans came out for the doubleheader; but they made up in noise what they lacked in numbers. The A's fans gave him a big hand every time he came to bat, and Williams responded with a great show.

His first time up, Ted singled sharply to right off Dick Fowler. His second time, still facing Fowler, he belted one of the longest home runs of the year, 440 feet over the right-field wall. When he came up for the third time, Connie Mack, the A's manager, yanked Fowler and put in Porter Vaughan, a southpaw. The left-handed Williams smashed Vaughan's third pitch through the box for his third straight hit. Vaughan was still pitching when Ted got his fourth hit, a sharp single over the first baseman's head. He reached base on an error his last time up. Williams' batting average had risen to .405 when the game ended. He had turned in a wonderful four-for-five performance with all the chips on the table, and nobody expected him to play the second game.

For the third time in a week, Cronin approached Williams and suggested he call it a season. "Nope," snapped Williams. "I'm going all the way."

Fred Caligiuri, a rookie right-hander, was on the mound for the A's. Ted had never faced him before. Caligiuri limited the Red Sox to six hits in the nightcap. Ted got two of them, a single and a double, in three official times at bat. For the entire day, he had been at bat eight times and collected six hits. His batting average for the season was a glittering .406, highest average since Rogers Hornsby hit .424 in 1924.

"Ain't I the best hitter you ever saw?" he shouted at the reporters who swarmed in on him in the locker room. Nobody disagreed!

Bobby Thomson's Home Run
October 3, 1951

As long as baseball lives, so will the name of Thomson. Although he hit hundreds of home runs in his career, it is one very special homer that made him immortal. Probably the most dramatic home run ever hit, it was all but impossible to believe—and certainly impossible to forget. It was the final touch of a miracle that brought an impossible pennant to the New York Giants.

After an incredible mid-August rally, the Giants suddenly found themselves in the final inning of the final pennant play-off game with the Brooklyn Dodgers. The Dodgers were ahead 4–1 when Alvin Dark and Don Mueller each singled off pitcher Don Newcombe. There was as yet no cause for alarm in the Dodger dugout. But when Whitey Lockman sliced a double to left, scoring Dark to make it 4–2, Charlie Dressen, Brooklyn's manager, called the bullpen.

He asked Clyde Sukeforth, the pitching coach, who was ready. Clem Labine was throwing out there but he had pitched the day before. Preacher Roe was throwing, and so was Carl Erskine. Sukeforth said Erskine's curve ball was flat while Ralph Branca's fast ball was exploding. "Branca's the man," growled Dressen.

Sukeforth was right. Branca looked extremely fast in his warm-ups. His first pitch to Bobby Thomson was a fast ball, over the inside corner, exactly where catcher Rube Walker had asked for it. Umpire Lou Jorda called it a strike.

Walker signaled for another fast one, up and in on Thomson to push him back a little. Branca didn't get it in far enough, and Thomson, seeing his chance, swung and met the ball squarely. The ball traveled in a low line toward the left-field fence. The fans held their breath. Bobby Thomson held it longer than anyone, with the possible exception of Andy Pafko, who stood helplessly watching the ball sail into the stands not far above his head at the 315-foot mark near the foul line.

Hardly a titanic drive, the homer nonetheless unleashed a tidal wave of emotion. Thomson led a delirious throng as he joyfully circled the bases and arrived at home plate to be welcomed by even greater hysteria. While every member of the Giants and half the spectators tried to embrace the hero of the hour, the Dodgers stood dazedly in their positions, not believing what they saw. A moment ago the Dodgers had the game won. Now the scoreboard showed New York 5, Brooklyn 4. How did it happen? Or did it really happen? Somehow they got to the clubhouse. Ralph Branca didn't quite make it, though. At least not for a while. The picture of him lying across the clubhouse steps, crying his heart out, like Thomson's homer itself, is something never to be forgotten.

Don Larsen's Perfect World Series Game
October 8, 1956

Don Larsen, the Yankees' tall, unflappable right-hander, had been the losingest pitcher in the American League (3–21) in 1954. Now, with eight perfect innings behind him, he stood on the mound in the sixth game of the 1956 World Series against the Brooklyn Dodgers.

The Yankees were ahead, 2–0. Twenty-four Dodgers had stepped up to the plate, and all twenty-four had returned to the bench. Only three outs stood between this fun-loving no wind-up pitcher and the first perfect game in World Series history. An error, a walk, a hit batter could ruin everything. In the stands tension crackled like high-voltage electricity among the 64,519 incredulous spectators.

The umpire gave the signal and it was time to play ball. Brooklyn outfielder Carl Furillo was first up. He fouled off four pitches before raising a routine fly to Hank Bauer in right. Roy Campanella, after hitting a long drive that curved foul at the last second, grounded to Billy Martin, who, having picked up the ball, squeezed it for a split second, just to be sure, before he threw it to Joe Collins.

The next batter was Dale Mitchell, a left-handed pinch hitter summoned by Manager Walter Alston to bat for pitcher Sal Maglie. Now, with but one out to go, Larsen was no longer nonchalant. The burden of baseball history was on his big-boned, slouching shoulders as he turned his back to the plate.

"I was so weak in the knees out there in the ninth inning," Larsen recalls, "I thought I was going to faint. When Mitchell came up I was so nervous, I almost fell down. My legs were rubbery, and my fingers didn't feel like they were on my hand. I said to myself, 'Please help me out, somebody.' "

Larsen's first pitch to Mitchell was wide. Don came back with a slider, and Babe Pinelli, umpiring his last big-league game behind the plate, called it a strike. Mitchell swung at the next pitch, a fast ball, and missed. Strike two. Larsen threw another fast ball. Mitchell fouled it into the stands. It was Larsen's ninety-sixth pitch of the game. The crowd by now was roaring with every pitch he threw.

Yogi Berra, behind the plate, signaled for another fast ball. Mumbling a prayer to himself, Larsen wound up for the first time in the game and let go. The ball nipped the outside corner. Mitchell started to swing but changed his mind. Umpire Pinelli thrust his arm through the air in a strike motion, ending the game such as no one had ever pitched before. Mitchell started to complain that the pitch was outside, but nobody would listen to him.

Certainly not Pinelli, who retired after the Series. Certainly not Berra, who was already racing toward the mound. Certainly not Larsen, who had climbed the heights he had never thought to reach.

Yankee Stadium had become a madhouse. Berra had hurled himself into Larsen's arms. Yankee players came pouring out of the dugout and the bullpen. Frenzied fans came tumbling down from the stands. They had witnessed something that no one had ever seen before and that, quite likely, no one would ever see again.

Harvey Haddix'
12 Perfect Innings
May 26, 1959

When Pittsburgh Pirate Harvey Haddix went out to win his fourth game of the season on May 26, 1959, there was little reason to think the thirty-three-year-old left-hander would go the distance. He was nursing a cold, he hadn't been pitching well, his teammates hadn't gotten him many runs in recent games, and he was facing the same Milwaukee Braves (1957 and 1958) who had already won two pennants and would lose out in the play-off for the third later that season. The weather, cold and damp following an afternoon of rain, was no help. Neither was Milwaukee manager, Fred Haney, who stacked his Braves' lineup with seven right-handed batters, including pitcher, Lew Burdette. The only left-handed hitters were Eddie Mathews and Wes Covington.

Using a fast ball and slider, the two pitches that would be almost his entire repertoire that night, Haddix quickly disposed of Johnny O'Brien, Mathews, and Henry Aaron in the first inning. In the third, Johnny Logan drilled a hard liner that shortstop Dick Schofield caught with a short leap. In the sixth, Schofield fielded a Logan grounder in the hole and threw him out.

In the meantime, the Pirates were getting hits off Burdette but wasting them. They put together three hits in the third, but Roman Mejias was cut down trying to go from first to third. It started to rain in the seventh but nothing seemed to bother Haddix. Three up and three down! Three up and three down! By the time the ninth inning came around the crowd of 19,194 knew it was seeing something special. The trouble was, Pittsburgh couldn't seem to score.

Haddix had pitched a perfect game for nine innings. When he retired O'Brien in the tenth, he became the first pitcher ever to retire twenty-eight men in a row. The score was still 0–0, and until his teammates got him some runs, the frustration would continue. And continue it did—through the tenth, eleventh, and twelfth. By then Haddix had made history again. No one had ever pitched a perfect game for more than nine innings and no one had ever pitched a no-hit game for more than eleven innings.

Burdette had given the Pirates a twelfth hit in the thirteenth inning but no run resulted. Haddix seemed tired as he came out for the thirteenth. Felix Mantilla was on second and Henry Aaron on first when Joe Adcock stepped up to the plate. Haddix threw a slider, low and away. The little southpaw threw another slider. As soon as the ball left his hand he knew it was higher than he wanted it to be. Adcock swung and the ball sailed toward right center field. Bill Virdon, the Pirate center fielder, leaped but the ball dropped over the fence for a home run.

At least, that's what everybody thought it was. All but one. Aaron, who had rounded second, thought the ball had hit the fence and was still in play. Seeing Mantilla cross the plate, he figured the game was over and headed for the dugout. Adcock, running with his head down, passed Aaron and was declared out. After some confusion, the umpires ruled that the Braves had won, 2–0. It wasn't until the next day that league President Warren Giles ruled the official score should be 1–0, as only Mantilla scored.

Whatever the score, it was a heartbreaking defeat. "It still hurts," says Harvey Haddix today.

Bill Mazeroski's World Series Homer
October 13, 1960

Pittsburgh Pirate Bill Mazeroski's ninth-inning home run in the final game of the 1960 World Series climaxed one of the strangest World Series ever played. Throughout the contest the New York Yankees shattered records by the dozen, overwhelmed the Pirates in three games by the fantastic scores of 16–3, 12–0, and 10-0, batted .338 as a club (to Pittsburgh's .256), and got thirty-one more hits and six more home runs than their opponents. Yet, when it was all over, Pittsburgh carried off its first World Championship in thirty-five years.

The turning point of the Series came in the eighth inning of the seventh game. The Yankees were leading 7–4 as the Pirates came to bat. With no outs, Gino Cimoli singled off pitcher Bobby Shantz. Then came the break of the game. Pirate Bill Virdon slashed an apparent double play ball at Yankee shortstop Tony Kubek, but it struck a pebble, came up hard, struck Kubek in the throat, knocked him to the ground and sent him to the hospital.

Suddenly, instead of two out and the bases empty, there were none out and two on. Dick Groat singled in a run to make the score 7–5. Jim Coates replaced Shantz on the mound. Needing two runs to tie, Bob Skinner sacrificed the two runners along. Rocky Nelson hit a short fly to Roger Maris for the second out. Roberto Clemente hit a chopper to Bill Skowron at first for what should have been the third out. But Coates was slow covering first and Clemente beat it out for a hit while Virdon scored the sixth run. Then Hal Smith smashed a tremendous home run over the left-field wall and the Pirates were ahead 9–7. Mickey Mantle and Yogi Berra tied things up for the Yankees, and the stage was set for one of the most exciting World Series finishes in years.

Ralph Terry, last of five Yankee pitchers, was on the mound as the Pirates came to bat in the last of the ninth. Mazeroski, who had hit Pittsburgh's only Series homer up to this game, was the batter.

Mazeroski recently looked back on that moment. "I'd been up in the seventh inning with a runner on first and one out," he recalled, "and I tried too hard. I wasn't after a homer then but I did want to hit the ball hard and I overswung. I grounded into a double play. In the ninth, I really did want a home run and I remembered that double play and reminded myself not to overswing."

He didn't. The stocky second baseman met Terry's second pitch, a chest-high slider, squarely and drove it high and far in the direction of left field. Yogi Berra, playing left field for the Yankees, took one step backward, looked again, patted his glove, and began trotting toward the clubhouse.

The crowd of 36,633 knew, too. It sent up a roar that almost tore Forbes Field apart. Mazeroski also knew it. After rounding first, he leaped high, waved his arms, and swung his cap in the air. Fans, delirious with joy, jumped out of the stands and Maz ran into a welcoming committee at third base. He was met at home plate by wildly cheering teammates.

It was hours before the park emptied. Outside cars honked and blared. Trolley cars clanged. Impromptu parades snake-danced in the downtown streets. The city of Pittsburgh had gone absolutely crazy. The police admitted that they were licked. The boulevards and tunnels were closed. Inbound motorists were turned back. There was simply no room for them. Bill Mazeroski and his bat had literally closed the town.

Roger Maris' 61st Home Run
October 1, 1961

It was Sunday, October 1, 1961. As twenty-six-year-old Roger Maris got out of bed that morning he knew he had a problem. All season long the tension had been building as the young Yankee right fielder approached Babe Ruth's great benchmark of sixty home runs in a single season.

As he got closer and closer, the pressure became all but unbearable. Life had become an ordeal as reporters, autograph hounds, photographers, and telephones constantly vied for his attention. And then there were those people who did not wish him well, people who resented him and scorned his attempt to surpass the most coveted record of the most popular ballplayer who ever lived. Finally, there was the ruling by Ford Frick, then Commissioner of Baseball, that if Maris was going to break Ruth's record he would have to do it in the same number of games the Babe did, 154. Any homers hit after that limit would be stigmatized with an asterisk to indicate that they came in the extended eight games.

Maris disagreed. "A record is a record," he said. "I didn't make the schedule. A season is a season. If I hit more home runs than Ruth in a season, that's it."

Well, game number 154 against Baltimore had ended with Roger hitting his fifty-ninth homer, one short of the mark. The very next game, again with the Orioles, Maris drove a 2–2 pitch by Jack Fisher into the third deck of Yankee Stadium. Home run No. 60, with four games to go.

Maris sat out the first one and failed to even come close to hitting one out of the park in the next two. And now here it was, the final day of the 1961 season. It was a now-or-never situation. As he faced Tracy Stallard, the tall, hard-throwing Boston rookie, he had good reason to be concerned.

Things did not go well his first time at bat. Perhaps the long months of pressure that reached its maximum intensity that afternoon were to blame. Maybe Roger was trying too hard. Whatever the reason, his first time at bat ended with a weak fly.

Tracy Stallard remembers the occasion well. "I was aware of the record, of course," he recalls. "I didn't want to be remembered as the guy who gave up the big homer."

Maris led off in the fourth inning, and Stallard did his best to stop him a second time. But Maris was not to be denied. He smashed a tremendous drive into the lower deck in right field about 360 feet away. Roger Maris had done it. For the first time he let his emotions show as he grinned broadly on his way around the bases.

"If I never hit another home run," he said later, "this is one they can never take away from me!"

Sandy Koufax's
Perfect Game
September 9, 1965

It is doubtful if there ever was a more remarkable game than the one played on September 9, 1965 between the Chicago Cubs and Los Angeles Dodgers. It is the only game in major league history with just one hit. Sandy Koufax, the Dodger pitcher, hurled a no-hitter, a perfect game. Bob Hendley, the loser, permitted only one hit—and that didn't even figure in the lone run the Dodgers managed off his left-handed delivery.

Hendley was a run-of-the-mill pitcher. His record for that year was four victories and four defeats. His lifetime totals were a modest 48-52. Koufax, in sharp contrast, was enjoying one of his greatest seasons. He was to win 26 and lose only eight that year. Already acknowledged as one of the greatest pitchers of all time, Koufax was in the midst of a sensational six-year span during which he pitched four no-hitters, led the National League in earned run percentage five times, in strikeouts four times and in victories three times. Three times he struck out 300 or more batters and three times he won the Cy Young Award as baseball's best pitcher.

So it surprised hardly anyone at Dodger Stadium as Cub after Cub went down before the southpaw slants of Koufax. But to see Hendley match the Dodger ace pitch for pitch was a stunner. It was not until the fifth inning that Hendley allowed the first base runner. Lou Johnson walked, advanced to second on Ron Fairley's sacrifice and, with Jim Lefebvre at bat, stole third and continued home on catcher Chris Krug's high throw. Hendley then fanned Lefebvre and threw out Wes Parker on a soft tap back to the mound. But the damaging run was home.

Meanwhile, facing a lineup stacked with right-handed batters, Koufax mastered the Cubs with only three anxious moments. In the first inning, Glenn Beckert hit a sharp drive over third base which landed inches foul. In the second Willie Davis in center grabbed Pidge Browne's hard liner and in the seventh

Koufax fell behind 3-0 to Billy Williams, the only left-handed hitter in the Cub lineup. But he slipped over two quick strikes and induced Williams to hit a soft fly to Lou Johnson to close out the inning.

It was Johnson who authored the only hit of the game, a bloop double into short right in the seventh that just managed to elude first baseman Ernie Banks' outstretched glove. Johnson was the only base runner in the entire game.

Koufax fanned 14, including the last seven batters he faced. In the eighth Ron Santo was called out on strikes and Ernie Banks and Pidge Browne went down swinging. Chris Krug fanned to start the ninth. Joey Amalfitano, batting for Don Kessinger, also struck out; Harvey Kuenn, another pinch hitter, also swung at the third strike, and Koufax had his perfect game in becoming the first pitcher to register four no-hitters.

Koufax went on to strike out 382 batters, a National League record, despite an arthritic elbow that forced him to soak his left arm in ice water after every game. Koufax had one more season left, his best and most painful. In 1966, he won 27 games, setting up a National League record for the most victories in a season by a left-hander. His last victory, on the final day of the season, clinched the National League pennant for the Dodgers. He led the pitchers in practically every department, including victories, complete games, innings pitched, strikeouts, shutouts and ERA.

During the winter that followed Koufax announced his retirement fearing that arthritis in his left elbow, which had grown progressively more painful since its inception three years earlier, might leave the arm permanently damaged.

To the surprise of hardly anyone, Sandy Koufax was elected into the Hall of Fame in 1972, the first year he was eligible and at age 36, the youngest player ever to be so honored.

Willie Mays'
Farewell
September 25, 1973

"Ladies and gentlemen, Willie Mays . . . "

The cheers drowned out the rest. Long, loud, and lingering . . . thirty seconds . . . a minute . . . ninety seconds. There was no letup. The fans who filled New York's Shea Stadium were pouring down their cheers . . . and their love . . . and their thanks to the most exciting baseball player of his time and most likely the best as well.

It was Willie Mays' farewell to baseball . . . the game he loved so much . . . the game that brought him so much joy. . . . "I like to be happy," he once said, "and playing baseball makes me happy."

For twenty-two years the "Say Hey Kid," whose childlike enthusiasm and ingenuousness made him the darling of the baseball world, was finally and reluctantly saying farewell to the game and the tears poured down his cheeks. "This is a sad day for me," he said and could go no further. Three times the fans stood and roared their hearts out for Willie, waving banners that could have been Valentine cards.

"We love you, Willie. We always will," one of them read.

"We who are about to cry, salute you," read another.

And cry, indeed, they did. The pennant race was forgotten. The game was to have started at 8:05. It was now 8:55. Nobody seemed to mind. Willie Mays was more important than any old pennant race. Then came the words that were the most touching of all. Willie spoke of his love for baseball, and how sorry he was that he could no longer help the Mets, and how he wanted to help kids play the game now when, fighting back the tears, he turned in the direction of the Mets dugout and apologized to the players for intruding on their time. "I say to the Mets players, forgive me," he said. "I hope you go on to win the flag for the New York people. I know this is a delay for you. But this is my farewell, I thought I'd never quit, but I know there always comes a time to get out. The way these kids are playing tells me one thing: 'Willie Mays, say good-bye!' "

Willie Mays had enjoyed better years than the last one. Much better years. But this may have been his most beautiful moment, and the people responded. The cheers were deafening; the tears flowing.

They remembered lots of things . . . when he hit a home run in his first time at bat at the Polo Grounds . . . when he returned to New York after fourteen years in San Francisco and won the first game he played for the Mets with a home run . . . against the Giants . . . when he slammed four home runs in one game . . . when he made that miraculous catch against Vic Wertz in the 1954 World Series. When he made that incredible throw to nip Brooklyn's Billy Cox at the plate, causing the Dodger manager to exclaim, "I saw it, but I don't have to believe it." Willie Mays could do everything and do it better than anyone else. None had Mays' flare for the game, his grace in pursuing a baseball. And none was ever more exciting stealing a base or going from first to third.

Willie Howard Mays, Jr., No. 24, the man of the patented "basket" catch, the great arm, the explosive speed, and the quick bat leaves his superb talents in record books. In twenty-two years, Mays batted over .300, collected over 3,000 hits, hit 660 home runs, established five major-league records, tied seven others, was the National League's Most Valuable Player twice, and played in twenty-four All-Star Games. He could no more be kept out of the Hall of Fame than a breakwater could stop a tidal wave.

"We who are about to cry, Willie Mays, salute you!"

Lou Brock
Shatters Stolen
Base Record
September, 1974

Lou Brock of the St. Louis Cardinals now holds the record for the most bases stolen in a single season. His 118 thefts surpassed the previous one-season record (104 by Maury Wills) by an incredible 14 bases. Even more incredible, Lou stole more bases in that 1974 season than seventeen major-league clubs combined. And he did this at the age of thirty-five. "That," remarked teammate Dal Maxvill, "is like a ten-year-old horse winning the Kentucky Derby."

Brock didn't start out like he was about to better his own previous high—74 stolen bases in 1966—let alone establish a new modern high when he was nailed by Pittsburgh's Mike Ryan on his very first attempt of the season. But he made it his next 28 times in a row—and there was no stopping him after that. By July 1, 1974, he had 48 steals in 53 attempts and the chant "Lou! Lou! Lou!" had become infectious with Busch

Stadium crowds whenever Brock reached base.

By August 1 he had accumulated 65 stolen bases for an even 700 career figure. Then he really opened up. He swiped 29 bases in August, bringing his total to 94. On September 1, he stole 4 more in San Francisco. The Cards came home to St. Louis for an eight-game stay and Lou really wanted to break Wills' record before the home fans. But after seven games he was still two short of the mark.

Right-hander Dick Ruthven was on the mound for the Phillies on the night of the final game, and Bob Boone, son of former major-league star Ray Boone, was the catcher. Brock, leading off, singled in the first inning, and the chant began: "Lou! Lou! Lou!" On the second pitch to Ron Hunt, the next batter, Brock took off and slid in under Boone's throw for a clean steal. That was No. 104 and it tied him with Wills. Lou failed to

reach base in either of his next two at-bats.

In the seventh inning, with Ruthven still on the mound, Lou cracked a single to right. The chant began again. Batter Ron Hunt fouled off the first pitch. The chant grew louder. On the next throw, Brock took off and stole his 105th base.

The stadium exploded with the cheers of over 27,-000 fans. The game was halted and Brock's teammates rushed out to congratulate him. A member of the grounds crew dug up second base. James "Cool Papa" Bell, a St. Louisian who was a speedster in the old Negro Leagues and a Hall of Famer, was given the honor of presenting the bag to Brock. "I might as well give this to you," Cool Papa remarked. "If I didn't, you'd steal it anyway."

Henry Aaron's Home Run No. 715 April 8, 1974

For thirty-nine years Babe Ruth's great lifetime home run record of 714 had stood, beckoning but unreachable. Thousands of players had tried to equal it, but few even came close. Then, on April 8, 1974, the entire world watched as Henry Aaron swung his mighty bat and made the 360-foot jaunt around the bases and into baseball history. Home run No. 715. It was an occasion not to be believed.

Aaron had equaled the Babe's record with the first swing of his bat in the season's opener at Cincinnati. But the celebration there was nothing compared to the pandemonium that reigned in Atlanta Stadium that day. A hometown crowd of almost 54,000 was joined by a national television audience of millions, the governor of the state, the city's mayor, Sammy Davis, Jr., Pearl Bailey, and media people from South America, Europe, and Japan. There were bands and balloons, skyrockets and streamers. It was truly the homecoming of a local

hero. All that was needed was home run No. 715.

Aaron's first time at bat was a disappointment to the crowd. Hank never got his bat off his shoulder as Los Angeles lefty Al Downing threw a ball, a strike, and then three more balls. The crowd booed as Aaron took his base.

Then it was the fourth inning. The Braves were trailing, 3–1, and rain was falling. Downing's first pitch was inside, a ball. Then came the second pitch, a fast ball waist-high, in the strike zone. Henry took his first swing of the game. *Whack!* The crack of the bat resounded throughout the stadium. There was never any doubt. The ball rose high toward left center as the crowd rose to its feet. It cleared the fence 385 feet from home plate and was caught in the Braves bullpen by relief pitcher Tom House.

Suddenly the sky was filled with fireworks as the scoreboard lights flashed their gigantic message: "715

. . . 715 . . . 715." As Aaron rounded third he saw the entire Atlanta team waiting for him at home plate. But it was Henry's father, sixty-five-year-old Herbert Aaron, Sr., who had jumped out of the family's special field-level box and outraced everybody to greet the man who had just broken Babe Ruth's record. Not far behind came Henry's mother, Estella, tears in her eyes but a wide, rapturous smile on her face. "I knew, I knew," she explained later. "I knew Henry wouldn't break the record until he got to Atlanta where I could see it."

In the decades to come the memory of the inning, the count, or the score that night might blur. But the sound of Henry Aaron's bat as he connected with the ball, the clamor of the crowd, and the ecstatic scene at the plate as Hank was hoisted on the shoulders of his delirious teammates will remain crisp and clear for as long as the game of baseball is played.

Nolan Ryan Hurls 4th No Hitter
June 1, 1975

They call him the Ryan Express. They say he can throw a baseball harder than any one in the world. One of his pitches has been clocked at 100.9 miles an hour, faster than any human being has ever thrown a baseball before. Never in baseball history has there been a pitcher of such magnetic quality about him—a quality that lures people in tantalizing anticipation of witnessing something special. Early in 1975, he pitched his fourth no hitter, in a little over two years. He also has pitched four one-hitters, seven two-hitters and 13 three-hitters. On the final day of the 1973 season, he struck out 16 batters. The last strikeout was his 383rd of the season, a new major league record. He also struck out 329 batters in 1972 and 367 in 1974 to become the first pitcher ever to fan 300 or more batters in three successive seasons.

No wonder Harry Dalton, the general manager of the California Angels has advocated that the Baseball Writers Association of America, which annually awards the Cy Young trophy to the best pitcher in baseball, resurrect the immortal Hall of Fame pitcher and present him with the Nolan Ryan award. It was Dalton who had succeeded in pulling off something resembling the Brinks robbery in November of 1971 when he spirited Nolan Ryan away from the New York Mets. Incredibly Ryan was one of four players Dalton delivered to California in exchange for Jim Fregosi, the man who was supposed to solve the Mets' third base problem.

It was while with New York that Ryan was a spectator on September 13, 1969 when Steve Carlton, then of the St. Louis Cardinals, established a major league record by striking out 19 Mets. Ryan was still a Met, on April 22, 1970 when Tom Seaver, a teammate, fanned 19 San Diego Padres to equal Carlton's record. On August 13, 1974, at Anaheim Stadium, Ryan was present again as another pitcher etched his name into baseball's record book with 19-strikeout performances. That pitcher's name was Nolan Ryan.

"I guess I'm the only guy in the world to have seen all three of them" Ryan drawled in his Texas twang after he had thrown a strike past Boston's Bernie Carbo.

It was on June 1, 1975, however, that Ryan savored his greatest moment. On that day he hurled his fourth no-hitter in only his 220th major league start. Only Sandy Koufax of the more than 5,000 pitchers who have worn a major league uniform had ever turned that trick. And Sandy has 314 starts. Consider that 197 no-hitters have been pitched in 225,036 opportunities going into the 1976 season—that's once every 1,142 games—and you get an idea of the magnitude of Ryan's accomplishment.

Ryan pitched his first no-hitter on May 15, 1973 in Kansas City when he no-hit the Royals. Exactly two months later, he did the same in Detroit, embellishing his second no-hitter with 17 strikeouts, a record for a no-hit performance. His third no-hit came on September 28, his final start of the 1974 season, vs Minnesota. The fourth, a 1-0 triumph over Baltimore, was the most taxing—and most gratifying. It was not only Ryan's 100th major league victory but his wife, Ruth, was one of the 18,492 thrilled spectators at Anaheim Stadium.

"I just felt he was going to do it, that's all," said the beauteous Mrs. Ryan. "I can't explain it, but I had a strong feeling about it today."

"I guess I started thinking about it in the fifth inning, Ryan recounted later, "but I never really got the feeling, even in the ninth inning. I didn't feel very confident because I knew I had to face Tommy Davis and Bobby Grich and those two are the toughest outs in the Baltimore lineup."

Ryan recalled that the last time he faced the Orioles he held them hitless until the eighth inning only to lose 2-1. Now, as he retired the Orioles in order in the eighth, the home crowd gave him a standing ovation. That left three outs to go. Al Bumbry was an easy out in the ninth, on a soft fly to Morris Nettles in left field. That brought up Tommy Davis, the veteran who had gotten the closest thing to a hit when he opened the seventh with a high chopper over second base. But Jerry Remy, the rookie second baseman, raced to his right, gloved the ball and barely got Davis, a slow runner, at first. The decision drew a brief protest from the Baltimore bench.

There was no protest this time as Davis meekly bounced out to Remy for the second out. The crowd, on its feet now, was cheering every pitch as Ryan got a curve ball over for a strike to Grich. Then came a fast ball that was inside, another curve for a strike, a foul, a fast ball outside for ball two and another foul. Finally, the final pitch was a change-up on the outside that completely fooled Grich for the third strike.

"I expected a fast ball," Grich explained afterwards. What else can you expect from the Express—unless it's another no-hitter!

Rennie Stennett
7 For 7
September 16, 1975

Back in 1892, Wilbert Robinson of the Baltimore Orioles, yes, the same Uncle Robbie who later was to manage the Brooklyn Dodgers, hit safely seven times in seven at bats in a nine-inning game. Since then, close to 11,000 major league players, including Ty Cobb, Rogers Hornsby, Honus Wagner, Babe Ruth, Stan Musial, Ted Williams, Willie Mays, Hank Aaron and other great hitters have taken dead aim but failed to duplicate that mark. A number have gotten six straight hits and one, unhearalded Cesar Gutierrez, did collect seven hits in seven times at bat, but they came in a 12-inning game.

It was not until September 16, 1975, 83 years later, that Robinson's feat was duplicated. Imagine that! As columnist Dave Anderson of *the New York Times* put it: consider that if it takes that long for another major leaguer to do it, the deed will occur in the year 2058, perhaps on the moon.

"I knew somebody had six hits but I didn't know who," said Rennie Stennett, the player who accomplished the seven-for seven feat. "But I didn't know whether anybody else had seven or not. I never even heard of Wilbert Robinson until after the game."

Frankly, not very many people had heard of Rennie Stennett, although the slender second baseman of the Pittsburgh Pirates had been a vital cog in the team's pennant drive. The trouble with Stennett has been that he does everything with so little flair that he is hardly noticed. Pittsburgh manager Danny Murtaugh is fully aware of his talents, however. When the Pirates had to choose between him and Dave Cash as their second baseman, they traded Cash to the Phillies for Ken Brett, a left-handed pitcher. Cash has helped the Phillies but with Rennie Stennett at second base, the Pirates won the National League East title two consecutive seasons.

Oddly enough, Manager Murtaugh was undecided whether to play Stennett because of an ankle sprain Rennie had sustained a week before. It was heavily taped. "I decided to play him a few innings and rest him," said Murtaugh. "But he kept getting hits. . . ." Murtaugh finally did take out Stennett after the eighth inning. By then, he had collected a triple, two doubles and four singles. He doubled and singled in a nine-run first inning and doubled and singled in a six-run fifth. That tied him with three other players who had made two hits in an inning twice in one game. The other holders of that record are Max Carey (Pirates, 1925),

Johnny Hodapp (Indians, 1929) and Sherman Lollar (White Sox, 1955).

Stennett's tattoo of base hits was not a one-man assault, by any means. The Pirates assaulted five Chicago Cubs pitchers for 24 hits in the widest shutout margin in modern baseball history. The score was 22-0. For trivia lovers, it was the biggest rout ever started and finished by brothers. Rick Reuschel faced nine batters in the first inning and eight of them scored. Paul Reuschel pitched the last two innings, both scoreless, marked only by Stennett's record-tying eighth inning triple. In between, Tom Dettore, Oscar Zamora and rookie Buddy Schultz took their lumps.

Stennett had a double off Reuschel and a single off Dettore in the third. Then in the fifth, he doubled off Dettore and singled against Zamora. Schultz was the fictim of a single in the seventh. There were two out in the eighth when Stennett slammed a Paul Reuschel hit over Champ Summers' head in right field for a triple.

"I had to be lucky," said Stennett. "There are a lost of guys capable of getting seven hits in a game if they are lucky enough to get up seven times."

True. But only Rennie Stennett has done it.

160

GIANTS OF THE GAME

THE ALL-TIME ALL-STAR TEAM

BY JOE REICHLER

Nineteen seventy-six is jubilee year in America. The National League is celebrating its hundredth anniversary. The American League is capping this anniversary with its own seventy-fifth birthday. And the United States is proudly proclaiming its bicentennial. What better time than this to select baseball's All-Time All-Star team?

Timely? Certainly. Wise? Highly debatable. Picking a handful of athletes out of more than eleven thousand eligibles, playing in different eras, under different conditions, with different equipment, is about as difficult as splitting the atom. And just as dangerous. At best, it's a no-win situation. No matter whom you select, you're bound to get an argument. Somebody always has someone better at each position.

What this author will attempt to do is to select two American and two National League teams, one each for the period between 1900 and 1940, up to the start of

World War II, and one each from 1941 through 1975, or the postwar era.

Is there a just and accurate way to compare the quality of athletes of the early 1900s to the athletes of the 1970s?

Probably not. But the following selections, by positions, were made by one pure of heart if not of mind, without malice or wisdom, devoid of favoritism and, according to some, bereft of facts, too. Trimming the field to forty did not lessen, to any great extent, the herculean task of selecting one All-Time All-Star team. The fact that the selector saw all of these All-Stars in action, excepting Honus Wagner, was hardly a handicap. Ten of the twelve all-time greats chosen, as well as the All-Star manager, John McGraw, are members of the Hall of Fame. The others—Willie Mays and Brooks Robinson—are as certain as the setting of the sun to join them.

AMERICAN LEAGUE

NATIONAL LEAGUE

Lou Gehrig	1b	Mickey Vernon
Eddie Collins	2b	Bobby Doerr
Jimmy Collins	3b	Brooks Robinson
Joe Cronin	ss	Lou Boudreau
Ty Cobb	lf	Ted Williams
Tris Speaker	cf	Joe DiMaggio
Babe Ruth	rf	Al Kaline
Bill Dickey	c	Yogi Berra
Walter Johnson	rhp	Bob Feller
Lefty Grove	lhp	Whitey Ford

Bill Terry	1b	Stan Musial
Rogers Hornsby	2b	Jackie Robinson
Pie Traynor	3b	Eddie Mathews
Honus Wagner	ss	Pee Wee Reese
Paul Waner	lf	Hank Aaron
Edd Roush	cf	Willie Mays
Mel Ott	rf	Roberto Clemente
Gabby Hartnett	c	Roy Campanella
Christy Mathewson	rhp	Bob Gibson
Carl Hubbell	lhp	Sandy Koufax

FIRST BASE

Lou Gehrig, the great Iron Horse of the Yankees, was selected over George Sisler, Bill Terry, Jimmy Foxx, Hank Greenberg, and Jim Bottomley. He was the greatest clutch hitter the game has ever known. No one in baseball history has a more productive runs-batted-in average per time at bat than Gehrig. A lifetime .340 hitter, Gehrig holds the major-league record for grand-slam homers, with twenty-three, and was chosen the American League's Most Valuable Player four times. Larrupin' Lou, who played with the Yankees from 1923 until his diamond career was cut short by illness in 1939, was the game's most durable performer. He set an all-time consecutive game record of 2,130 contests before he was struck down at the height of his career.

SECOND BASE

Rogers Hornsby, perhaps the game's foremost right-handed hitter, was selected over Eddie Collins, Napoleon Lajoie, Frankie Frisch, Charlie Gehringer, and Jackie Robinson. He is one of three players to hit over .400 three times. His .424 average in 1924 is the highest of the twentieth century. In one span—from 1921 to 1925—he hit .397, .401, .384, .424, and .403. He won seven batting titles, and twice won the Triple Crown. His lifetime batting average is .358.

THIRD BASE

Brooks Robinson. Until Robinson came along, Pie Traynor spread-eagled the field that included such greats as Jimmy Collins, Frank Baker, Buck Weaver, Bill Bradley, Stan Hack, Eddie Mathews, George Kell, Jimmy Dykes, Joe Dugan, Pepper Martin, Harry Steinfeldt, and Ken Keltner. An incredible defensive player, Robinson holds the major-league career records at his position for most games, most assists, most put-outs, most total chances, most double plays, highest fielding average. He has won fourteen straight Golden Glove awards as the American League's outstanding fielding third baseman. A candidate for the 3,000-hit club, Ro-

binson is one of baseball's best clutch hitters. No third baseman has ever amassed more hits, and only Eddie Mathews has hit more home runs or driven in more runs. An All-Star for fifteen straight seasons, Brooks is one of the most durable players in history, playing in over 95 percent of the Orioles' games over a sixteen-year span.

SHORTSTOP

Honus Wagner stands out all alone like the Rock of Gibraltar. Despite his bulk and awkward appearance, he was one of the speediest men ever to wear spiked shoes. He led the National League in base-stealing five times, was the league's batting king on eight occasions, and had a lifetime batting average of .329. He was unequaled as a fielder. He had the range of Marty Marion, the anticipatory sense of a Lou Boudreau, the agility of a Pee Wee Reese or a Luis Aparicio, the swiftness of a Phil Rizzuto, the shovel hands of an Eddie Miller, and the throwing arm of a Travis Jackson. No shortstop came close to him as a hitter. A durable competitor, he saw twenty-one years of service on the playing field.

CATCHER

This is the toughest of all, with *Bill Dickey* as the choice. There have been numerous great catchers. Two of baseball's greatest, Roger Bresnahan and Johnny Kling, caught Christy Mathewson and Mordecai Brown, respectively. Then came the famous American League trio of Ray Schalk, Wally Schang, and Steve O'Neill. In time they were replaced by Mickey Cochrane and Bill Dickey, while Gabby Hartnett, Jimmy Wilson, Bob O'Farrell, and Al Lopez dominated the National League. The best two catchers in the last two decades have been Yogi Berra and Roy Campanella. It comes down to two—Mickey Cochrane and Billy Dickey. Both were magnificent receivers with almost identical lifetime averages. Dickey hit the longer ball, but Cochrane was faster afoot. Dickey caught over 100 games thirteen successive seasons and was on a pennant winner eight times. He is among the leaders in catchers with 1,969 hits, 202 home runs, and 1,209 runs batted in.

LEFT FIELD

Apart from his many records, *Ty Cobb* was a human dynamo, a man who played baseball with every ounce of energy in him. His many records virtually fill a book. He led the A. L. twelve times in batting, nine years in succession. He had an incredible lifetime average of .367 over a twenty-four-year-span. He had three .400 seasons. He leads all major-leaguers with 892 stolen bases. He ranks over Ted Williams, Joe Medwick, Fred Clarke, Joe Jackson, Al Simmons, Zack Wheat, and Stan Musial.

CENTER FIELD

Willie Mays or Joe DiMaggio or Tris Speaker. Mays gets the nod because of his durability, greater speed, and power. DiMaggio, a man of grace and leadership, was perhaps more consistent and more reliable in the clutch. Speaker may have been the best defensively, but neither Mays nor DiMaggio was a slouch in the field. Willie was the most spectacular. Willie gets the nod because of his 660 home runs, 1,903 runs batted in, and record for most games and most putouts by an outfielder. This trio stood apart from other center-field luminaries such as Mickey Mantle, Edd Roush, Max Carey, and Duke Snider.

RIGHT FIELD

Babe Ruth. Who else? The Babe holds nearly all single-season and lifetime slugging records. Almost every baseball fan knows that Babe Ruth hit 60 home runs in a 154-game season and 714 in a twenty-two year career. The Babe led the American League in home runs twelve times and in runs batted in five times. He hit 15 home runs in World Series competition. His lifetime batting average is .342. As an outfielder, he had hair-trigger reflexes and intuitive intelligence. He had a strong arm and was surprisingly fast for a big man. He ranks above Hank Aaron, Ross Youngs, Enos Slaughter, Paul Waner, Al Kaline, Roberto Clemente, and Mel Ott.

It was a colossal task to sift through the many pitchers who could qualify for such a team. There were such right-handers as Cy Young, Christy Mathewson, Walter Johnson, Grover Cleveland Alexander, Mordecai Brown, Bob Feller, Red Ruffing, Addie Joss, Ed Walsh, Jack Chesbro, Bob Gibson, Juan Marichal, Dazzy Vance, Don Drysdale, Red Faber, and Tom Seaver. The lefties include Rube Waddell, Lefty Grove, Vernon Gomez, Herb Pennock, Eddie Plank, Nap Rucker, Hal Newhouser, Rube Marquard, Carl Hubbell, Warren Spahn, Wilbur Cooper, and Sandy Koufax.

The precarious picks are *Walter Johnson* and *Christy Mathewson* as right-handers and *Lefty Grove* and *Sandy Koufax* as left-handers. Johnson probably was the fastest of all pitchers. He won 416 games, struck out 3,508 batters and hurled 113 career shutouts. He won 20 or more games twelve times and 30 or more with a high of 36 in 1913. He was thirty-six and in his eighteenth season in the American League in 1924 when he helped pitch the Senators to their first pennant with a 23–7 performance.

Christy Mathewson was a real pitching artist. No pitcher ever so fully combined a great physique with a brilliant flexible mind. He won 20 or more thirteen times, 30 or more three times, with a high of thirty-seven in 1908. His 373 victories ties him with Alexander for high in the National League. He reached his peak of artistry when he shut out the champion Philadelphia Athletics three times in six days in the 1905 World Series.

Lefty Grove, in seventeen years with the Philadelphia Athletics and Boston Red Sox, won 300 games, including sixteen in a row. He lost only 141. His .682 won-and-lost percentage is the second best among pitchers with 200 or more victories. He led the American League in ERA nine times and in strikeouts seven times, all in succession. He was the

mainstay of the A's pitching staff that carried the team to three straight pennants. He won four of six World Series decisions.

Sandy Koufax didn't win 20 games until he was twenty-seven years old, but once he reached that charmed circle for pitchers there was no stopping him. Over a four-year period, from 1963 through 1966, Koufax virtually dominated the game, winning 97 while losing only 27. In three of those years, he led the Los Angeles Dodgers to the pennant. His won-and-lost records for those years were 25–5, 19–5 (out for a time with an injured finger), 26–8, and 27–9. His ERA for those seasons were 1.88, 1.74, 2.04, and 1.73. He pitched four nohitters, including a perfect game, struck out 2,396 batters in 2,325 innings, including 382 in 1965, and fanned ten or more batters in a game ninety-seven times. He won the Cy Young Award as baseball's best pitcher three times, and at thirty-six, was the youngest player ever to be elected to the Hall of Fame.

A team of that caliber doesn't really need a manager but one will be named nevertheless. The choice is *John McGraw,* the legendary Little Napoleon who stormed through a riotous thirty-year career during which he brought ten pennants to the New York Giants. The name "Giants" had little meaning until he took over the club in the middle of the 1902 season. No manager dominated the game in more complete and dictatorial fashion. He smashed his way to more pennants than any other manager except Casey Stengel, who won as many. McGraw was a pioneer, an innovator, a creative manager. He gave the game the hit-and-run play that revolutionized baseball. He changed baseball from a mere contest of power and skill to psychological warfare. He developed the use of the bunt. He was the first manager to hire a ballplayer for the sole duty of serving as a pinch hitter. He was the first to relegate a pitcher exclusively to the bullpen.

HONUS WAGNER

BY JOE REICHLER

The first thing you noticed about him were his bowlegs. It was said of Honus Wagner that his legs took off at the ankles in a curving sweep to meet in surprise at his waistline. The next thing you noticed were those long arms that hung at his knees. "He is the only man" Lefty Gomez once said, "who can tie his shoestrings without bending."

He was a strange-looking figure, indeed. With that thick neck, broad shoulders, and barrel chest, he looked more like a wrestler than a baseball player. Authorities such as Ed Barrow, who discovered him, Fred Clarke, who managed him, and John McGraw, who observed him throughout his long career, always insisted he was the greatest player of all time.

There was never any question about his rating as a shortstop. He was the greatest shortstop by so wide a margin that his selection on any all-time all-star team is unchallenged. Selectors simply jot down the name of "Wagner," alongside the position "shortstop," then ponder over the other selections. Along with Ty Cobb, Babe Ruth, Christy Mathewson, and Walter Johnson, Honus was in the first group of five players to be elected to baseball's Hall of Fame.

Wagner had no weakness at the plate—unless it was a base on balls. It was practically impossible to walk him. He'd even chase a waste pitch. The rule change defining the batter's box was adopted because of his refusal to let anything go by. And he made no distinction among pitchers. He batted .324 in 327 times up against Christy Mathewson. His mark against Cy Young was .375, Kid Nichols .352, Rube Marquard .327, Nap Rucker .356, Hooks Wiltse .372, Vic Willis .369, and so on up and down (mostly up) the line.

The only pitcher who ever bothered him consistently was a Chicago right-hander named Jack Taylor who got him out with slow, twisting stuff that exasperated Honus more than it fooled him. Wagner got so furious one day that he turned around, batted left-handed, and swatted a two-bagger. It was one of the few hits he got off the Chicagoan.

In the field, Wagner was just as hard to get a ball by as he was at bat. On his stumpy bowed legs, he scuttled over the field with the agility of a sand crab. His huge hands were like scoop shovels. Those hands of his were so big that once when he reached for a plug of tobacco one of them got jammed in his hip pocket. Honus calmly caught a throw with his free hand, called time, went to the dugout, and was cut loose. Wagner had a rifle arm and an instinctive sense for the right move. He played every position except catcher. Wagner did not become a shortstop on a permanent basis until 1903, his sixth year in the major leagues.

The Flying Dutchman, as he was affectionately called, joined the Louisville club in the National League in the middle of the 1897 season. Ed Barrow, who had signed him to his first contract, for a munificent $35 a month with Steubenville, Ohio, of the Tri-State League, sold him to the big leagues for $2,100.

The years just prior to the turn of the century were rugged ones in baseball, especially for bushers, and Wagner, an amiable, gentle person despite his fierce-looking appearance, got his share of abuse, even from his own teammates. "Get outa my way, kid, or I'll split your skull," a Louisville player bellowed as Wagner tried to edge into the batter's box for some pre-game licks. And Honus obligingly retreated to the dugout. Then there were teams like the Baltimore Orioles, as rough and tough a gang that ever sharpened its spikes. In his very first game, Wagner learned a little how the Orioles operated. "On my first time up," Honus loved to recall, "I got a single. The next time I might have had a triple, but Jack Doyle gave me the hip at first, Hughie Jennings chased me wide around second, and John McGraw blocked me off at third, then jammed the ball into my belly, knocking the wind out of me."

When Wagner returned to the dugout, still dazed from the going-over, he received a cussing-out from his manager, Fred Clarke. "Are you going to stand there like a dummy and take that?" fumed Clarke. "You want to stay in the big leagues, don't you? Then fight back!"

Wagner didn't get his chance until a couple of days later. He drove one deep into center that was good for extra bases. He dumped Doyle on his behind at first, left Jennings in the dirt at second, and trampled all over McGraw's feet coming into third. Clarke was so tickled seeing McGraw fuming and cussing that he came over to the coach's box and said, "Nice day, ain't it, Muggsy?"

It didn't take long for word to spread around the National League that the big Dutchman was no man to be trifled with. At bat, on the bases, and in the field, he proved his quality every day—at Louisville and at Pittsburgh, to which owner Barney Dreyfuss shifted his franchise in 1900 when the National League was pared from twelve to eight clubs. The American League learned the same lesson in the 1909 World Series which brought Wagner to grips with Ty Cobb for the first and only time. The first meeting of the two absolutely fearless competitors was a memorable one. Cobb had reached first base and shouted over to Wagner, "Hey, Krauthead, I'm comin' down on the next pitch. Get out of the way or I'll cut you to pieces!" "I'll be waitin'," replied Wagner.

As good as his word, Cobb set sail with the next pitch. The ball and Ty's feared spikes came almost simultaneously. But before the steel could dig into Wagner's shins, Honus smashed the ball into Cobb's mouth. The bleeding Tiger had to leave the game to have three stitches in his torn lip. In that Series, Wagner completely outplayed Cobb. He batted .333 and stole six bases, while Cobb was held to a .231 average and only twice got away with larceny.

Although he was twenty-three, a comparatively ripe age for a rookie, when he broke into the majors, Honus played twenty-one seasons. He was forty before he ever fell below .300 in batting. His eight batting titles and seventeen straight .300 seasons are National League batting records. His 3,340 base hits, 651 doubles, 252 triples, 4,893 total bases, and 1,740 runs rank him with the giants of the game. He hit more than 200 home runs in the era of the Dead Ball. A free swinger who gripped the bat with his hands held about two inches apart, Wagner specialized in screaming line drives, which he hit with equal power to all fields. Perhaps his most surprising statistic is his 722 stolen bases. He was no model of grace but he possessed incredible speed. He led the league in stolen bases five times, reaching as high as sixty-one thefts in 1907.

Wagner slowed down appreciably in his waning years, and, finally, in 1917, he hung up his spikes. On July 1 of that year, Dreyfuss fired Jimmy Callahan, his manager, and appointed Wagner. Hans gave up the post after four days, saying, "This is not for me." He had taken the job unwillingly and gave it up because he was not suited for it and he knew it. His one weakness in baseball was that he couldn't tell anyone else how to play the game. But no one ever had to tell John Peter Wagner.

TY COBB

BY JOE REICHLER

Ty Cobb made his first appearance in a major-league ball park on August 30, 1905, at Bennett Field, in the city of Detroit. His name was not even on the score-card. He arrived at the plate unknown, an angry faced, jut-jawed, mean-eyed, eighteen-year-old kid who held his bat like a club, left hand high, right hand low. Facing him was Jack Chesbro, New York's greatest spit-baller, winner of forty-one games the previous season. The rookie twisted his mouth scornfully, taunted Chesbro with a few derisive words, then whacked out a double, driving in two runs; this set the pattern for the twenty-four years to come.

Cobb was undoubtedly the greatest and fiercest competitor any sport has ever known. He was at his best when the pressure was on. He gloried in the clutch. His most brilliant plays generally came when the odds were heavily against him. He was one of the worst losers anywhere, and this bitter dread of defeat made him a spectacular winner. He could endure almost anything but failure. There was no amount of drudgery he would not undergo to reach his goal.

To Cobb, baseball was not an athletic contest. To him a baseball game was a relentless fight. He fought players, umpires, even the fans, with his fists and even with his spikes. He was attacked on city streets. His life was threatened. But nothing slowed him up. If a pitcher threw a beanball at Cobb, as many of them did, Ty was sure to bunt the next pitch down the first-base line, in an effort to lure the pitcher directly in his path and run him over.

"I was their enemy," Cobb once said. "If any player learned I could be scared, I would have lasted two years in the leagues, not twenty-four." Cobb always denied that he was a dirty player. He felt the base paths belonged to him, the runner. He hit every base at full speed, feet first. His spikes were sharp, and if the baseman got hurt, that wasn't Cobb's fault.

Cobb's reputation as a knifing runner was based mainly upon his spiking of Frank "Home Run" Baker of the Athletics in 1910. It became the most discussed spiking incident of all time. It happened in Detroit when the Tigers and Athletics were battling furiously for the American League championship.

"Everyone said I deliberately spiked Baker," recalled Cobb, not without a trace of bitterness. "The picture of the slide showed I couldn't have done it deliberately. Baker didn't even lose an inning but I got thirteen threatening letters and one of the bums threatened to shoot me from a window outside the park."

The anger of the fans against Ty Cobb reached an all-time high in 1912. In a game in New York, Cobb, while trotting to his position in left field, suddenly began to run at full speed toward the bleachers where a longtime heckler of his was sitting. Cobb vaulted the rail, pushed his way through a mass of spectators, and proceeded to administer a thorough drubbing to his tormentor. Cobb had to fight his way back to the playing field, where his teammates protected their star standing along the rail with brandishing bats.

Cobb, of course, was suspended. The Tigers met and decided to go out on strike. It was not out of affection for Cobb but affection for his .400 batting average. On May 18, 1912, Detroit was scheduled to meet the Athletics in Philadelphia. Rather than forfeit $5,000, Manager Hughey Jennings hired a group of Philadelphia semipros and sandlotters and fielded them against the A's. The Athletics won, 24–2.

Hatred for Cobb was universal. It was a toss-up who hated him the most, the opposing players or his teammates. There was almost a coalition of fans and baseball players whose sole mission was, win or lose, to stop Ty Cobb. It was in 1910 that Cobb and Napoleon Lajoie were battling for the American League batting title. On the last day of the season, Cobb led Lajoie by several points. Lajoie's Cleveland Naps were playing a doubleheader against St. Louis on the final day of the season. He collected eight hits, seven of them bunts down the third-base line. The St. Louis third baseman was purposely laying deep on Lajoie allowing the great second baseman to beat out bunts in an effort to deprive Ty Cobb of the batting title. Cobb fooled them. He went three for four and beat out Lajoie by one percentage point.

H. G. Salsinger, best of Ty Cobb's biographers, wrote about him: "He was the outstanding phenomenon of baseball. Some players had more mechanical ability, some could field better, some could throw better, some could run faster and some could hit the ball farther, but none ever matched him for speed of mind, for coordination, for aggressiveness and daring, and for flaming competitive spirit. He stands alone as the fiery genius of the game. There was never another like Cobb and it's not probable that there will ever be another with a similar combination of talents. He was not the fastest runner of his time, yet he still ranks as the greatest base runner of all time. He was not a natural hitter and still he created the most impressive lifetime batting average ever compiled. He was never much better than an average fielder and still he was the most spectacular outfielder the game has ever known, and the most dangerous."

Cobb was an artist with a bat and he drove the opposition crazy. If they played deeply, he bunted. If they inched in, he slashed hits past them and over them. Never should it be forgotten that he averaged .367—not for one season but for over the course of twenty-four years. Twelve times a batting champion, three times a .400 hitter.

As a base runner, he was in a class by himself and the figures prove that, too. They show 892 stolen bases in a lifetime and a season high of 96. Yet even they are deceptive because they don't reveal enough. Cobb on the base paths transmitted a mass case of jitters to the enemy operatives. They never knew what to expect and he heightened their fears by his tantalizing actions.

"I often tried plays that looked reckless, maybe even silly," he once confided. "But I did it to study how the other team reacted, filing away in my mind any observations for future use."

And that's how he was able to score the winning run from first base on an infield out. Cobb was on first when Sam Crawford dribbled one to Hal Chase, the first baseman, on a hit and run. In full speed even before bat nudged ball, Cobb was tearing into third as Chase stepped on first and fired across the diamond to Jimmy Archer. From past experience Archer knew that Ty would round the bag and scramble back. He speared the ball and swooped low for the tag. This time, though, Cobb was not scrambling back. He was sliding home.

Proud of his eminence, he grew nettled when Babe Ruth's home run bat began to take away the headlines. "What's so difficult about hitting home runs?" snarled Cobb. "I can hit them anytime I want to." He hit three that day and two the following day to set a record never surpassed.

But homers never interested him. He wanted hits and made 4,191 of them. Once he singled on the first pitch, stole second, then shouted a warning that he would steal third and proceeded to do so. Then with two strikes on the batter, Cobb broke for the plate. The pitch was little high, and before the catcher could pull it down, Cobb had slid home. The man at the plate hadn't swung at the ball, but Cobb had gone all the way around the bases.

That was Ty Cobb.

CHRISTY MATHEWSON

BY JOE REICHLER

Twenty-seven thousand fans jammed the Polo Grounds on October 14, 1905. They filled every seat and were lined ten deep along the outfield ropes. Some daring fellows clamored on the grandstand roof; others perched on the fences. Every fan in New York, it seemed, had tried to get in for this game, which could decide the first World Series on Manhattan soil. And what a Series! Four games, four shutouts, and the Giants led the Athletics, three games to one.

The Giant management had provided a band. But this crowd hadn't come for a concert. Tension mounted as the minutes ticked slowly away toward game time. At last the Giants burst from their dressing room. The bleachers erupted. "Pitch Matty! Pitch Matty!" the bleachers implored. "Let's clinch it today." And Matty it was. The crowd went wild when the beloved right-hander, Christy Mathewson, with indolent grace, began lobbing the ball to his favorite catcher, Roger Bresnahan.

Big Six (the nickname was coined by Sam Crane of the New York *Journal,* who dubbed Matty the "Big Six of pitchers," alluding to the champion engine of the New York Fire Department) was Broadway's darling. He'd won thirty, thirty-three, and thirty-one games in the last three years. He'd pitched the Giants to two straight pennants, their first since 1888 and 1889. And he'd shown Connie Mack's bully boys that there was still life in the old league yet. The Boston Red Sox of the brash young American League had whipped the Pittsburgh Nationals, five games to three, in the first World Series, two years before. The leagues did not get together in 1904, but the A's were cocky entering this postseason encounter—at least, they were until they met Matty. Big Six had whitewashed them, 3–0, on four hits, in the opener at Philadelphia, beating Eddie Plank, his old college rival from Gettysburg. In New York, the next day, the A's had evened the Series, 3–0, as Chief Bender outpitched Iron Man Joe McGinnity. After a

one-day break, Matty had put the Giants on top again, with a 9–0 victory over Andy Coakley. It was another four-hit breeze. Then McGinnity had redeemed himself and horse-collared the Athletics, 1–0.

So the stage was set. Could Big Six, working his third game in six days, come through again, against the well-rested Bender? The stands buzzed about Manager John McGraw's daring gamble. It was a pitcher's duel from the start. Matty, working easily, had base runners to cope with in all but one of the first six innings. But Big Six was invincible in the clutch. No one advanced beyond second. Bender was mowing them down, too. In the fifth, Bender's control wavered. Two bases on balls, a sacrifice bunt, and Billy Gilbert's fly drew first blood for the Giants. They got another in the eighth. Matty calmly reeled off the last three outs in the top of the ninth and the Giants were world champions. If Christy Mathewson accomplished nothing else, his name would live for those three shutouts within a six-day span. In them, he allowed just fourteen hits and one walk.

But this unmatched achievement marked just one brief passage of glory in the seventeen-year career of the "perfect pitcher," who captivated the public as no other ballplayer except Babe Ruth has before or since. Big Six stood on a solitary peak in pitching's greatest age.

An All-American fullback at Bucknell, where his phenomenal dropkicking caught Walter Camp's eye, Matty came to the Giants in 1900 after two minor-league way-stops and, with the arrival of John McGraw in 1902, became their keystone. One of the first college graduates to adopt baseball as a career, Matty brought to the game more than outstanding athletic qualifications. He was known for his keen sportsmanship and sense of fair play. Handsome, intelligent, and clean-living, he was held up as a model to American youth. Over his career, abbreviated by a mysterious side ailment, he won 373 games (a National League record later matched by Alexander) while losing only 188. He won twenty or more games twelve straight years (1903–14). His 37 victories of 1908 is still a league high. He helped the Giants win five pennants.

Mathewson's control was legendary. He gave only twenty-one walks in 306 innings in 1913 and only forty-two in 391 innings in 1908. In 1913 he pitched 68 consecutive innings without passing a batter. He could put the ball wherever he wanted to, consistently. Out in front, Big Six was not inclined to bear down. But no one could turn it on harder when he had to. Although not a strike-out pitcher, his 2,511 career strikeouts and 267 whiffs for a season in 1903 still rank among the best.

Mathewson was best known for his famous fade-away pitch, the screwball of today. A reverse curve thrown by the big right-hander, it broke in and down on right-handed batters and away from left-handers. Matty was at his best in times of stress. McGraw once summoned him from the shower to check a ninth-inning

Cub rally. Chicago, one run behind, had filled the bases with one out. With his blond hair dripping wet, his hat awry, and his shirttails flapping loose, Matty without even bothering to lace his shoes struck out the last two batters and went back to finish his bath.

Matty was not so fortunate in World Series play. Although he pitched 101 and 2/3 innings, a figure topped only by the Yankees Whitey Ford, his Series record shows five victories and five defeats, four of them by one run. Four of his triumphs were by shutouts.

Mathewson's competitive mishaps were minor tragedies, however, in view of the sad end to the stirring saga of Big Six. In 1917, a year after leaving the Giants to manage Cincinnati, Matty enlisted in the army. As a captain in the chemical warfare division, he soon went overseas and, in combat on the western front, he was gassed. His lungs never fully recovered, and soon after the war, from which he returned to coach the Giants, he became critically ill. A long convalescence at Saranac Lake followed. Then, in 1923, against better advice, he accepted the presidency of the Boston Braves. Under the strain of his work, his health broke again. A sorrowing nation learned of his death, at the age of forty-five, on October 7, 1925. The news cast a pall over the 1925 World Series. His memory remained alive, however, and eleven years later, the Baseball Writers Association of America, in their first election, enshrined him in the Hall of Fame.

WALTER JOHNSON

BY SHIRLEY POVICH

In the summer of 1907, the Washington Senators were assailed by continual letters from a fan in far-off Idaho, a persistent one-way pen pal who identified himself only as a traveling salesman. The theme of his unanswered letters was always the same: "This boy Walter Johnson is the strikeout king of the Snake River Valley League, and worth a look. His pitch is faster than Amos Rusie's and his control is better than Mathewson's. He's a phenom."

In a subsequent letter he wrote Senator's Manager

Joe Cantillon, "This boy throws so fast you can't see 'em, and he knows where he is throwing the ball, because if he didn't there would be dead bodies strewn all over Idaho." Surely, the fellow was telling traveling salesman's jokes.

He wasn't. When Cantillon finally unbent and sent scout Cliff Blankenship to Weiser, Idaho, to assess the Snake River Valley League strikeout king, Blankenship brought back a pitching prize unmatched in all major-league baseball history.

For the next twenty-one years, Walter Perry Johnson pitched for the Senators, winning more games in the American League than any pitcher who ever lived. He demolished all American League strikeout records and pitched more shutouts than any other man. Yet the man who was throwing the most-feared fast ball in the big leagues was the gentle strikeout king, admired for his "aw-shucks" modesty and warmth of nature. No baseball athlete ever achieved a higher place in the affection of the nation's fans. They, too, were melancholy when it took him seventeen years to pitch for a pennant winner. They rejoiced when, at last, he appeared in a World Series.

The details of that day when Johnson became the property of the Senators bear retelling. Blankenship's first glimpse of Johnson was as a losing pitcher. He was beaten, 1–0, by a teammate's error in the twelfth inning. At the game's end, Blankenship wrote out a quick contract on a piece of wrapping paper. It called for $350 a month, but the Senators scout was also flashing $100 in bills as a cash bonus. But the young pitcher said he must first consult his dad. He returned to ask Blankenship for a special security benefit. He asked a guarantee of return fare from Washington to Idaho if he was released by the Senators. He got his release more than two decades later, when he asked for it.

Johnson's acquisition was announced with great excitement, including exclamation points by the Washington Post baseball writer in a dispatch from New York where the Senators were playing: "Manager Joe Cantillon has added a great baseball phenom to his pitching staff. The young man's name is Walter Johnson. The premier pitcher from Idaho was signed by Cliff Blankenship. Cantillon received word telling of the "Capture!" Johnson pitched 75 innings in Idaho without allowing a run! Blankenship is very enthusiastic, but fails to say whether the phenom is left- or right-handed."

Ten thousand curious fans assembled in Washington's American League Park for Johnson's pitching debut on August 2, 1907. They quickly learned he was right-handed and long of arm, and that he looked every inch his 6'1" and 200 pounds. But they gasped at his first delivery against the Detroit Tigers. This couldn't be the fierce fast-baller they had heard about. This chap was pitching sidearm, with a long sweeping delivery that was almost underhand, defying the popular image of what great fast-ballers are made of, fellows who come in overhand with their best speed.

But the Tigers, including Ty Cobb in his third season in the majors, were coming to respect Johnson's speed. Quickly they resorted to bunting. Three of the six hits they made off him were bunts, two by Cobb. Two bunts figured in the winning run before Johnson left the game trailing, 2–1, in the eighth inning.

In his second start, Johnson beat the Cleveland Indians with a four-hitter. He would win 415 more games for the Senators before he retired in 1927, and 113 of them would be shutouts. In 1913, the first year earned run averages were kept, Johnson set the record of 1.09. Exactly 3,500 others were to be claimed as his strikeout victims after he fanned the first one.

There would have been more strikeouts, Johnson's teammates always claimed, if Johnson were not a confirmed loafer. He never set strikeout goals for himself, liked to get a lead and experiment with a curve ball that he never did master.

The person who feared his fast ball most was Johnson himself. He was constantly inhibited by his dread of maiming or even killing a batsman who couldn't duck one of his inside pitches. After one of his pitches hit Frank "Home Run" Baker, turning that fellow's cap around, he vowed to trainer Mike Martin that he would never again brush back a batter. In later years Ty Cobb confessed that he exploited Johnson's fear of hitting a batter, saying, "I crowded the plate on him, knowing I'd never get a pitch on the inside." Cobb also agreed that he had little success in hitting Johnson even with that advantage.

For ten consecutive years, Johnson was a 20-game winner, most with hopeless Washington teams. He was at his zenith in 1912 and 1913 when his won-lost records were 32–12 and an incredible 36–7. In 1912 he won 16 consecutive games. In 1913 he pitched 56 scoreless innings, in a record streak that came to a halt unfairly when he was charged with a run left on base by the pitcher he replaced in a relief stint.

There was universal dismay when Johnson, getting his first chance to pitch in a World Series, was beaten by the Giants in his first two starts in 1924. But joy came in the seventh game. The desperate Senators called him in for relief and he delivered four shutout innings to emerge as the winning pitcher in the twelfth.

The Big Swede, he was frequently called by writers and fans during most of his career. Actually, Johnson was German-Dutch but he never once denied he was Swedish. "They're nice people, the Swedes," he said, "and I don't want to offend them."

Walter Johnson didn't want to offend anybody, including the fan who buttonholed him one day in a St. Louis hotel lobby. When Johnson finally detached himself, teammate Joe Judge, who was waiting to accompany him to a movie, asked, "What took you so long?"

Johnson said, "Oh, that fellow wanted to talk. He said he knew my sister in Kansas."

Judge said, "I didn't know you had a sister."

"I don't," Johnson said.

RUTH, GEHRIG, AND DIMAGGIO

BY ROBERT W. CREAMER

A generation or so ago, when the stock market was on a sustained upward march and pennants came to the New York Yankees with the regularity of the autumnal equinox, a disgruntled wit one day muttered something to the effect that following the Yankees must be like rooting for U. S. Steel. The *mot* was widely repeated and, along with such profundities as "Tell it like it is" and "the impossible dream," became one of the enduring cliches of sports. It meant, presumably, that following the Yankees was safe and satisfying and even profitable, but it certainly was not exciting. Oh, how often you heard that line in those days. "Being a Yankee fan," one man would say to another, his tones indicating that something significant was about to be revealed, "is like rooting for U. S. Steel." And the other, wishing he had said it first, would nod and reply, "That's true. That's true."

But it was not true. Rooting for the Yankees in their glory years was a terrific feeling. There is deep, vicarious satisfaction in seeing superb athletes do things well, and what excites a baseball fan most is watching his heroes come through, when they do the great things man is capable of, when they make the watching fan feel that he, too, is part of this splendid and accomplished human race. The player hitting the home run, making the superb catch, racing across the plate with the winning run, is me, triumphant. There is no better feeling in sports than watching your hero doing heroic things, which is why being a Yankee fan was so much fun—because Yankee fans had more and better heroes than anyone else.

Here we will discuss three of them. Their proper names are George H. Ruth, H. Louis Gehrig, and Joseph P. DiMaggio, but if I had written Babe, Lou, and Joe, you would have known who I meant. For more than thirty years, they *were* the New York Yankees. Anyone who thinks it was not an extraordinary feeling to see them on a ball field, anytime you went to a ball park, does not know what baseball is all about.

Take Babe Ruth. What can be said about him that has not been said a hundred times before? When he was sold by the Boston Red Sox to the Yankees in January 1920, he was already the most famous ballplayer in the land. He was twenty-six (he was actually a year younger than that, as a birth certificate disclosed when Babe applied for a passport in the 1930s, but he always went by the older age) and had been a big-leaguer for five and a half years. At twenty he had gone directly from the reform school where he had spent most of his youth to the minor-league Baltimore Orioles; four months later he was in the major leagues. He was a left-handed pitcher then, and a superb one. In 1915, his first full season, he won eighteen games, seventeen of them from June onward. In 1916 and 1917 he was the best pitcher in the American League, better in those years than the renowned Walter Johnson, whom he regularly defeated in head-to-head pitching duels. At the same time he was beginning to show his extraordinary prowess with the bat, hitting enormous home runs in an era when home runs were hit neither very often nor very far. In 1918, when team rosters were depleted by the departure of players to the armed services of World War I, Ruth, who was deferred because he was a married man, began to play first base and the outfield on days he was not pitching. By the end of the 1919 season he had put pitching aside and was a full-time outfielder and unparalleled slugger. He had shared the American League home run championship (with 11) in 1918, but in 1919 he won it outright and in so doing broke all existing records for most home runs in one season. His total, 29, seems amusingly modest today, but it was breathtaking then.

Baseball in that first year after the war enjoyed unprecedented popularity, and Ruth was in the forefront of that enthusiasm. He was the king, the best, the most famous player of all, better known to the country at large than Ty Cobb, Tris Speaker, Home Run Baker, and all the others who had been revered by the keenly interested but relatively small sector of the population that followed baseball before the war. The Babe broke new demographic ground for baseball; everybody, including your old Aunt Mabel, knew who he was, and most of them wanted to see him play.

And then Boston sold him to the Yankees, a deal that remains the single most astonishing player transaction in baseball history. It revolutionized the game. It certainly made the Yankees. Before Ruth, the Yankees had been a desultory, mostly second-rate team. In existence since 1903, they had never won a pennant, had finished as high as second only three times, and more often than not finished in the second division. In New York, they were distinctly inferior to John McGraw's Giants. But in 1920 Babe turned everything around.

In that first season of his with the Yankees, the first in which he was not obliged to mix regular pitching chores in with his batting, Ruth was utterly sensational. He hit 54 home runs, almost double the earthshaking

record he had set a year earlier, had the Yankees in the pennant race until September, and attracted 1,289,000 spectators to Yankee home games, the first time a major-league club had drawn a million or more people. In 1921 he was even better; what he did with his bat that year remains the finest single season any player has ever had: 177 runs scored, 170 batted in, a .378 batting average, 457 total bases, an .846 slugging average, 205 hits, 119 of them for extra bases, 59 of those for home runs, breaking his record again. No one was close to him: the second-best home run total in the American League was 24; the best in the National was 23. If you wanted to see homers hit, you went to see the Babe.

But it was not just the sheer majesty of his skill that made Ruth unique. His personality was irrepressible; he became a totally public figure. He was loud, profane, vulgar, cheerful, awful, marvelous—and he was visible. Everybody seemed to know where he was all the time. He made a vast amount of money and spent just as much. He gambled extravagantly, he drank too much, he chased women. His undisciplined behavior brought him into conflict with Judge Landis, the first Commissioner of Baseball, who because of the Chicago Black Sox scandal had been given absolute authority over all aspects of the game. Landis suspended Ruth for the first six weeks of the 1922 season, a year that turned into a succession of disasters for the Babe: he slumped badly at the plate; he had furious quarrels with umpires; he fought with a teammate on the bench during a game; he was suspended five different times that year. His popularity—as America's cheerful hero—dropped to a depressing low.

But Ruth was resilient. He came back from that awful year to play splendidly in 1923 and 1924, regaining the home run championship he had relinquished in 1922, winning a batting title, gaining the Most Valuable Player award. And then another disaster hit in 1925 when, with his marriage coming to an end, his constant drinking and carousing led him to physical collapse, an abdominal operation, a dismal season at bat, a run-in with the Yankee manager, Miller Huggins, and a showdown in which the diminutive 5′ 6 1/2″ Huggins stood up to the powerful Ruth, suspended him indefinitely, and brought him to heel when Babe, at long last humbled, apologized and dutifully returned to the fold.

From then on Ruth was unstoppable. Critics had written him off as finished after 1925, but he came roaring back in 1926 to lead the Yankees (a seventh-place team in 1925) to the first of three straight pennants. In 1927 he hit his famous 60 home runs. In 1928 he batted .625 in the World Series, hit 3 home runs in one Series game for the second time, and established once and for all that he was the king of baseball.

Time inevitably got to Ruth, and by 1932 he was in decline. He failed to win or share the home run championship for the first time since 1917 (except, of course, for 1922 and 1925, when he was out of the lineup for extended periods). He played fewer games and was quite ill late in the season, which led to reports that he might not play in the World Series. But, of course, he did, and, of course, that was the Series in which he hit the most famous home run of his career, the "called-shot homer" against the Chicago Cubs. The argument still rages over whether or not Babe actually pointed to a spot in the center-field bleachers and then hit the ball there. That terrible movie with William Bendix playing the role of Babe indicated he did; but Ruth certainly did not do what Bendix did in the film. Just as certainly, in the back-and-forth jockeying between the Yankees and Cubs, Ruth brazenly defied his opponents, did indicate he was going to hit one—as brash ballplayers often have promised—and then, by God, did hit one. Even if the legend exaggerates the precise facts of the incident, it nonetheless reflects a basic truth: that Babe did call his shot, did hit a home run under pressure before 40,000 people in the ball park and before millions more "watching" around the country.

There was never another like Ruth. Even in his final, sad year, 1935, after he had left the Yankees and put in a brief, depressing two months with the eighth-place Boston Braves, his last hurrah was almost unbelievable. In Forbes Field in Pittsburgh, probably the least inviting home run park in the majors, Ruth, fat and sick and forty-one, hit three home runs and a single in one game. His third homer that afternoon, the last he was ever to hit and the last base hit of his career, was the longest ever seen in Pittsburgh, the first ever to clear the towering right-field roof in that ancient park. A week later he was finished, done, through. But never forgotten, not even now.

By contrast with Ruth, Lou Gehrig in retrospect seems a placid, unexciting player. Massive, broad-shouldered, big-bottomed, heavy-legged, he had none of Ruth's flair, none of his bouncing personality. Ruth had been more or less alienated from his parents, who had put him behind the walls of St. Mary's when he was eight years old. Gehrig was always devoted to his. "Mom" Gehrig was as much a part of his life as the number 4 on the back of his uniform, or the big bats he swung with so much success. Unlike Ruth, Gehrig was modest, well behaved, disciplined to a fault. He never caused trouble with management, never was suspended, never complained about his pay, although his biggest salary was less than half of Ruth's best. He did his work like a dutiful factory hand, day after day, year after year. When Ruth suggested one year that they hold out together, Lou nervously rejected the suggestion.

Gehrig broke in with the Yankees in 1925, when Ruth had been a major-league star for ten seasons. Babe always looked upon Lou with condescension; Lou was a kid, Babe the big brother. They were great friends for a while—Ruth almost always had a rookie, a young ballplayer, as a close pal—but later they had a grievous falling out over a real or imagined difficulty between Mom Gehrig and Ruth's wife, Claire, and they barely spoke to one another for years after that.

Through it all, through the years of being overshadowed by Ruth, of being patronized by him, of being ostracized by him, Gehrig played ball magnificently. The paralysis that was to kill him ended his career when he was thirty-five years old. If he had been able to play three more seasons—until he was thirty-eight, say, although most of the superstars have played longer than that—and had batted only as well as he had in his last full season, (when the oncoming illness caused a drastic fall-off from his usual brilliance), Gehrig would have had well over 3,000 hits, 600 home runs, 2,300 runs batted in, 2,200 runs scored, figures that would be popping up in every story written as the Musials and Mayses and Aarons drift into that lofty statistical atmosphere at the end of their two decades of stardom.

Gehrig is surely the most overlooked of the truly great ballplayers. The one record most people remember him for is the ridiculous one of playing 2,130 consecutive games—he did not miss a game in thirteen straight full seasons. I say it is ridiculous because it causes Gehrig to be remembered for his attendance rather than his accomplishments. Look at the things he did. In 1927 when Ruth hit his 60, Gehrig matched him homer for homer most of the season—until Ruth's astonishing finishing surge—and ended with 47, which was more than anyone other than Babe had ever hit. Lou was the first player really to challenge Ruth's supremacy as a home run hitter, yet never has one athlete been so obscured by another. Consider Gehrig in the 1928 World Series, the one in which Ruth hit .625, still the best-ever World Series batting average. In that

Series, Babe had 3 home runs, 9 runs scored, 4 runs batted in. Gehrig had 4 home runs, 5 runs scored, 9 runs batted in—and his batting percentage was .545, which is the highest ever in Series play except for Babe's the same year. In the 1932 Series, when Ruth hit his called-shot homer, Gehrig batted .529 (to Ruth's .333), had 3 home runs (to Babe's 2), scored 9 runs (to Babe's 6), and batted in 8 (to Babe's 6). Yet 1932 is remembered as Babe's Series. In 1934, Ruth's last with the Yankees, Gehrig won the Triple Crown (which Babe, for all his accomplishments, was never able to do) by leading the league in home runs with 49, in runs batted in with 165, and in batting percentage with .364. More stories were written about Ruth that season—about his declining skills, his ailments, his running feud with Manager Joe McCarthy—than about Gehrig's marvelous performance at bat.

After that season Ruth was gone, and Gehrig stood alone—for one year. Then Joe DiMaggio came to the Yankees, and Gehrig found himself overshadowed again. In 1936, DiMaggio's rookie year, Gehrig hit 49 home runs (Lou twice hit 49 but never a glamorous 50), batted .354, and drove in 152 runs, but everyone was talking now about the fabulous youngster whose presence seemed to account for the Yankees winning the pennant again after failing to do so since 1932, Ruth's last important season. DiMaggio's rookie year was indeed remarkable—.323, 29 home runs, 125 runs batted in—but Gehrig was named Most Valuable Player, if anyone remembers. The next season DiMaggio led the league with 46 homers to Gehrig's 37 and had 167 RBIs to Lou's 159. The year after that, weakened by illness, Gehrig slumped. A year later he was gone from the majors and two years after that, not yet thirty-eight years old, he was dead.

Gehrig's abrupt decline and departure may account for the curious lack of personal popularity that the highly accomplished DiMaggio commanded during his first several years with the Yankees. The sportswriters loved Gehrig; Lou was a decent, friendly man, a New Yorker born and bred who spoke with the local writers on their own terms and who saw them, frequently on a friendly basis, during the off-season. DiMaggio, from the other side of the country, was aloof, silent, indifferent to the press. And DiMaggio—like Ruth, unlike Gehrig—staged fairly spectacular holdouts in his quiet way, fighting the tightfisted Ed Barrow, the Yankees' tyrannical general manager, for more money. Barrow much preferred the Gehrig type, grateful for the chance to be in the majors, dutifully accepting whatever pay he was offered. DiMaggio, who had spent three long seasons as a top-level minor-leaguer before being brought up to the majors, wanted full dollar for his rare skills; he did not hesitate to resist the irritated Barrow until he got what he deserved, or a lot closer to it than Gehrig ever received.

DiMaggio won the home run title in 1937 and back-to-back batting championships in 1939 and 1940, and he

was the key reason why the Yankees of 1936–39 won four straight pennants and four straight World Series, the first time that had ever been done. But it was not until 1941 that DiMadge—which was his nickname, not Jolting Joe—captured the imagination and affection of the fans. That was the year of his consecutive-game batting streak, and for sustained, day-in-and-day-out interest there has been nothing else like it in baseball. A batting streak is such a precarious thing—just one bad day at bat, or one unlucky day—and there it goes. The sports pages were aware of the streak fairly early and gave widespread attention to it when it reached 25 games or so. As it edged toward 30, records were dug into. The shining target was George Sisler's 1922 mark of 41 straight. As Joe approached that, someone came up with Willie Keeler's more ancient 44 in a row, set in 1897. Inexorably, DiMaggio rolled toward and past Sisler, toward and past Keeler, and did not stop. Seldom has a baseball achievement better reflected a player's personality: DiMaggio was the epitome of efficient, sustained skill, the unflappable ability to meet a challenge. It was not merely the breaking of the old records that excited the imagination of people all over the country; it was the way DiMaggio kept the streak going after he had passed all the old marks. Ultimately, he extended it to 56 straight games.

The way his streak ended was as fitting as the way he kept it alive. New York Met fans, fascinated by rookie Mike Vail's batting string late in the 1975 season (which stopped at 23, just short of the record for a rookie), will recall that Vail's streak ended in a fourteen-inning game in which the youngster had eight chances at bat to keep it going. That seemed like fate; Vail was destined to be stopped in that game. DiMaggio's, on the other hand, was broken only because Cleveland third baseman Ken Keltner made superb plays on two hard DiMaggio smashes that should have gone through for hits. And after that night, with the big streak ended, DiMaggio went on to hit safely in 16 more games in succession, itself a string of admirable length. No wonder they sang, that summer, "Joe, Joe, DiMaggio, we want you on our side."

When DiMaggio returned to the Yankees after three years of army service during World War II, he was not quite the ballplayer he had been. Plagued by ailments, particularly a bone spur in his heel, he hit well enough but—with the exception of 1948, when he had 39 homers and 155 runs batted in—not at the superla-

tive level he had maintained before the war. In 1949 he was unable to play at all through the first part of the season, but that set up a performance that forever endeared him to baseball fans generally and Yankee fans in particular. His return to the lineup in June, in a series against the league-leading Red Sox in Boston, was a melodramatic tour de force in the tradition of Ruth. DiMaggio had missed the first sixty-six games of the season, and his timing should have been off, to say the very least. But in his first time at bat in the first game of the three-game set he hit a ringing single, later added a home run that lifted the Yankee bench into paroxysms of delight, hit two more homers in the next game and a fourth in the final game of the series. The Yankees swept all three and, although ravaged all season by injuries, fought the Red Sox to the wire, beat them two straight at the very end of the year to win the pennant, and routed the Dodgers in the World Series. That was the first of five consecutive World Series triumphs for the Yankees, an unprecedented and still unmatched accomplishment.

In 1950 DiMaggio overcame a slump to play well enough, but his performance was not up to the level he expected of himself; after he missed three dozen games in 1951 because of age and infirmities (and hit only a dozen homers) he decided he had had enough. He played all six games of the World Series that fall and hit a home run (his eighth in Series competition) and then announced his retirement, even though the Yankees offered him $100,000 to play again the next year.

Unlike Ruth, who hung around too long, yearning for past glory, and Gehrig, whose end was so tragic, DiMaggio left baseball as he had played it, with grace and dignity and control. Where Ruth survived his playing career by little more than a dozen years and Gehrig almost not at all, it has been baseball's good fortune to have had the retired DiMaggio in and around the game for a quarter of a century now since he stopped playing ball. The special appeal of his presence at such functions as Old-Timers' Games is more than the tug of nostalgia, the idea of "Where have you gone, Joe DiMaggio?" Rather, it is that same old feeling of vicarious pleasure, the one we experience when we see another human being performing well, giving pride and, yes, class to us all.

U. S. Steel, indeed.

STAN MUSIAL

BY BOB BROEG

The hokiest movie Hollywood *never* made began twenty-eight miles south of Pittsburgh in western Pennsylvania's industrial Monongahela Valley, where a grimy little town of Donora crawled up a four-hundred-foot rise to escape the belching blasts of giant smokestacks that lined the western bank of a slow, silt-laden river.

To survive in a community gray from years of blast furnaces, the inhabitants had to be rugged. Most migrated from Russia, Germany, and Poland, including a wiry little man from a farm near Warsaw. He was Lukasz Musial.

Lukasz' wife, Mary Lancos, was a large handsome woman with a hearty laugh. A second-generation Czech who went to work housecleaning at eight, she rowed her father across the Monongahela River in a skiff early each day to his job as a coal miner and then rowed him back again in the evening. At fourteen, sorting nails in a wire mill, she met the shy little Polish immigrant, Lukasz Musial, who worked in the shipping department, wrestling hundred-pound bundles of wire into freight cars.

Lukasz spoke no English, but Mary understood Polish. Four years later they were married, at a time when Lukasz was bringing home eleven dollars pay every two weeks. They paid four dollars a month rent and raised six children, the next to last of whom was the first son, born in November 1920.

He was Stanley Frank Musial who became baseball's Horatio Alger, the poor Polish immigrant's son who struck it rich by playing a boy's game better than most men and by enriching lives with his attitude even more than his athletic aptitude.

Signed to play professional baseball for only sixty-five dollars a month when still in high school, Stan Musial faced a critical crossroads only three years later. Over his father's objections, he had turned down prospects for a college scholarship to play basketball, but now, married and with his first child on the way, he was a Class D pitcher, dead-armed as the result of an injury suffered as he tumbled to make a catch when playing part-time outfield for Daytona Beach, Florida.

Here is where not even Hollywood in the pretelevision period when it turned out movies by the bundle would have had the imagination—or gall—to produce a Grade B film in which the apple-cheeked, ample-nosed, good-looking kid would become a superstar overnight, a sensation in one year who endured through twenty-two record-smashing seasons to become a living legend, a homer-hitting grandfather at nearly forty-three.

A trim athlete and a good family man, Musial made news on the field, seldom off it. Yet he reached the public everywhere with his talent, team consciousness, and even temperament. He was indeed, as former commissioner Ford Frick described him in ceremonies at St. Louis' old Sportsman's Park the day Stan the Man hung it up with base hits his last two times up on the final day of the 1963 season:

"Baseball's perfect warrior . . . baseball's perfect knight," an accolade that is inscribed on the marble base of a bigger-than-life bronzed statue of Musial outside Busch Memorial Stadium in downtown St. Louis.

Elected rousingly to the Baseball Hall of Fame immediately when eligible, 1969, Stan was a superstar without a first-person complex. He was dedicated to doing things the team way, refusing, for instance, to fly by himself when he couldn't sleep on trains because he didn't want to leave the ball club. He shared gifts and samples with his teammates, making certain that the rawest Redbird rookie was favored as often as his longtime road roommate, Red Schoendienst.

Stan and his wife, the former Lillian Labash, his high-school sweetheart, had three daughters after their only son. It was the birth of Dick's first child that Grandpa Musial celebrated with a home run in Stan's last season, his lopsided grin widening as he told the press:

"That one, gentlemen, was for Jeffrey Stanton Musial, and I'll bet not many kids' grandfathers ever hit a big-league home run the day the boy was born."

His lifetime major-league batting average was distinguished by getting as many hits on the road as he had at home (1,815). As testimony to Musial's durability, he had the clutch facility of hitting higher in wearisome September (.344) than any month other than October, in which his brief regular-season appearances came out to a savage .438. He had 475 career home runs and was the first big-leaguer to reach 6,000 total bases.

He also hit a record six All-Star Game homers, including one that won the 1955 game at Milwaukee in the twelfth inning, 6–5. Musial and Ty Cobb are the only men ever to get five hits in a game four times in the same season. Stan did it in 1948, the year he missed by a washed-out home run, of leading the National League in runs, hits, doubles, triples, homers, RBIs, and average (.376). One time that season he went five for five with two strikes each appearance, the last time when, ripping tape from injured wrists, he took just five swings to get five hits.

Stan the Hundred Grand Man did all this from a crouched batting stance that included a humorous wiggle of his fanny, part of an instinctive effort to relax at the plate. He looked, someone once said, like a guy peeking around the corner to see if the cops were coming.

Spoiled by playing on four pennant-winning ball clubs his first four full seasons in the majors, Musial suffered the frustration of trying eighteen more times to match in maturity the youthful joy of competing for baseball's big apple in October. When the Cardinals rallied in September 1963 to win nineteen of twenty games before falling short against the Dodgers, the old man who earlier had announced his plans to retire finished strongly. But realistically unable to run as fast or to field as well as he once had, The Man stayed with his commitment to quit while he was still ahead.

When the Cardinals obtained Lou Brock from Chicago in a memorable mid-June deal in 1964 and then rallied to a pennant in which Brock was most prominent, The Man proved that although he had played in the past, he would not live in it.

"The Cardinals," he said, simply and honestly, "couldn't have won the pennant with me in left field."

In 1968 Musial stepped in as the Cardinal general manager and immediately was rewarded with a World Championship. Once again, good and lucky, a great combination, he stepped aside and summed up a look at himself and at baseball when he was inducted into the Hall of Fame two years afterward.

In that scenic, sylvan setting in Cooperstown, far from the grimy town in which he grew up and even farther from the maddening crowds before which he played the game as few before or after him have played it, Stanley Frank Musial said:

"I believe I played in the most exciting era of big-league baseball. I saw the game change from day to night, from regional to national, from long train rides to short plane flights, from cabbage leaves under the cap in hot weather to air-conditioned dugouts.

"I say baseball was a great game, is a great game, and will be a great game. I'm extremely grateful for what it has given me—in recognition and records, thrills and satisfaction, money and memories. I hope I've given nearly as much as I've gotten from it."

Now, how could Hollywood top that one?

TED WILLIAMS

BY SHIRLEY POVICH

In the exacting skill of hitting a pitched ball, few men have been so heroic as to give his name to an era of the game. Honus Wagner was an undisputed giant of the batter's box. Later, along came Ty Cobb, the thinking man's hitter. After Cobb, the role belonged to Babe Ruth, the carefree home run king with the unmatched batting thrust. They dwarfed their contemporaries with their feats with the bat.

Into this shining, if limited, company walked, in 1939, a tall, skinny, twenty-year-old Californian, called the Kid by his Boston Red Sox teammates. He immediately won the American League batting championship in his rookie year. Twenty years later, with a tenacity that taxed belief, and despite service in two wars, he was still putting together American League batting titles, back to back, still the extreme perfectionist whose name stood for awe as well as admiration. Ted Williams, too, carved himself an era.

There is doubt that a more scientific hitter ever lived, unless it was Ty Cobb. There is no doubt that any batter strived as much for excellence as Ted Williams, or that any batter was as prideful as the Kid, who was later to become known as the Splendid Splinter and, in his heftier, later years, as the Big Guy.

Even when Williams broke the .400 barrier in 1941, the line that was supposedly impregnable for modern hitters, he was not fully content with his .406 that outdistanced his nearest rival by 50 points. Just how much he demanded of himself was indicated by Williams when he once told a friend, "I do four out of ten jobs right, and they call me a great hitter."

Williams' pride was always present, often to an impractical degree. When opposing teams ganged up on him with their version of the Boudreau Shift, invented by Cleveland Manager Lou Boudreau in 1946 to foil Williams' strong penchant for pulling hits into right field, he spurned the chance to hit through the vacated left side of the infield or lay down a bunt. How many batting points he sacrificed by that stubbornness cannot be calculated, yet he hit .342 that season, .343 the next, and .369 the next.

He was haughty, too, about such things as giving satisfaction to pitchers who tried to brush him back, knock him down. Confident of his own dexterity at ducking a pitch, he was the last major-leaguer to resist wearing a batting helmet, under penalty of fine. He would perform torso acrobatics in the batter's box to remain upright, rather than go down from a close pitch, sometimes using his bat as a crutch, as if preserving his personal honor.

He often reduced Fenway Park fans to schizo-phrenia. Half of them cheered his every appearance; the other half often took to jeering him as a spoiled prima donna. In 1940 he stopped tipping his cap to the crowds after his home runs and never resumed it. He was the unrepentant individualist who, off the field, appeared only in sports shirts, would never wear a tie. "Ties," he said, "get in your soup."

Yet he was hero to most of the nation's fans. "Put a camera on him, and he performs," his business manager, Fred Corcoran, once said of Williams. True. When the American League All-Stars were desperate, two out in the ninth and a run behind, Williams hit a three-run homer off the third deck of Detroit's right-field stands, where no homer had ever been hit before. In the 1946 All-Star Game at Fenway Park, he made history as the only man to hit a home run off Rip Sewell's famed lazy blooper pitch, supplying all his own power.

He went off to war the first time, as a Marine flying cadet in 1943. Navy doctors who reported on his eye test had news that American League pitchers could appreciate. Williams, they said, was gifted with an excellence of vision noted only once in every 100,000 cases. His grasp of aerodynamics was also notable. He got high marks on qualification tests that few college-bred candidates could pass. The Marines say he still holds gunnery records involving sleeve targets. This was the fellow who batted .300 or more for nineteen consecutive seasons and had a .344 career mark at the finish.

Seven years after his discharge, Williams was back in service for the Korean War. He escaped with his life in one flaming plane crash, then took up batting again, for the Red Sox. Williams, the indestructible, won two more batting titles in the next three years. He was still winning them at thirty-nine, a new record, and a year later broke that record for batting title seniority when he won his sixth league title.

No hitter since Ruth generated as much fan excitement as did Williams in his twenty-year career with the Red Sox. Like Ruth, he created a "what-will-he-do?" suspense. Would he make the pitcher come in with the exact offering he wanted? Would he go for the long ball? Would he break down and tip his hat if he hit a homer? Why does he keep talking to the catcher so much? He commanded all eyes. He was part of American folklore.

He ducked the Red Sox victory party when they clinched the pennant in 1946. He shied away from the fans' adulation during the season and went into seclusion in his Florida fishing grounds in the off-season. Yet, there had been much evidence of his charity, even as a loner, especially his work for the Jimmy Fund (cancer research) in Boston. And at his own induction into the Hall of Fame at Cooperstown in 1966, it was Ted Williams who first publicly declared that "the great Negro stars like Satchel Paige and Josh Gibson and the others who didn't get a chance in our league should be honored here too."

SANDY KOUFAX

BY SETH G. ABRAHAM

They packed the parks to watch him pitch in his prime. Around the National League circuit fans queued up at ticket windows for hours before game time for a chance to see Sandy Koufax on the mound. After all, over a four-year period, from 1963 through 1966, he was the dominant pitcher in baseball. He overwhelmed batters with a fast ball of such exceptional velocity that it brought fans out to measure his blazer against their memories of Walter Johnson, Lefty Grove, and Bob Feller, three fastest of the fast.

Every Koufax start during those years offered the promise of a no-hitter or a new strikeout mark, and it seemed as if some sort of record tumbled every time the Dodger southpaw pitched.

When Koufax was pitching, it was not unusual to see fans leave the park after he yielded his first hit or run. Koufax used to say that he started every game with the hope of pitching a no-hitter. He fulfilled that hope four times, making him and, later, Nolan Ryan the only holders of this record. Pause to contemplate this achievement. The four no-hitters by Koufax equals the combined output of no-hit games by Johnson, Christy Mathewson, and Carl Hubbell, who, together, won over 1,000 big-league games. Consider the formidable pitching talents of Grove and Grover Cleveland Alexander. Neither ever pitched a no-hit game.

There are two postscripts to Koufax's no-hit record. He pitched them in four consecutive years, 1962–65, and the last one, against the Chicago Cubs on September 10, 1965, was a perfect game.

But if the no-hitter was a Koufax hallmark, then the strikeout was his trademark.

During his great years the strikeouts would come in bunches after Koufax eased into the steady, fluid pattern that pitchers call "rhythm." Pitch after pitch the motion hardly varied. But the compact windup and smooth delivery belied the power behind the pitches.

Fresco Thompson, the late Dodger front office man, used to say that Koufax's fast ball "takes off like a jet fighter." Leo Durocher, who saw many a fast-ball pitcher in his time, called Koufax "faster than any pitcher I've ever seen." According to Durocher, Koufax made the "ball look smaller" when he threw the fast one.

To many, though, Koufax built his reputation as a strikeout pitcher on more than just a fast ball, explosive as it was. Fresco Thompson said Koufax knew how to use his curve and change-up to keep the batters guessing.

"The batters trying to get their bats out front to outguess Koufax's fast ball," Thompson said, "are made to look stupid when he comes in with the curve."

Durocher used to point to Koufax's great control in those years. When Koufax settled into his rhythm, Durocher said, his pitches "were never more than a quarter of an inch off the plate."

Koufax broke all kinds of strikeout marks before an arthritic elbow ended his career at thirty-one in 1966. He finished a twelve-year career with 2,396 strikeouts in 2,325 innings, making him the only pitcher in baseball to average more than one strikeout per inning over a career. Over that period he fanned ten or more batters in a game a record ninety-seven times, including two eighteen-strikeout games. He broke the season's strikeout mark, owned for nineteen years by Bob Feller, with 382 in 1965. A year later Koufax became the first pitcher to register 300 or more strikeouts in a season three times.

The strikeout and no-hit marks were only part of the record that made Koufax a pitcher apart from all others during the mid-1960s. From 1963 through 1966 Koufax won 97 games, with records of 25–5, 19–5, 26–8, and 27–9. His earned run averages in those seasons were 1.88, 1.74, 2.04, and 1.73. His consistent performances helped the Dodgers win three N.L. crowns (1963, 1965, 1966) and two World Championships (1963, 1965). In 1963 he was the N.L.'s Most Valuable Player as well as the Cy Young Award winner as baseball's outstanding pitcher. He won that award twice more, in 1965 and 1966.

The Dodgers brought Koufax to their spring training camp at Vero Beach, Florida, in 1955, where his wildness plagued him and terrorized the teammates who batted against him. What was worse was the frequent disappearance of the Dodger catchers when it came time for Koufax to warm up.

Years later, when he had perfected his craft, Koufax recalled that "Dixie Howell wouldn't talk to me. His shins were blue from trying to catch me."

Once, the Dodgers took Koufax out behind the camp's barracks to throw in privacy with a catcher of his own. The move was probably made to protect the Dodger batters as well as preserve Koufax's confidence that he could get the ball somewhere near the plate. People in the Dodger camp began to regard Koufax as just another one of those nameless lefties who come up for a time to the majors with exceptional speed and then follow the erratic path of their fast balls straight to a minor-league outpost on their way out of baseball.

But the Dodgers stayed with Koufax, reasoning that he really only needed experience, a difficult prerequisite when the Dodgers had a pitching staff with arms that belonged to Newcombe, Erskine, Maglie, et al.

Koufax's major-league debut against the Braves foretold of things to come, good and bad. His wildness loaded the bases with no one out, but he pitched out of the jam by striking out the next three batters with fast balls.

Koufax had similar flashes of brilliance in his early years, some of which he even sustained over nine innings. His chronic wildness, however, seemed to be as much a part of his pitching makeup as his fast ball.

Koufax thought about quitting baseball at the end of the 1960 season. He had pitched poorly; too many walks contributed to an 8–13 record. During the off-season Koufax discussed his future with the Dodger management. He said he wanted more starts.

The 1961 season was the turnaround year for Koufax.

He made no mechanical adjustments in his pitching but rather changed his pitching philosophy. Beginning in spring training games Koufax no longer tried to blow the fast ball by every hitter. He began to use a wicked curve and a change-up with increasing effectiveness. His fast ball was suddenly under control as he learned to throw it less hard, but with the same velocity.

He brought his emotions under control, too. Koufax now took to the mound a plan, a way to pitch to every batter, instead of rearing back to throw the fast ball.

"I learned that I couldn't always challenge the hitter," he said. "Now I can go out to the mound and not only think about what I should do with each batter, but I can execute my idea most of the time."

Koufax's 1961 statistics, 18–13 and new strikeout records, showed that he was making the transformation from thrower to pitcher.

Koufax retired from baseball after the 1966 season, the victim of an arthritic elbow that had plagued him since 1964. Koufax said the decision was made after doctors told him he risked permanent injury to his left arm if he continued to pitch.

But even in retirement, Sandy Koufax rewrote one more baseball record. In 1972 the thirty-six-year-old Koufax was elected to the Baseball Hall of Fame, the youngest player ever to be so honored.

WILLIE MAYS

BY SHIRLEY POVICH

One man, more than any other, exemplified the pure joy of playing baseball, the dash and delight of it. In his exuberance, Willie Mays caught more fly balls than any outfielder who ever lived, knocked more major-league home runs than any player except Hank Aaron and Babe Ruth, and stole far more bases than sluggers of his breed were expected to steal. He may also have been the National League's best bunter for most of his career. That he had one of the most-feared throwing arms is generally agreed.

The name of Willie Mays conjures visions. A favorite is the memory of Willie daring so often to go from first to third on a single to left and making it, leaving his cap somewhere on the far side of second base. His bareheaded arrival at third base was, according to option, the perfect hook slide or the dive for distance.

That any single feat could stand alone among the heroics of Mays in his twenty-two-year career is a tribute to the sheer breathlessness of the catch he made on an October afternoon at the Polo Grounds.

That was the day Vic Wertz won a World Series game for the Cleveland Indians—almost. With the bases full, he hit a ball over the heads of everybody, including center fielder Willie Mays of the Giants. But the race was not over yet. Never looking back, Mays outsped the ball, with his face to the wall, and gloved it in one hand, on instinct, in the deepest extremity of the Polo Grounds. Of the most-remembered catch in all baseball history, Mays said simply, "It wasn't that hard. It was the only way to catch it."

Willie Mays played baseball like a zealot. He had prophesied the 1954 pennant for the Giants when he was drafted in 1952 for two years of military service. Leaving for basic training, he told the Giants "Hold 'em boys, till I get back." He came back, hit forty-one home runs, led the National League in batting (.345) and the Giants to that pennant he had promised.

It was by happy accident that the Giants signed Mays in the first place. The mission they gave their agent, Eddie Montague, was to scout the Birmingham Barons of the Negro League and possibly buy Alonzo Perry, the Barons first baseman. When he watched the Barons nineteen-year-old center fielder get three extra base hits and make all catches in center field look easy, Montague quickly changed priorities. He bought Mays for $10,000, plus a $5,000 bonus to the surprised and grateful boy.

For the Giants, young Mays did not immediately appear to be a bargain. In his first twenty-six times at bat, he made only one hit. But showing patience beyond the call of duty, Manager Leo Durocher vowed faith in him. Suddenly, Mays became electric. He hit twenty homers in his rookie year, batted .274, made the difficult catches look routine, made others that were incredible, and began a career that made him perhaps the most famous National Leaguer of his time. On off days he could be found playing stickball with New York kids in the streets. He knew about kids. In Birmingham he had left nine half-brothers and half-sisters.

Mays' schooling had been very brief and informal. But of that, Leo Durocher once said, "Willie may not be a mental genius, but with that uniform on there's nobody smarter. He's alert, he's quick as a cat, gets every sign right. Once around the league, I never had to repeat anything to him again. In strict baseball terms I rate him with Eddie Stanky, Al Dark, and Pee Wee Reese as the smartest players I ever managed."

Durocher, who quickly foresaw Mays as one of the great players of the game, did not suffer from that confidence in him. For twenty consecutive years, Mays was voted on the National League All-Star team. He broke or tied twelve major-league records, nine National League records, and may have been the most-applauded player of his time.

Even with only ten letters in his name, Willie Mays has caused the publishers of record books to use up a lot of ink on his behalf. National League Rookie of the Year in 1951, Mays led the league in home runs in 1955 (with 51), in 1962 (with 49), in 1964 (with 47), and in 1965 (with 52). In 1961 he set the record for the most home runs hit in a nine-inning game (4). And in 1965, when he was chosen Most Valuable Player by the Baseball Writers Association of America, he set the record for homers hit in one month (17). Finally, as he finished out his second decade of major-league ball in 1971, he became the National League's all-time leader in runs scored when he crossed home plate for the 1,950th time to break Stan Musial's record.

Willie Mays was always the eager athlete, even after he had established himself as a batting champion and home run king. At the end of each inning he came in from the outfield in a tight gallop, as if he were trying to beat out an infield hit. It was the kind of hustle usually shown by a fellow trying to make the team, but rarely by a star of Mays' magnitude.

With arguments on the field, Mays had little patience. When they told him in his earlier years that certain pitchers would knock him down or brush him back with dust-off pitches, he pointedly disagreed. "You say they're gonna throw fast balls up around my head," he would respond. Then, taking an imaginary swing at waist level, "Well, they gotta throw some down here, too."

Another of Mays' aphorisms: "If you worry about one thing, pretty soon you start worrying about others. I don't worry about nothing." Nor, as it turned out, did he have any reason to.

HENRY AARON

BY SETH G. ABRAHAM

For the better part of two decades Henry Aaron was baseball's man in the gray flannel suit. He spent that time collecting glittering statistics in Milwaukee and later Atlanta, but other stars, most notably Willie Mays and Mickey Mantle, were collecting the headlines with their flashier play in New York.

Aaron had competition for the headlines even from his own teammates, particularly in Milwaukee. Frequently, the play of Eddie Mathews, Lew Burdette, or Warren Spahn overshadowed Henry's contributions.

A prime example was the 1957 World Series. The Braves dethroned the World Champion Yankees in seven games, with Aaron's bat their most potent war club. His rampage against New York pitching included three homers, seven runs batted in, and a .393 batting average. This impressive demonstration, however, took a back seat to the three complete-game victories registered by Burdette—a feat not turned since 1920.

Today, Henry Aaron breaks some kind of batting record every time he steps up to the plate. And invariably, the record he passes is his own. His armful of batting records includes games played, at-bats, extra-base hits, and career total bases.

But *the* record that ensures Aaron's place among the lineup of baseball's all-time greatest hitters and forever dispels any shadows still hanging over him is most home runs, lifetime.

Through the end of the 1975 season Aaron had hit 745 home runs in twenty-two seasons. To many, the actual number is less important than his achievement of breaking Babe Ruth's seemingly unbreakable record: 714. A generation of baseball fans grew up believing that that number was the upper limit of the universe when talking about home runs.

Aaron passed the Babe on the night of April 8, 1974, when he slammed his 715th home run off the Dodgers' Al Downing in Atlanta. He went on to hit 18 more homers in 1974, but most fans stopped counting after April 8. Only statisticians and lifelong Aaron watchers can tell you anything about Aaron homers 716 through 745.

The assault on the record is another story. It was the chase, after all, that brought Aaron the recognition from the press and public that was his rightful due. But no matter. Henry Aaron, by virtue of seasons of stunning consistency, was inexorably moving up to hallowed ground where only the Sultan of Swat had gone before.

191

Aaron finished 1972 with 34 home runs, putting him within two-season striking distance of the Babe. The next year a thirty-nine-year-old Aaron hit 40 homers, putting him exactly one swing of the bat away from George Herman Ruth.

And one swing was all it took. The very first time the bat left Aaron's shoulder in the 1974 season he reached the 714 mark. After watching four pitches go by, Henry homered off the Reds' Jack Billingham on April 4, 1974, in Cincinnati. The record-breaker came four days later in Atlanta.

Aaron first drew the attention of big-league scouts in 1952. He was tearing up the Negro Leagues that year, batting .467 for the Indianapolis Clowns. In mid-season, representatives of the Giants and Braves approached Aaron, then a second baseman, about tryouts for the big leagues.

A Braves scout, after watching Aaron bat and seeing those wrists in action, quickly filed a succinct report to the Braves management. "I don't know if he can field," the scout wired, "but he's worth $10,000 just for that swing."

In June the Braves bought Henry Aaron's contract from Indianapolis and assigned him to their Eau Claire, Wisconsin, farm club. His ability to hit at Eau Claire and later Jacksonville, Florida, was apparent from the start. His whiplike swing was spraying baseballs all over the field. The final minor-league stop for Aaron was Jacksonville, where he led the league in batting, runs scored, hits, doubles, RBIs, and total bases in 1953.

All of these statistics are that much more remarkable because Aaron had to overcome some unusual hitting habits that lingered from his Negro League playing days. For openers, Aaron had spent his early years in the Negro Leagues batting cross-handed. That is, he would bat right-handed but hold the bat like a left-hander with his left hand over the right. Hundreds of times at bat with that grip made Aaron look uncertain at the plate as he became accustomed to the standard grip for right-handed hitters.

The early Aaron also had a hitch in his swing that some scouts feared would adulterate his natural power. There was another problem, too. Aaron had developed a tendency to swing at bad pitches.

Despite these unusual hitting habits, Aaron hit major-league pitching from the start. He finished his rookie year with a .280 batting average, displaying good power with 69 runs batted in and 13 homers in 122 games.

The slugger in Aaron emerged the next season as he hit 27 home runs and drove in 106 runs with a .314 batting average. Over the next eighteen seasons Aaron was the model of consistency. From 1956 through 1973 he averaged 37 home runs and 106 runs batted in per season, capturing four home run crowns (1957, 1963, 1966, and 1967) and four RBI titles. His batting average over that period was .311, with two batting championships: .328 in 1955 and .355 in 1959.

Aaron's superb record has finally earned him the recognition and public adulation that went to others during so many of his great years. Everywhere he goes he is noticed, cheered, and besieged for autographs.

In July 1975 Aaron, a Milwaukee Brewer now, made his debut as an American League All-Star in Milwaukee after twenty-three appearances as a National League All-Star. When he was introduced to the fans, many of whom had watched him break in as a rookie in 1954, they cheered him with a standing ovation that lasted two full minutes. The crowd clapped in thunderous unison as County Stadium seemed to sag under the collective weight of 51,480 people on their feet. On the field, the players were lined up along the first- and third-base foul lines. As Aaron trotted onto the field to his introduction, the players joined the crowd in applauding this giant of the game.

He is no longer a superstar without headlines. Proof of that can be found halfway around the world in Moscow, where *Pravda,* the official Russian government newspaper, carried stories about the successful chase of Babe Ruth's record by Henry Louis Aaron.

THE GLORY

BASEBALL AS PART OF AMERICANA

BY JOSEPH DURSO

The New York Nine beat the Knickerbocker Club in the first baseball match on record. June 19, 1846.

In the generation after George Washington rode to the hounds in Virginia and the great stallion Messenger arrived by ship from England, the sporting life of the new American states spread with their frontier. And as the nation turned into the nineteenth century, the sporting life and the frontier both stretched farther across a continent that was being tamed by towns and the people who worked and played in them.

It wasn't that the New World proved easier than the Old World, where the philosopher Thomas Hobbes had observed that life was "nasty, brutish, and short." But as the migrations widened into the middle colonies and the South, much of the puritanical strictness of early America began to yield to the settlers' need for some recreation in a life that hopefully would grow less nasty, brutish, and short.

In New England it took the form of wrestling, running, and jumping. In the new cities down the Atlantic Coast: horse racing, bowls, ice skating, cockfighting, and cricket. In the countryside to the south: boxing matches, the breeding of blooded horses, and the raising of gamecocks.

And to the west, the Sioux and the Wichita tribes played field hockey in symbolic contests between the evil of winter and the revival of spring.

Spring . . . the time when everybody threw off the "evil of winter," clearing the land, planting the fields, organizing the towns. And in the early decades of the nineteenth century, one of the most enduring imports of all from the Old World was taking hold in the springtime of the United States: *base ball,* spelled in two words and derived from cricket, rounders, one old cat, and other games played with stick and ball in the English schoolyards.

In the Colonies, it began as town ball, a sort of mass-participation sport played by the villagers during town meetings in New England. There was no limit on the number of people on each side at first, so at times it escalated into a swirling crowd until the whole town seemed to be embroiled. By the middle of the 1830s some order was enforced when the combatants were limited to eleven or twelve to a side, and Robin Carver was printing woodcuts of boys playing the game on the Boston Common. Then Alexander J. Cartwright, a surveyor in New York, trimmed even that lineup to nine and began to fix the geometry of the "national pastime."

It was still a pastime for the well-to-do young men who had the leisure and the money to lavish on such things while more and more of their neighbors were being drawn into the dawn-to-dark rigors of life in the Industrial Revolution. Cartwright began playing ball with his friends on open land near Madison Avenue and Twenty-seventh Street in Manhattan. They called themselves the Knickerbocker Club, and they played the first "baseball" match on record on June 19, 1846, at the Elysian Fields in Hoboken, New Jersey, just across the Hudson River.

They were trounced for their trouble by a rival club, the New York Nine, by the untidy score of 23–1, with Cartwright serving as the umpire. Even in that role, though, he

Union soldiers, imprisoned by the Confederates at Salisbury, N.C., played baseball to help pass the time.

made history: fining one of the players six cents for "cussing." But by then, he already had made history by drawing up a set of rules that lasted: bases ninety feet apart in the shape of a diamond, unchangeable batting orders, three outs to a side in each inning, and no throwing the ball at a base runner to put him out, like a clay pigeon.

Three years later, the Knickerbockers added style to their sport: long blue woolen trousers, white flannel shirts, and straw hats. But by then, Cartwright himself was making history for the Republic someplace else. He bought a covered wagon, joined the gold rush of the Forty-niners, headed west, and wound up in Hawaii, an imposing figure with white hair and a long beard when he

died in 1892, two years after Casey Stengel was born in Kansas City.

After that, the game grew with the country. Union and Confederate soldiers played camp baseball games, sometimes against each other when prisoners of war were allowed a few hours' free time. The Nationals of Washington, D.C., took to the road after the War between the States, covering 2,400 miles and winning games by lopsided scores of 113–26, and by 88–12. They were subdued only when a teen-ager named Albert Goodwill Spalding outpitched them in Rockford, Illinois, by 29–23. The Red Stockings of Cincinnati went even farther, traveling 12,000 miles and winning sixty-five straight times after becoming the first "professional" ball club in 1869. The entire

196

country was in the turmoil of the Reconstruction Era then, and the Red Stockings joined the commotion by performing before 200,000 persons, including hordes of betting men who began to follow the team and make book openly on the sidelines.

Two years later, the National Association of Professional Baseball Players was formed, a governing body that tried to keep order against long odds. It did bestow a "championship streamer"—or pennant—on the Athletics of Philadelphia and then on the Red Stockings of Boston, a roaming team that detoured into Canada during its "pennant race." But the National Association was besieged in its short life by continued gambling and the raiding of players by rival clubs, and when the gate re-

ceipts started to decline along with the public's tolerance, stricter measures were taken. The result: the National League, created in 1876 with Morgan G. Bulkeley of Hartford as president, eight teams on the field and austerity in everybody's mind.

No Sunday baseball was permitted, no beer was allowed in the grandstand, and no ticket-scalping was countenanced. For all these reasons, perhaps, dissent was sure to set in, and it did. So for another generation, while the population of the United States was skyrocketing from 50 million persons to 75 million under waves of immigration from Europe, baseball moved on a twisting course through the days of the "beer and whiskey" clubs of the American Association, the challenge of the

Players League, the club-jumping of the Gay Nineties, and finally, at the turn of the twentieth century, the rise of the American League.

By then, it was firmly established as the game of the working class, and its rivals for the public's passion were few. Golf and tennis were the rich men's sports. Football and basketball became the colleges' sports. Racing had not yet developed into a leisure activity for masses of people. And prizefighting was outlawed in some states all of the time and in all states some of the time.

If there was ever a time for the working class to stop working and start playing, this was it. It was a time when cities replaced towns in the East, and towns replaced the wilderness in the West. A time when,

General Philip H. Sheridan calculated in 1866, about 100 million of the great American bison roamed the plains of Kansas and the Indian Territory; and, inside a quarter century, the herds were decimated until only a thousand or so of the one-ton buffalo remained. A time when Washington, Montana, and North and South Dakota joined the Union, and when the last armed conflict between the white man and the red man was fought at a place called Wounded Knee Creek. A time when the Census Bureau reported there was no longer a land frontier.

Small children, like John J. McGraw in Truxton, New York, recited out of McGuffey's Readers. Others, like William Henry Keeler of Brooklyn, watched Buffalo Bill's Wild West Show wind through the streets with elephants, spangled girls, and "bloodthirsty Indians." And in Baltimore, Henry L. Mencken noted that his father had installed the first steam-heating equipment in the row houses along Hollins Street, and observed: "The one sport my father was interested in was baseball, and for that he was a fanatic."

This was the quarter century following the assassination of Lincoln, a generation that revolutionized life through the Machine Age and that yearned for recreation to separate the men from the machines.

The typewriter, reinforced concrete, the Westinghouse air brake, celluloid, barbed wire—all made the scene in the decade after the Civil War. Then in 1876 came Bell's telephone, and in 1884 Mergenthaler's linotype and Parsons' steam engine. Edison started lighting the streets in the eighties. Daimler produced his high-speed internal-combustion engine in 1886. Eastman invented his hand camera in 1888, and Otis his electric elevator a year later.

In Manhattan, brush-arc lamps were replacing the gas lights, cable cars were chasing the stage coaches off Broadway, and the Third Avenue Elevated was already rocking the sidewalks of New York with trains that coughed up storms of black smoke over the cobblestone streets. America was moving from the frontier to the city, and machines were beginning to upstage and sometimes to upset men. Thomas B. Reed, the

Speaker of the House of Representatives and a three-hundred-pound "czar" of the national mood, was asked what was the greatest problem facing the American people at the time, and replied: "How to dodge a bicycle."

In 1878, as far as anyone could calculate, turnstiles were introduced into society—and three years later, twelve persons went through them to see Chicago play Troy in a driving rain on the final day of the baseball season. In 1882 umpires were told to stop soliciting the views of players and spectators, and to make up their own minds. In 1888 the actor DeWolfe Hopper recited "Casey at the Bat" for the first time on a stage. And in another move that spread the game before the public, A. G. Spalding took two teams on a tour of Hawaii, Australia, Ceylon, Egypt, Italy, France, England, and Ireland.

By then, the sport was spreading to the colleges, where baseball teams promptly did more scoring than the football teams. As early as 1859, Williams had played Amherst at Pittsfield, Massachusetts, and Amherst won by 66–32. That was ex-

KNICKERBOCKER NINE,
1864.

actly ten years before Princeton and Rutgers played the first football match, with Rutgers winning, 6–4.

Life was hard in those days, and baseball offered a diversion, and an inexpensive one. The railroads were too high-priced for the working class to take simply for trips or vacations, so people stayed home—and instead went to the amusement park, the picnic ground, or the ball field, which could be reached for five cents by trolley car. Town folk stayed in the towns, and they either hung around the livery stable in the evening or played a game of ball, and then town teams began playing *other* towns. No radio, no television, not even many national sensations like those that bombarded the public in the next century when mass communications created mass audiences.

The working class even had its own language then, or at least its own syntax, because many persons didn't finish the eighth grade. In fact, the first "baseball writer," Henry Chadwick, was English. Even years later, Shoeless Joe Jackson and Rip Russell were illiterate when they made it to the big leagues. It was a

time when country boys seized the chance to escape the farm by becoming ballplayers, farm boys like John McGraw, who went from upstate New York to the Iron and Oil Baseball League to the Three-I League to the Baltimore Orioles, arriving by day coach and toting a box suitcase and a baseball glove not much thicker than a mitten.

When McGraw reached Baltimore as a professional in August of 1891, he stepped into a city of high-tariff Republicans, Grover Cleveland Democrats, Gladstonian collars, cigar-store Indians, and chickens in backyards. He was only eighteen years old, and when he reported to the team's office, Manager Bill Barnie stared at him for a while and then said, "Why, you're just a kid. Can you play ball?"

Baltimore then was a place renowned for the quality of its crab cakes and the passions of its citizenry, and was not offended because it was known as "Mob Town." The mayor was General Ferdinand C. Latrobe, who became famous for his speeches at picnics and outings and who catered outrageously to the eth-

nic groups who were flocking into the cities along the Atlantic Coast. Mencken remembered that on various occasions Latrobe had claimed "not only Irish, Scotch, Welsh, Dutch, and other such relatively plausible bloods, but also Polish, Bohemian, Lithuanian, Swedish, Danish, Greek, Spanish, and even Jewish."

"The best he could do for the Chinese, who were then very few in Baltimore," he recalled, "was to quote some passages from the Analects of Confucius, which he had studied through the medium of a secretary."

Many of the ballplayers seemed to be Irish, though, probably because the potato famines had long since driven the Irish to the shores of America, where they joined the growing ranks of the poor. And baseball for generations was the pleasure of the poor. Besides McGraw, the Orioles were fortified with Hughey Jennings, Willie Keeler, Dan Brouthers, Ned Hanlon, and Joe Corbett, the brother of the heavyweight champion Gentleman Jim Corbett. Whether they were farm

Philadelphia fans line the right field wall at Shibe Park.

199

The Baltimore Orioles of 1894.

lads fleeing a life of drudgery or unskilled laborers fleeing a life of dull factory work, they turned to the intriguing world of fame and travel offered by baseball.

Besides, the message—as well as the opportunity—was refreshingly simple. "The main idea," said Mc-Graw, "is to win."

For a time, it was a game played from more or less stationary positions; Charles Comiskey, who left home to become a player, like so many of the others, was one of the first who played wide of first base on defense. But if the infielders were stationary for a time, the rooters were not. When "Oriole baseball" neared its peak of violent perfection in 1894, a crowd of 15,000 jammed the Baltimore park and strained against the ropes strung around the perimeter of the outfield. And the New York Giants, who had trained in Charleston, arrived with hundreds of fans and a dozen newspaper writers.

By the turn of the new century, no doubt remained that this was a national sport that reflected the national mood. The frontier heroes were gone, the Spanish-American War provided much of the patriotic lore, World War I had not yet produced its Rickenbackers and Persh-

ings—and ballplayers took their places on the public stage as the new stars. Their pictures appeared in cigarette packages, their feats were dramatized in play-by-play accounts of World Series games in newspapers, their praises were sung in popular tunes like "Slide, Kelly, Slide," and "Finnegan the Umpire" and even "The Baseball Quadrille."

In 1912, when the New York Giants played the Boston Red Sox in the ninth World Series, momentous events were swept off page one while everybody took sides. Less than six months earlier, the *Titanic* had been wrecked by an iceberg on her maiden voyage from Southampton. China became a republic and elected its first President. Captain Robert F. Scott and four companions reached the South Pole, only to perish on the return to civilization. Lieutenant Charles Becker of the New York police went on trial for complicity in the murder of Herman Rosenthal, a gambler who had accused him of being a silent partner. And Theodore Roosevelt, saying "I feel like a bull moose," broke away from the Republican party and fought both President Taft and Woodrow Wilson for the White House.

"This is to be a week of notable

The New York Giants and Boston Braves pose just prior to the season opener at the Polo Grounds in 1891.

incidents," *The New York Times* observed in an editorial. "As the third from the last week of the most bewildering Presidential campaign of recent memory, it should be full of political excitement. The greatest naval pageant in the history of the country will begin at the city's gates. A criminal trial of larger significance than any in late years will begin. Yet, who will doubt that public interest will center on none of these, but on the games of baseball at our Polo Grounds and in Boston?"

Whereupon Mayor Fitzgerald of Boston, renowned as "Honey Fitz" and later as the grandfather of John F. Kennedy, put on his stovepipe hat and led the boisterous bunch called the Royal Rooters aboard four special trains while two brass bands reached crescendos. When the cavalcade reached Manhattan, more than a thousand strong, they carried torchlights down Broadway singing battle hymns like "Tessie" and "When I Get You Alone Tonight," while Honey Fitz himself lifted his Irish tenor every couple of blocks in solo salutes to the finest baseball team in his world.

It was a time when ball parks were built, financed and owned by private citizens, who tended to be pioneer ballplayers like Connie Mack, Clark Griffith, and Charles Comiskey; when much ado was made of the fact that Christy Mathewson, Eddie Plank, and Eddie Collins had gone to college; when a handful of scouts or tipsters competed in the free-for-all for talent, discovering gems in the rough like Walter Johnson; when teams carried eighteen players on their rosters, and not twenty-five as in later years; when William Howard Taft would leave the sultriness of Washington in the summer, visit his home in Cincinnati, and throw out "the first ball" for his local team.

Games started late in the afternoon, between three and four o'clock; there was no tax on tickets; Friday sometimes was set aside as Ladies' Day, and women were admitted to the grandstand free; ushers retrieved baseballs hit into the stands; two umpires worked the games in-

stead of four; a man with a megaphone shouted the batteries for the day's game; players did not have numbers on their uniforms; and you could sit in the bleachers for twenty-five cents or in the boxes for one dollar.

By the Roaring Twenties, the public's fever for heroes was running high in the backlash of World War I, and heroes it got: Jack Dempsey in the ring, the Four Horsemen on the gridiron, Man o' War on the track, Bill Tilden on the tennis court, and Babe Ruth on the diamond. Then one spring day in 1923, a young singer from Washington named Graham McNamee took a stroll up lower Broadway during a recess from his duty as a member of the jury in Federal Court. At No. 195, he noticed a sign that read, "Radio Station WEAF," dropped into the little studio to see what was happening, and four months later he was describing the twentieth World Series by radio hookup along the eastern seaboard.

If anyone doubted the social significance of baseball's "fall classic," the doubt was dispelled in the endless columns of comments from public lions, odds quoted by brokerage houses in Wall Street, and predic-

tions from Broadway actors and actresses, who formed one of the sport's strongest claques. George M. Cohan quipped, "You know the old wheeze—New York will win the World Series." Leon Errol said, "Nothing to it but the Yankees." Florenz Ziegfeld said, "McGraw has demonstrated that he is the greatest manager in baseball." Charlie Chaplin said, "The Giants look good to me." And Kenesaw Mountain Landis, rising above the babel, said, "On that subject, the baseball commissioner is not permitted to think."

"Truly," the *Times* reflected, "baseball is the national game."

So it was, part of the national fabric and frenzy, from town ball and base ball and Cartwright's rules to the time of night games, the jet airplane, Jackie Robinson, and television via earth satellite. The game that gave the English language "the double play," "the squeeze play," "the heavy hitter," "out of their league," "knocked out of the box," "the foul ball," "the screwball," "the high, hard one," "touching all bases," and "the seventh-inning stretch." The summer game, the American game, the old ball game.

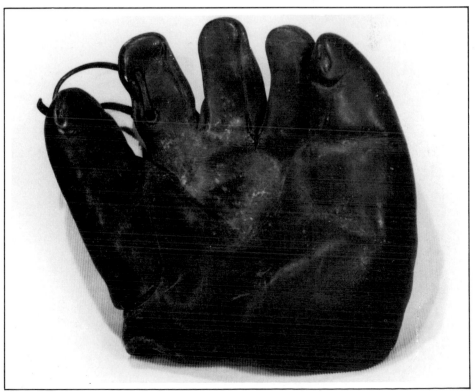

A far cry from the baseball gloves of the 1970's.

REFLECTIONS OF A FAN ON CHICAGO BASEBALL

BY JAMES T. FARRELL

Before World War I, Chicago was a great baseball town. It remained so after the war, but I am speaking here of the time when I was a little boy and first became aware of baseball. Whenever I would go home to visit my father and mother, who also lived in Chicago, my older brother, Earl, would talk baseball with me. In those days, pictures of baseball players, both major- and minor-league players, came with certain brand packages of cigarettes—Piedmonts, Sweet Caporals, and Sovereigns. Not just the stars but practically entire teams would be included in these pictures. My brother and I collected these, and even before I started school and could read, I could name the players on every picture. Earl and I used to stand in front of cigar stores and ask men as they came out to give us the baseball pictures in their cigarette packages. Before I ever saw a ball game, I must have known the names of two hundred or so major-league players, the position they played, etc. Some of the pictures I collected were of Tom Neeham, second or third Cub catcher; Billy Purtell, an infielder who never set ball games on fire; Del Howard, who played first base for Chicago when "the Peerless" Frank Chance didn't, which wasn't too

often; Lou "Big Finn" Fiene, whose lifetime major-league record spent with the Chicago White Sox was .308.

The first modern World Series was played in 1903. The third one was the first intercity World Series. The Chicago White Sox, called the Hitless Wonders, defeated the Chicago Cubs managed by Frank Chance in six games. I was not quite two years old then, but my older brother, Earl, went to one of the games with my father. In fact, in an old newspaper photograph of Chicago fans at the Series, my father and Earl can be spotted.

In the 1906 season, the White Sox hit poorly. The team batted a .234 for the season. In 152 games, the team hit six home runs. One of these was hit by Bill Sullivan, an outstanding catcher, whose batting average that season was .214. Fielder Jones, the Sox manager, hit two of the six home runs.

That year, the Cubs, winning their first pennant under Frank Chance, set a record by winning 116 games. They lost 36. They finished 20 games ahead of McGraw's New York Giants, which had won the World Series the previous year. The Cubs were the overwhelming favorites, but they lost the Series. This became

a baseball legend and the Hitless Wonders were remembered as such even while many of their members were still in the major leagues.

One was the Reverend Billy Sunday. He later became the famous evangelist who shadowboxed the devil at revival meetings. Billy Sunday played five of his eight major-league years in Chicago—1883 to 1887. His batting average against Satan must have been higher than it was against the National League pitchers. He finished with a lifetime batting average of .248.

The Cubs dominated the National League from 1906 to 1910. They won the pennant every year except in 1909 when their great catcher, Johnny Kling, one of the first Jewish baseball stars, did not play because of a salary difference.

The Cubs had a small park on the West Side of Chicago with wooden stands. The White Sox park was located at Thirty-ninth and Wentworth Avenue. The ride to the Cubs park from the South Side could take from one to two hours. It was the same for West Siders who wanted to see the White Sox play. I might add that Chicago is like three cities—the South Side, the West Side, and the North Side. At that time, there was no team on the North Side. This is why there is such rivalry between Cubs fans and White Sox fans, especially when the teams don't play in the same league. From the start of the two modern leagues, the Chicago teams seemed to be in different cities so far as their fans were concerned. This rivalry was intensified by the legendary victory of the Hitless Wonders in 1906. Then, for years, when one or the other of the Chicago teams was not in the World Series, a city series was played. The White Sox invariably won no matter how poorly the team may have played in the regular league season. This went on for years. One year the Cubs did win the first three games of the series, but as things turned out, they even lost that one when the White Sox took the next four in a row.

Hall of Fame catcher Ray "Cracker" Schalk.

204

Charles "The Old Roman" Comiskey.

The White Sox

On August 1, 1910, Comiskey Park, "Home of the White Sox," was opened. Twenty thousand spectators saw the first big-league game played in this ball park. It is still used by the White Sox and is the oldest ball park operated in the major leagues. It has been much changed and reconstructed from its original appearance. Charles A. Comiskey I, a man reputed to be a tightwad, had faith in baseball and in Chicago as a baseball town. This was why he built what was the most modern ball park of the era. It was made of steel and concrete except for the bleachers, which extended all around the outfield, seating some thousands. The prices were a dollar for box seats, seventy-five cents for the grandstand, fifty cents for pavilion seats, a section which extended from behind first and third base to right and left field respectively, and twenty-five cents for the bleachers. These prices, I might add, held during that decade.

However, with due respect to the architectural phenomenon of Comiskey Park, this was not the big attraction on that August first in 1910. The main attraction was a young man from Georgia, young Tyrus Raymond Cobb, often called the Georgia Peach or sometimes "sorehead." The game was the final one in a four-game series. Detroit had taken the previous three games in the old White Sox Park, four blocks south. Of course, the White Sox were going no-where but to the end of the schedule in 1910; but nevertheless, the reason they lost three in a row at the end of July in 1910 was Mr. Cobb. He was on his way to his first .400 season and he was doing everything according to legendary specifications and proportions.

Detroit was leading 5–1 by the fourth inning. The White Sox filled the bases in their half of the fourth. Lee Tannehill, one of the Hitless Wonders, came to bat. He was the White Sox shortstop. He hit one over the head of left fielder Davy Jones. Out in left field, there was a picket gate by the space separating the bleachers from the pavilion seats. Tannehill's hit took one bounce and went through the picket gate. The pickets were set too far apart with gaps wide enough for a ball to go through. By the rules of the day, Tannehill's hit was a home run, the first in Comiskey Park.

The second home run was predictable. The man in center field for the Detroit Tigers took one look at the picket gate through which Tannehill's homer had bounced. He dropped his glove on the field as players did in that period and trotted in to the bench. He was second up that inning.

With the score tied, Hugh Duffy, White Sox manager, put in Big Ed Walsh to pitch. According to Ring Lardner's account of this game, it seems that Mr. Cobb was mad at Mr. Walsh. Mr. Cobb was, of course, the man in center field for Detroit. The first Detroit hitter, Charley O'Leary, went out. Cobb came to bat. He got hold of one. It flew over the head of Pat Dougherty, another Hitless Wonder. Dougherty chased the ball and even kicked at it, but in vain. The ball bounced through two pickets of the same gate. Detroit won the game, 6–5. In commenting on the whole series, Ring Lardner remarked that it would have been different if Mr. Cobb had stayed in Georgia.

The White Sox had the best park in the big leagues. All they needed was a team. I should add that the first ball game I ever attended was that one on August 1, 1910. My father took my brother Earl and me; we sat in the pavilion seats. I was too young to follow the game and it was before I had glasses, and I needed them.

The old White Sox Park was taken over by the American Giants, a Negro team. The manager, Rube Foster, was an outstanding pitcher. A story has it that John McGraw once tried to "smuggle" Rube Foster into the big leagues as a Cuban but failed. Rube Foster looked like Jack Johnson, the then heavyweight champion. The resemblance was so strong that when Jack Johnson was under federal indictment and trying to get out of Chicago in order to flee the country, he posed as Rube Foster—and got away with it!

I saw the first no-hit game pitched in Comiskey Park on August 27, 1911. My brother Earl, who lived with my parents at Twenty-fifth and LaSalle, was coming home from mass when he found a box seat ticket to the game that day between the White Sox and the Boston Red Sox. He took me and we were admitted to grandstand seats. We sat on the third base, the White Sox side of the ball park. Big Ed Walsh pitched. Instead of his famous batterymate Billy Sullivan, Bruno Block, one of three White Sox catchers, was behind the plate.

The White Sox scored in the first inning. Boston went hitless. It started to rain. Canvas was stretched over the infield; there was a delay of about ten minutes. I waited, anxiously. I wanted the rain to stop. I prayed that it would, that the White Sox would win, that various White Sox players would make a hit in a pinch. The rain stopped. The game was resumed.

Lee Tannehill poled a ball to right center. Tris Speaker, center fielder for the Red Sox, and Olaf Hendricksen, in right field that day, ran for the ball. They collided and fell. Tannehill gained three bases on the hit. There was a sudden hush in the ball park. Speaker and Hendricksen were carried off the field on stretchers. It was feared that one, or both, had been seriously injured. The

Ty Cobb.

207

next day it turned out that they hadn't been.

Inning after inning passed without a hit. This produced a sense of drama in the stands. Eight innings passed. Still the Red Sox had not gotten a hit off Walsh and his spitball.

The ninth inning came. The first two batters were easy. Nunamaker, a third-string catcher, was sent up as a pinch hitter. If Walsh got by him, he would have a no-hit game. I was rigid with waiting. Nunamaker hit one between first and second base. Amby McConnell, the White Sox second baseman (and a former Red Sox player), made a sparkling play and threw Nunamaker out at first base. A howl went up from our side of the ball park. Ed Walsh had pitched a no-hit game. This was history. And I had seen it. Walsh had struck out eight men and issued one base on balls.

That was one of my biggest thrills in watching big-league baseball. For years, after I became a writer, I intended to introduce Ed Walsh's no-hit game in one of my novels. I did, in *A World I Never Made,* published in the fall of 1936. The book was hauled into court on a censorship charge, in New York City. Chief Magistrate Henry M. Curran issued a written decision, clearing my novel, and pointing out that I went into much detail concerning every phase of the novel. He cited as an example my detailed account of Ed Walsh's no-hit game.

Until 1912, I had not seen a major-league game in which the catcher used shin guards. These were invented by the Hall of Fame catcher Roger Bresnahan. In the 1912 season, one of the Sox catchers was a young player named Walter Kuhn, who appeared in seventy-five games. He was the first White Sox catcher to wear shin guards. Kuhn looked as though he had won the job as first-string White Sox catcher until late in the season. At that time, a small youth who looked more like a bat boy than a big-league catcher reported to the White Sox from the Milwaukee Club of the American As-

Catcher Roger Bresnahan—the inventor of the shin guards.

sociation, a Triple-A league. His name was Ray Schalk. On his first day, he was sent in to catch Doc White, the southpaw who, for a few years, had been a nemesis of Ty Cobb. Schalk caught a creditable game, made a hit, and threw out Stuffy McInnis, of the Philadelphia Athletics, when he tried to steal second.

From then on, Schalk was the major White Sox catcher. Kuhn sat on the bench, appearing in very few games, for the next two seasons. Then he disappeared from the big leagues. By the end of the 1913 season, Schalk, small as he was, was acknowledged to be a great catcher. Up to this time, most catchers were big and heavy; a number of them were human truck horses. Schalk helped revolutionize catching. He followed the runner down to first base. He was fast and sure on foul balls. He once even made a putout at second base. Even after he was recognized as a great catcher, he was once ejected from morning practice at Comiskey Park by a guard because the other players, playing a joke on him, told the guard that he was just a kid who didn't belong in the ball park. On that same afternoon, when Schalk appeared at the park and the guard learned whom he had booted, he was overwhelmed with humiliation.

The White Sox won the 1917 pennant and World Series. They were one of the great teams of baseball history. In their daily lineup, there were five great players, all of them Hall of Fame stature. There was Joe Jackson in left field, Happy Felsch in center; Buck Weaver at third and shortstop; Eddie Collins at second base; Ray Schalk, the catcher and spark plug of the team; and three great pitchers—Eddie Cicotte, Red Faber, who won three games in the 1917 World Series, and Lefty Williams.

Another pitcher on the 1917 team calls for mention—Reb Russell. Russell was a southpaw. I saw him break in, pitching a relief role, in 1913 against Cleveland. The first two batters he faced were Joe Jackson and Larry Lajoie. He struck them out. He was an effective starter but

Frank Chance, "The Peerless Leader" played and managed for the great Cub teams of the early 1900's.

his arm went after the 1917 season. According to Ray Schalk, Reb Russell was the model, or one of the models, for Al Keefe, the busher of *You know me, Al,* Ring Lardner's great baseball novel.

(I might add that Ring Lardner wrote this novel in the same neighborhood in which most of the action of my trilogy *Studs Lonigan* takes place. Lardner lived at 6002 Prairie Avenue in Chicago.)

In 1918, World War I disrupted the White Sox. Jackson, after playing in seventeen games, went to work in the shipyards. He was followed by Lefty Williams and Birdie Lynn, second-string catcher, but second string only because Ray Schalk

was on the club.

An incident in 1918 resulted in one of the most bitter feuds in baseball history. The White Sox brought up Jack Quinn, born John Quinn Picus. He had pitched for New York and then been returned to the minor leagues. At the end of the season, New York claimed Quinn. Ban Johnson, president of the American League and father of the league, awarded Quinn to New York. Charles Comiskey never forgave Johnson. There had been friction between them before this but the Quinn case was the backbreaking straw and the two men became enemies.

When Comiskey, afraid that his

"Shoeless Joe" Jackson compiled an impressive .356 batting mark in 13 big league seasons.

players were throwing the 1919 season, went to Johnson, Johnson turned cold on him and was reported to have said that Comiskey was "whining" because his team was losing.

Baseball men were worried when the 1919 season opened. They had cut the schedule to 140 games. The White Sox won the American League pennant easily. The Cincinnati Reds, a team which in comparison to the White Sox seemed a lucky bunch of castoffs, won the National League pennant.

We know now that the Series was fixed. I have written of it elsewhere—*My Baseball Diary*—and also Eliot Asinov in *Eight Men Out*.

One incident connected with the scandal: I saw the "Say it ain't true, Joe" incident involving Joe Jackson. On a Sunday late in September, two days before the scandal broke with the confession of Eddie Cicotte, I saw the White Sox beat Detroit. I was standing by the clubhouse under the stands watching the players come out. When Jackson and Felsch appeared (they had already been named in the press as two of the involved players), a crowd of men and boys followed them all the way to the right-field exit near a soccer field which was behind the right-field bleachers. Many of them kept calling to Joe Jackson:

"It ain't true, Joe. Say it ain't true, Joe. Say it ain't true."

Neither Jackson nor Felsch looked back.

The Chicago Cubs

The Cubs were trounced 4–1 by the Philadelphia Athletics in the 1910 World Series. This was really the end of the reign of Cub Manager Frank Chance. Gradually, the players of his championship team were let go, and after 1912, Chance went to New York as manager. Then Hank O'Day, an umpire, managed them for a year. Then they acquired Roger Bresnahan, the Hall of Fame catcher in 1913; and in 1915 he was playing manager of the Cubs. Heinie Zimmerman, who had been a substitute on the championship teams, bloomed into stardom. In 1912 he led the National League in batting with .374. When Zimmerman died, his obituary in *The New York Times* failed to mention this.

Zimmerman was a hotheaded player with great natural ability, and —incidentally—an old-time favorite of Casey Stengel. He was traded to the New York Giants for Larry Doyle, the second baseman who one year led the National League in batting.

Through these years, they had a great catcher named Jimmy Archer. Archer was born in Ireland. There was something wrong with his arm and he developed the squat throw. He would throw to the bases with a snap of the wrist while still squatting. The first time Casey Stengel played with Archer catching, Stengel got on first base. He took a lead of only a few feet. Archer, without looking at first base, snapped the ball to the first baseman and Stengel was picked off.

The Federal League operated in 1914 and 1915. There was a Chicago team, the Whales, who were also called the Chifeds. They were managed by Joe Tinker, the old Cub shortstop; and in 1915 Mordecai Brown, the great pitcher of the days when Frank Chance, "the Peerless Leader," was on the roster. A new park was built on the North Side at Addison and Webster. The owner of the Chicago club was Weeghman, who ran a chain of inexpensive restaurants in Chicago.

After 1915, the Cubs, whose West Side park was antiquated, moved to the North Side and began playing in what is now Wrigley Field. The first game I ever saw there was late in the season of 1916. It was the last time that Christy Mathewson and Mordecai Brown, who had faced each other in so many tense and crucial games, pitched against one another. Mathewson was manager of the Reds. The Reds won a free scoring game. When Brown left the field, he was in tears. Cincinnati had a left-handed second baseman named Hal Chase. He played second base in sixteen games that season and he also led the league in hitting with an average of .339.

After the close of the 1917 sea-

Hall of Fame pitching immortal Grover Cleveland Alexander.

son when the Cubs finished fifth, they bought the great battery of Grover Cleveland Alexander and Bill Killifer from the Philadelphia Phillies. Alexander had won thirty or more games for three seasons in a row—ninety-four games in all.

With these acquisitions, the Cubs looked like a sure pennant contender for 1918. The manager was Fred Mitchell, who in a seven-year career in both major leagues had pitched, caught, played every infield position, and the outfield.

In addition, they had acquired Lefty Tyler from the Boston Braves. He had been one of the three pitchers who had hurled the 1914 Boston Braves to their miraculous pennant and their four-game sweep of the Philadelphia Athletics in the 1914

World Series.

Early in 1918, they suffered a serious blow. Alexander was drafted He pitched only three games in 1918, winning two and losing one. I took off from school and went to Wrigley Field to see him pitch his last game before going off to war. He won easily over the St. Louis Cardinals. He pitched fast, threw a heavy ball with remarkable control, and kept the batter off balance. The only good hit made off him was a two-base blow to left field by a Cardinal infielder named Rogers Hornsby.

Despite the loss of Alexander, the Cubs went on to win the pennant that year. But it should be noted that the 1918 season was an abbreviated one. Secretary of War Newton D. Baker issued a "Work or Fight" order which included baseball players as well as men working in other categories. The big leagues closed their season after Labor Day. The World Series was played in September. The Cubs won the pennant. Their outstanding hurler was left-handed Hippo Jim Vaughan, one of the best pitchers in either league. The Cubs also had Claude Hendrix and Shuffling Phil Douglas to help Vaughan and Tyler. But the principal reason the Cubs won was the play of their shortstop, Charlie Hollocher. It was his first year in the big league. He was twenty-three. From the very start, he was clearly a star. He could field, throw, and was a .300 hitter. He batted left-handed, choked his bat by a few inches, chopped and placed his hits to all fields, many of them on the ground. That season he hit .311. Hollocher was one of the best shortstops ever to play for a Chicago team, but his was a short career because of ill health. A song was written about him during the 1918 World Series.

After seven years he retired because he was too weak to play. He died in 1940. I feel sure that had he had good health, the name Charles Hollocher would be enshrined in the Hall of Fame today.

The 1918 Cubs team was mainly one of veterans, men who were steady and solid ballplayers but no more than that. Les Mann, who was with the 1914 Miracle Braves, was in left field. His was always the dirtiest uniform among the Cub players, just as Buck Weaver's was on the South Side of Chicago. Fred Merkle, called Bonehead for his failure to touch second in 1908, had a good year as first baseman. Charlie Deal, who played third base for the 1914 Braves because the regular third baseman was injured, was on third. And Dode Paskert, who had been with the pennant-winning Phillies in 1915, was in center field.

The Boston Red Sox and the Cubs played in the 1918 World Series. For the games in Chicago, the Cubs moved to Comiskey Park because it could hold a larger attendance. They might as well have

stayed on the North Side; the attendance was poor. It was a pitcher's series and Boston won in six games. I saw the first one. Babe Ruth shut out the Cubs 1–0 with Hippo Vaughan opposing him. The winning run was driven home by my friend, Stuffy McInnis, a great first baseman in his day. He dumped one of his typical Texas League singles to center to bring home the only run.

There was a threatened strike in Boston before the Series ended because of the poor attendance and the low rewards going to the players as their share from the receipts of the first four games, but it never came off.

Babe Ruth made one hit in this series—a triple. He pitched and played in the outfield.

After 1918, the Cubs had a long haul before winning their next pennant in 1929, but this is another story.

In the first two decades of this century, baseball was not only popular in Chicago but it seemed, to

A major league second baseman for a quarter of a century, Eddie Collins was the pride and joy of the White Sox from 1915 through 1926.

many, to be as important as history. There were good teams, championship teams, great players, great games. Games were watched and cheered with great enthusiasm. I sat and watched many of them and I would say that the crowds were as enthusiastic as Brooklyn Dodger crowds used to be, or as Met crowds are when the Mets are in contention for the pennant.

In those years, baseball filled my boyhood with dreams and with a passionate, almost devout, interest.

Baseball provided me with many hours of suspense, thrills, and pleasure. I remember endless plays: Babe Ruth in 1917 coming in to relieve Dutch Leonard. The White Sox had the bases full. Ruth struck out Eddie Collins, Joe Jackson, and Happy Felsch. Joe Jackson making a great shoestring catch in the first game of the 1917 World Series. Eddie Collins, almost every time I saw him play. Hal Chase fielding a bunt. Buck Weaver running. Ty Cobb making six hits on infield

grounders or bunts in a doubleheader in 1917.

Much of the best part of my early years was baseball. I bow in memory to all of the players whom I saw in those days and who are no more, except as names in *The Baseball Encyclopedia* or in the box scores of old newspapers.

I was, and I remain, a baseball fan.

PORTRAIT OF A FAN

BY DICK SCHAAP

The white-haired fan had been coming to Fenway Park to watch the Boston Red Sox play baseball for more than fifty-five years, and for more than fifty-five years he had dreamed of seeing the Red Sox win a World Series. As a youngster he sat out in right field with his father in a grandstand seat, but now, as the Red Sox threatened to break out of a scoreless tie in the bottom of the third inning of the seventh game of the 1975 World Series, he was sitting in a front-row box seat, just to the left of the Boston dugout. He was in a perfect spot to call out encouragement to his friend Carl Yastrzemski, who was coming to bat, and to all Yaz's teammates, to urge them to make the Red Sox world champions for the first time since 1918.

The white-haired fan had missed the 1918 World Series—he was not quite six years old at the time—and he had missed the first two innings of the seventh game of the 1975 World Series because he had been delayed at his office in the city of Washington, D.C. A consumer bill was up in front of the Congress of the United States, and his vote had to be recorded, and so Thomas P. O'Neill, Jr., Democrat, Massachusetts, the majority leader of the House of Representatives, had hustled back and forth between his own office and the floor, finally casting his vote and then hurrying off to the airport with Silvio Conte, Republican, Massachusetts, so that they could climb into a friend's plane and make the 70-minute trip to Logan Airport in Boston. "We had to wait on the ground in Washington for forty minutes," said O'Neill later. "I was ready to fly the plane myself."

214

Congressman Tip O'Neill (left), Mrs. O'Neill and Massachusetts Senator Edward Brooke applaud the Red Sox during the 1975 World Series.

At Logan, the two Congressmen jumped into a cab, and the cab driver took one look in the rear-view mirror and spotted Thomas P. O'Neill, Jr., of North Cambridge, Massachusetts, and said, "Hiya, Tip," and knew without asking that he should drive his fares to Fenway Park. The cab drivers in Boston know Tip O'Neill and they know he is a baseball fan. Other politicians go out to the ball park during a World Series because it might be worth a vote or two or even a hundred thousand—if John V. Lindsay had not been persuaded to attend the games of the New York Mets in 1969 and if the Mets had not sprayed him with champagne after they won the World Series, he might not have been re-elected mayor of the city, which probably would have spared him a lot of grief—but Tip O'Neill goes to the ball park because he likes it there, because he likes baseball. He is as comfortable sitting in the stands with his Daniel Webster cigar and his scorecard—filling in 6-3 and K and HR, and even recording each pitch sometimes for an important game—as he is in the smoky cloakrooms of Washington, D.C., wheeling and dealing and getting bills passed and bills killed and being one of the maybe half-dozen most powerful politicians in the United States.

Tip O'Neill reached his seat in Fenway Park at 8:59 P.M. on Wednesday, October 22, 1975, and less than fifteen minutes later the Red Sox had runners on first and third, only one out, and Carl Yastrzemski coming to bat. "Gullett's struggling," said Tip O'Neill, nodding toward the starting pitcher for Cincinnati. "Now's the time to get to him."

Tip O'Neill is a superfan, the best kind of baseball fan. He has rooted long and hard for one special team, the Red Sox, and yet he has always appreciated excellence on opposing teams. He grew up on baseball. Shortly after World War I, his father, Thomas P. O'Neill, Sr., founded the North Cambridge Knights of Columbus baseball team, a semi-pro club; and Tip can recall crowds of ten and twelve thousand turning out on a Sunday afternoon and making a small donation to watch North Cambridge, with its college stars and local heroes and thriving young men doing so well they couldn't afford to go into professional baseball, take on rivals from all over the East. He remembers a team coming in from Gardner, Massachusetts, to play North Cambridge for the unofficial semi-pro championship of the world, and he remembers that interest in that series was second only to interest in *the* World Series. Gardner won, three victories to two, mostly because of a gifted pitcher whose name was unfamiliar, but whose style was not: The pitcher was Eddie Cicotte, one of the Chicago Black Sox, banned for life from professional baseball but playing for Gardner (supposedly for $1,000 a game) under an assumed name.

Young Tip O'Neill went to his first big-league game when he was seven, in 1920, and that first game was a memorable one. "I think it was in June," says O'Neill now, fifty-five years later. "Walter Johnson pitched a no-hitter." O'Neill's memory is miserable. He is one whole day off. Walter Johnson pitched a no-hitter against the Boston Red Sox in Fenway Park on July 1, 1920. Six years later, Tip O'Neill saw his second no-hitter, pitched by Ted Lyons of Chicago against the Red Sox, and then twenty-four years passed before O'Neill witnessed another no-hitter, the last he's seen, thrown by Vern Bickford of the Braves against the Dodgers. That was a long time ago: The Braves were in Boston, the Dodgers were in Brooklyn, Tip O'Neill was in the Massachusetts legislature and a young Congressman named Richard M. Nixon was just starting the career that Tip O'Neill, as a driving force behind impeachment, would help end a quarter of a century later.

As a youngster, he was a member of Boston's Knot Hole Gang. O'Neill went to baseball games almost every day during the summer, and later, after he was graduated from Boston College and plunged into politics, he still spent a lot of time at the ball park. He tried each year, when the Braves were still in Boston, to see every major-league team at least once, so that he could form strong and knowledgeable opinions of the players and of their clubs. He saw Ty Cobb play for Detroit, and Tris Speaker for Cleveland, and George Sisler for St. Louis, and Babe Ruth and Lou Gehrig for the Yankees, and later he watched Feller and DiMaggio and Williams and Musial and Mays and Mantle and Aaron, and now, in his mind, he can create instant images of the superstars of today and of the superstars of twenty or thirty or forty years ago, and he can measure those superstars against each other. Tip O'Neill is proud of his baseball opinions, and he has been known on occasion to back up those opinions with small, friendly wagers.

O'Neill's dedication to baseball is so complete he will even tell you, with only the mildest prompting, that he was nicknamed after a ballplayer, a man who batted .435 for St. Louis in the American Association in 1887. The player's full name was James Edward O'Neill, but he was called Tip because, in that season, bases on balls counted as base hits, and O'Neill used to foul-tip a lot of pitches on his way to walks that fattened up his batting average. In the 1880s, explains the modern Tip O'Neill, a wave of Irish immigrants swept over the United States, and one of the things the immigrants liked best about their new country was baseball. Naturally, the Irish quickly became fans of James Edward O'Neill, the great batsman—he also led the American Association in home runs in 1887—and in honor of James Edward, the O'Neills among the immigrants began calling their offspring Tip. The practice persisted right into the twentieth century.

Thomas P. O'Neill, Jr., the consummate politician, will also tell you that he and many other Irishmen are nicknamed Tip because of roots in Tipperary, if you prefer to hear it that way.

In 1975, because the respon-

The "other" Tip O'Neill as he looked as a St. Louis outfielder in 1889.

sibilities of being the majority leader of the House of Representatives occasionally interfere with more pleasurable activities, Tip O'Neill was able to attend only seven Red Sox games during the regular season. He went to four of them in Baltimore and three at Fenway Park. The Red Sox won all seven of those games. The Red Sox also won the first game of the 1975 World Series, but they broke O'Neill's personal winning streak at eight when they lost the second game of the Series in the ninth inning. Then the Red Sox went off to Cincinnati for a few days, and O'Neill hurried back to Washington, to devote himself temporarily to the business of the nation. By the time the Series resumed in Boston, on a Tuesday night, after three days of rain-outs, O'Neill found himself in a terrible bind: He had committed himself to a speech to the Academy of General Dentistry in Chicago. Speeches to dentists are the sort of thing that enables politicians to afford to be politicians.

If the Red Sox had won the second game of the Series, to keep O'Neill's winning streak alive, he probably would have cancelled the speech in Chicago. But since his good-luck charm had apparently worn off, Tip figured the club could get through one game without him. When he finished his speech in Chicago, he ran up to his hotel room and found out that the Red Sox were leading Cincinnati, 3-0. He felt confident that the Red Sox would even up the Series at three victories each team and that he would see a seventh game in Boston the following night.

O'Neill was getting a lift from Chicago to Washington in a friend's plane, and by the time he had to leave his hotel room, his confidence had waned. Cincinnati was ahead, 5-3, and the prospects for a seventh game seemed bleak. They seemed even bleaker by the time O'Neill reached the airport. Cincinnati's lead was up to 6-3.

The private plane took off from Chicago and landed twenty-five minutes later in South Bend, Indiana, to pick up Senator Birch Bayh, who had selected that day and that spot to announce his Presidential candidacy. But Bayh, O'Neill and his companions discovered, was going to be delayed in South Bend, so they were told to go ahead to Washington without him. As the plane prepared for takeoff, O'Neill asked the pilot if he'd happened to hear the final score of the World Series game. "It's the eleventh inning," said the pilot, "and the score's six-six."

"Let me off," said O'Neill. "I've got to see the end of the game."

O'Neill dashed off the plane and into a cocktail lounge in the South Bend terminal, just in time to see Boston's Dwight Evans make a sensational catch, inches in front of the right-field fence, depriving Cincinnati's Joe Morgan of an extra-base hit and depriving Cincinnati of at least one run and the lead. Evan's throw back to the infield doubled Ken Griffey off first base.

O'Neill watched Boston go down

217

Boston Red Sox hero Carl Yastrzemski.

Republican, Massachusetts. Senator Brooke was on the far side of his daughter, seated on the aisle, directly opposite the Commissioner of Baseball, Bowie Kuhn. The commissioner, a good host, had just sent out for hot dogs and soft drinks for the Congressional delegation. "C'mon, Yaz, you can do it," shouted Senator Brooke. Tip O'Neill cheered silently, measuring Yaz's aging reflexes against the remarkable swiftness of young Don Gullett. O'Neill didn't have to cheer loudly to let Yaz know that he was with him. In O'Neill's Washington office, the walls are decorated exclusively with paintings celebrating the Bicentennial (one shows Paul Revere on his rounds), with only a single exception: Carl Yaztrzemski's plaque from an All-Star game, a gift from the Red Sox veteran to the Capitol Hill veteran. (Yastrzemski's Most Valuable Player trophy from 1967 is in the Lyndon B. Johnson Museum in Texas, transmitted from MVP to President through Tip O'Neill.)

Yastrzemski grounded a single to right field, sending home Bernie Carbo with the game's first run, and Denny Doyle who had been on first base, raced all the way around to third. Alertly, on the throw to third, Yaz moved up to second base. "Head's up play," said O'Neill, more impressed by Yastrzemski's hustle than by his base hit.

When Gullett walked three of the next four Red Sox batters to force home two more Boston runs, O'Neill prayed that a 3-0 lead might produce his team's first world championship in 57 years. For five innings, Bill Lee shut out Cincinnati, occasionally throwing the Reds' batters off-stride with a very slow, very high-arching curve ball that reminded O'Neill of the blooper pitch Rip Sewell used to throw for the Pittsburgh Pirates. "I'll never forget when Ted Williams hit a home run off Sewell in an All-Star game," said O'Neill.

In the sixth inning, with two men out, Tony Perez of Cincinnati hit a home run off Bill Lee's blooper, and in the next inning, Pete Rose

in order in the bottom of the eleventh, watched Cincinnati threaten but fail to score in the top of the twelfth and then let out a big cheer when Carlton Fisk, leading off in the bottom of the twelfth, drove a home run off the foul screen in left field and drove the World Series into a seventh game.

The majority leader jumped back into the private plane and hurried off to Washington so that he could get the affairs of state out of the way in time to attend the seventh game.

Now, in the third inning of the seventh game of the 1975 World Series, Tip O'Neill was one of 35,205 spectators, the legal limit, crowded into Fenway Park. He was seated between his wife, Millie, and the daughter of Senator Edward Brooke, singled home a run to tie the score at 3-3. In the bottom of the eighth inning, with the score still tied, with two men out and no one on base, O'Neill was surprised to see Darrell Johnson, the Boston manager, send up Cecil Cooper to bat for Jim Willoughby. For one thing, Willoughby had retired the only four Cincinnati batters he had faced without allowing a ball to be hit out of the infield; for another, Cooper had gone one for eighteen in the World Series. Cooper made the third out, and when Jim Burton came out to pitch the nintn inning for Boston, O'Neill was again surprised. "I thought Johnson would go with Drago or Cleveland," the Congressman said later, "someone a little more experienced than Burton."

Unlike many equally ardent fans, Tip O'Neill is very hesitant to second-guess a manager, partly because he is a politician and largely because he identifies with the manager. "It's as tough being a manager today," said O'Neill, "as it is being a political leader. There's a new breed of baseball player just as there's a new breed of politician. Kids come up to the majors these days without any seasoning in the minors or with very little. They don't know discipline. And it's the same thing in my field. Nearly half of the first-term Congressmen are holding their first elective office. They haven't come up through the state legislatures, through the minor leagues of politics. And they're not always too good on party discipline, either."

When Cincinnati scored in the top of the ninth inning and moved ahead, 4-3, on a looping single by Joe Morgan off Jim Burton, O'Neill said he sensed the same sinking feeling in his stomach he experiences whenever a bill he favors goes down to defeat. Yet he refused to quit on his team. Even when the first two Red Sox batters went out in the bottom of the ninth, O'Neill *knew* that if only Yastrzemski could get on, then Fisk would get on, and then Freddy Lynn would do something, and the Red Sox, who had won so many games during the regular season in the

ninth inning, would manage to win, would manage for the first time in Tip O'Neill's game-going lifetime to capture a World Series.

But Yastrzemski flied out to center field, and when the ball settled into Cesar Geronimo's glove, and when Geronimo leaped high in the air, in the joy of victory, O'Neill was one of the 35,000 fans who sat stunned and silent in Fenway Park, their dream shattered once more. "It reminded me of a wake," said Tip O'Neill a few days later, back in Washington, back at the business of the nation.

O'Neill shook his head sadly, glanced at the Yastrzemski plaque on

his wall and then, like a million other fans in a million other offices, thought of next year and brightened. "For a young club," said the majority leader, with a smile, "they did a great job. And that Series did more for baseball than anything I can think of in recent years. And we're going to be back there next year. And all we've got to do is get a couple of pitchers . . . that's all we need . . . a couple of pitchers . . ."

And the smile grew wide and the white-haired fan looked forward to his 57th season of watching his team, knowing that this year, finally, he would see a winner.

"Superfan" O'Neill.

The Milwaukee Brewers host the Angels on Opening Day, 1970.

THE SUNSHINE GAME

BY HARRY REASONER

There are three things about baseball that I find particularly rewarding—other admirers of the game would find three others, I assume. First of all, to love and enjoy baseball and to talk about it to others, you don't have to know all that much about the physical nature of the game. You need to know about scoring and statistics and things like ERAs (earned run average) and RBIs (runs batted in), but you don't have to know where a pitcher puts his fingers to throw a knuckle ball.

I can tell reasonably well if a pitch is exceptionally fast or exceptionally slow, but, frankly, I get lost when the experts start talking about sliders and drops and "taking a little bit off the ball." It's all right, though, since the explosive moments of action and the matching of wits with the manager that are the delight of watching the game don't depend upon your knowing *how* it's done.

You notice, for example, a shortstop move five paces to his left for a given hitter. A minute later you see him stop a grounder he would otherwise have missed. You don't have to know *how* he decided to change his position; the move is just as pleasant for you in its result as if you knew what the shortstop knew. (Or, conceivably, if it's the other guy's shortstop who moves five paces to the left, it can be a pleasure to see the ball skip by him on his right. Baseball *is* a partisan affair.)

Secondly, you don't have to have a winning team to enjoy baseball. You'll hear baseball fans talk about going out to watch "The Game," and they mean a very precise and important thing by that. *The Game* is enough, a round and full entity of its

221

own; it doesn't have to be a game affecting the pennant race; it doesn't have to be played by superstars; it doesn't even have to be major league. The game is a microcosm of human conflict and effort, all by itself, and there is always something to make it interesting.

A team may no longer have any hope of postseason play, but its fans will still go out to the park, because there is still the Game. Even late in the season there are always things to watch and things to speculate about, records being set, promises for next year being defined by late-season performance. In 1975, long after my team (the New York Mets) had been eliminated from the pennant race, I thought about which pitcher—Tom Seaver or Catfish Hunter—would finish the season with a better record. About whether Mike Vail, the Met rookie who hit safely in twenty-three straight games after being called up from the minors, would continue to live up to our expectations and become the next Pete Rose.

Even the Chicago Cubs, with only two weeks in the 1975 season remaining, fifteen games out of first place, managed to nail down a spot in the record books. The Cubs lost 22–0 to the Pittsburgh Pirates, a shutout score never equaled in modern history. It's something to talk about—and baseball fans like to talk about their teams, even when it's not good news.

Those of us who belong to the New York Mets are particularly conscious of this. We went through seven years of jokes. *The New Yorker* ran a cartoon of a fresh-faced boy in a Mets uniform sitting on the bench among his colleagues. "Gee," he says, watching the field, "we sure get to play some wonderful teams." Those were the days when Casey Stengel said, "Can't anyone here play this game?" And when two Mets partisans met on the street, one said, "Did you see that game last night? The Mets got seventeen runs!" "Wonderful," his friend exclaimed. "Who won?" But through it all the folks went out to watch the game.

The American League Champion St. Louis Browns of 1944.

The third thing I like about baseball is that you don't have to be at the ball park to love it and be part of it. There is a society—or at least there was a few years ago when I interviewed its president—dedicated to bringing the St. Louis Browns back to St. Louis. The Browns were one of the most charmingly ineffectual teams in baseball history; only once in their long career did the Browns win a pennant, and that was during World War II when most healthy players were in the armed services. But people who never saw the Browns might have been depressed if they had gotten nostalgic about them.

Similarly, my devotion to baseball began in Iowa in the middle thirties, listening to a Des Moines radio station relay telegraphic reports on how the Chicago Cubs were doing, listening with my sister and keeping

222

home-made box scores. When I finally saw a major-league game, it looked just as it had looked in my head. The announcer on those games, incidentally, was a capable young fellow named Dutch Reagan. He later left sports announcing to become an actor, and, after that, governor of California, and still later, a possible candidate for President of the United States.

The best place to be is the ball park. But a lot of us can't get to a ball park very often, and for us, television has been a great boon. And if you can't get television, radio is fine. And if you can't get a radio report on your team, you still read about it the next day—and see it all, in your head.

These three things about baseball stand out in my mind, but there is much more that appeals. Oh, there is no doubt that baseball is the best game of all. It stands alone. Baseball is to football as chess is to checkers— incredibly more complex, contemplative, mature, intellectual. Part of it is its consistency, I suppose—the almost perfect balance between offense and defense, the continuity of rule and tactic through the years. You can't guess how Bronko Nagurski would do in football these days because the game has changed so. But rejuvenate Ty Cobb, give him a couple of innings to get used to the slightly different weight of the ball, and he'd be as good as ever.

And part of it is the satisfying quality that baseball has of adding everything up. Sure, a football coach can study the films of a game for hours and get a pretty good idea of who did what and how well. But even to knowledgeable fans a lot of football is a mob scene—the guy who spoiled the play or made it work is often lost under a confusing pile of bodies. In baseball, the physical law of action and reaction applies; you not only know exactly what everyone contributed for good or bad in a game, you can go back ten years later and check it. Every effort is evaluated—it is hit or out or walk, assist or putout or error. There is something peculiarly pleasant in a philosophical way about a human enterprise where, if you always pay for your mistakes, you also always get credit for your achievements.

I have said nothing about the beauty of baseball. It is, as Roger Angell titled his great book about it, *The Summer Game.* It is played outside in pleasant weather (for purposes of this generality, I will ignore the Astrodome, and forgive it, considering the nature of Houston's weather). Its athletes are graceful—people who have seen it say there never was anything as pretty as watching Joe DiMaggio take one look as a fly ball left the bat, turn and run easily without another glance to the place his genius told him that ball was going, turn, and catch it. It is, as noted, contemplative: there is a long enough period in a dramatic situation before the final, concentrated explosive action for you—and the athletes—to consider all possible alternatives and be ready for them

MY BASEBALL MEMORIES

BY EDWIN NEWMAN

Yankee hurler George Pipgras.

With perhaps one exception, I have made no lasting contributions to baseball. That exception came on the *Today Show* when Joe Garagiola was talking about the number of times he had been traded, and I said, "Joe, you were never traded. Your club always threw you in."

Apart from that indispensable bit of setting the record straight, I have done nothing for baseball. On the other hand, baseball has done much for me. For one thing, though I am occasionally daunted by the

number of teams, and by the growing legal complexities surrounding contracts (I still don't understand how or why Catfish Hunter became a Yankee), it is an interest that I have maintained since I was a boy. Who wins no longer concerns me, but I still find much to admire—or be outraged by, which is almost as useful—on the field. There is little continuity in American life; baseball provides some. Then, too, baseball enables you to wallow in nostalgia. For some, few words in the language (especially since what usually happens is a foul ball and you get to contemplate alternatives all over again). It is a sport that welcomes all shapes and sizes—you have to be *good,* but you don't have to be preternaturally tall or grossly heavy. Just good.

And there is one thing about baseball that seems significant to me. It has recently been discovered about football that if you write down some of the more revolting locker room language of its players you can sell books—but no other sport but baseball has stimulated so much *fine* writing.

Not only big efforts, but quick, sure lines like the one in a story about Johnny Bench a few years back. The writer was explaining how, in a tight situation with a man on first, Bench, like any catcher, wants a pitch thrown high and outside, so he can get a quick throw off to second. The pitcher wants to throw it low and inside to lessen the chance of a big hit. "In baseball," the writer said, "this dilemma is usually resolved in this wise: the catcher calls for high and outside and the pitcher throws low and inside."

Well, that's the writing, one of

the nicest aspects of this delightful sport. From Ring Lardner to Red Smith, fine writers have found it inexhaustible. And the writing, like the memories of green and sunshine and summer sounds in your head, like the lazy December talk, is something you can keep with you about baseball through the winter, and through all the winters of your life.

Ernie "Schnozz" Lombardi.

are as depressing as "I remember seeing . . ." when those words come from somebody else. But for the one who is saying them, they are immensely satisfying.

When I was a boy in New York, I was a Yankee fan. This probably began because Babe Ruth was a Yankee, though Lou Gehrig ("Biscuit Pants," the New York *Daily News* disrespectfully called him) was my particular favorite. The Yankees were so powerful for so long that I remember (Here I go!) one World

Series when George Pipgras started the third game. Pipgras had won thirteen games that season, and I could not understand how a pitcher who had won only thirteen games could rate a Series start.

And of course there was Babe Ruth and that certain dignity and sense of proportion about the way he would not go out to right field for the ninth inning when the Yankees were far ahead. Sammy Byrd would take his place and would often make catches that the Babe, in his late

years, could not have.

The Polo Grounds, where the Giants played in those days, I considered enemy country. Ebbets Field was not enemy country; it was not taken seriously enough to be. But there were Giants whose talents I respected.

One day at the Polo Grounds I remember seeing Carl Hubbell at his peak, pitching against the Cincinnati Reds with two men on. Ernie Lombardi hit a ball to the bleachers in dead center. It was caught, as I re-

Bob Feller.

next eight innings, my man was Buster Maynard (lifetime average .221).

The closest I've ever come to seeing a no-hitter was watching Earl Whitehill of the Washington Senators, known to some as Pineapple Head, pitch eight and a third innings without a hit. Up came Ben Chapman, with whom Whitehill had fought not long before when Chapman slid high into Buddy Myer at second. Chapman singled on the ground to left. It was a close game; Whitehill was tired; and having given up one hit in eight and a third innings, he was taken out.

I was in the bleachers at Griffith Stadium when Joe DiMaggio passed George Sisler on his way to setting a new record for hitting in consecutive games. It was so hot the soda pop vendors were selling water in used bottles.

I saw Bob Feller as a rookie, and I remember Red Ruffing, pinch-hitting, grinning, and making a dipsy-doodle gesture to the umpire after a Feller fast ball whizzed by. I saw Grove, Foxx, Simmons, Dickey, Rowe, Greenberg, Averill, Dean, Gehringer, Gomez, Reiser, Blackwell, Stratton, Crowder, Terry, Luque, Lyons, Hornsby, Wyatt, the Waners, Pennock, Durocher, Frisch, Traynor, Roush, Hafey. I saw Koufax, Drysdale, Keller, Walters, Derringer, Mantle, Maris, Doby, Mize, Wills . . . sometimes I think I saw everybody.

And of course there were things that took place off the field. I remember seeing Waite Hoyt, then a right-handed pitcher for the Yankees, appearing on the stage of the Audubon Theatre in New York. Hoyt had a very pleasant singing voice, and he enjoyed performing. The only problem, he said, was that he got nervous. People used to ask him how he could possibly be nervous on the stage when he could go out on the field before tens of thousands of fans and not be nervous at all. Hoyt had, I think, a very clever reply. "The thing is," he would explain disarmingly, "on the field, I know what I'm doing."

One day, during a high school

call, by Hank Lieber. Lieber fell as he caught it but tossed it to the left fielder, Joe Moore. The Reds' base runners, one of whom was outfielder Kiki Cuyler, were hopelessly late getting back to their respective bags. When it was all over, Lombardi had hit a ball off Hubbell five hundred feet into a triple play. By the way, I thought Lieber would have become one of the great players of his time had he been able to shake off the effects of an early beaning.

I was at the Polo Grounds on another occasion with a group of friends when each of us drew a player. The arrangement we had was that at the end of the doubleheader, the owner of the player with the most total bases would carry off the pot, each base being worth ten cents. I drew Mel Ott and rejoiced. But on his first time at bat, Ott complained a bit too vigorously about a called third strike (it *was* way outside) and was thrown out of the game. For the

Waite Hoyt.

lunch recess, some members of the Giants were discovered near the school. They lived there. One was Mel Ott. I was about fifteen at the time, and it took all my courage to ask him a question. Why, I wondered, since John McGraw had just stepped down as manager (Bill Terry had replaced him), had he, Ott, not been chosen? Ott cracked a smile. "Well," he said thoughtfully, "I guess I'm just too young." I was impressed by his having replied to me ("Being

a reporter may not be so hard," I thought), and still more by his Louisiana accent. It was unlike anything I had ever heard before.

The older memories are more vivid. That's natural. But I had the good fortune to be in Atlanta to interview Hank Aaron on the days he hit his 699th and 700th home runs. The year the Mets won the World Series, I said on the air—it was disguised as news analysis—that the Mets were an elemental force loose in

the world and that nothing the Orioles could do could keep them from winning. It proved to be so.

On the other hand, not many years earlier, I had gone on the air with the cry, "Break up the Mets." That is sometimes heard when a team is too good. My argument was that it should be done with the Mets because they were too bad and no fans had done anything to deserve them. They turned into a winning team sooner than I expected.

229

Some of the memories are melancholy. One day in the summer of 1972, Jackie Robinson came into my office to keep an appointment. "Let the old man sit down," he said. It was only half in jest. A few months later, he was gone.

I miss nicknames: Big Poison and Little Poison Waner; Shanty Hogan, a catcher and a good hitter who on his way around the base paths always seemed to be running in place; Harry "the Horse" Danning, another catcher with the same problem; Gabby Hartnett; Chief Koy, a non-Cleveland Indian and an outfielder; Ducky Medwick; Mule Haas; Bing Miller; Dazzy Vance; Lefty Grove; Lefty O'Doul (of course, left-handers are more common now); Hack Wilson; Rube Walberg; Blondy Ryan; Fatty Fothergill; Jumbo Jim Elliott; Boom Boom Beck; King Kong Keller; Biff Berger; Socks Seibold; Jumping Joe Dugan; Duke Snider; Frenchy Bordagaray; Pie Traynor.

Some of the names had a fine rhythm and euphony—Lefty O'Doul, for example. Others told everything anyone had to know about a player. Thus Boom Boom Beck, whose fame as a right-handed pitcher rested on the sound his pitches produced when bat and ball violently met, as they so often did when he was on the mound.

We need more nicknames.

There are some things about baseball now that don't appeal to me: artificial turf, domed stadiums, so many night games, the profusion of home runs and fences moved in to make home runs easier, the endless parade of relief pitchers, gloves the size of snowshoes, and the rate at which managers are hired and fired these days.

To me, baseball should always be played as it was when I was a boy. That, of course, is a dream. But not a bad one.

Carl Hubbell, left, chats with Lou Gehrig.

Opposite: Jackie Robinson.

THE GAME'S UNIQUE APPEAL

BY AL SILVERMAN

Boston's Grand Pavilion on Alleghany Street.

Like a dream borne on a tide, baseball plunges in and out of my consciousness. It is always there: in a fragment of conversation with a friend, in a casual glance at the box scores in the morning newspaper, or an inning or two observed on television, that most incompatible medium for this best of all sports.

I sit with my father in the living room of his apartment, watching with him, not irritated now by what happens to baseball on television; caring, rather, and relieved that my father can lose himself for a while in the game, knowing that this link of love that has stretched through the years still quivers between us.

The house is old and the room is faded, facing on a blighted street in the city of Lynn, Massachusetts, where I was born and grew up and where baseball was a passion of my youth and where so many of those early years were filled with images and fantasies about baseball. My father sits there, watching his beloved Red Sox, alert and aware, hoping that this will be the year. It is perhaps the last passion of his life, too. My father is old and sick and defeated, his hands and wrists are swollen and misshapen, his ankles, too, edema from a heart that grows weaker on him every day. Pain guards him at all times. He sits and watches and my mother sits with him. She tries, but she is not connected to the world as he is, her mind floats. She remembers me, knows him, little fragments of reality swirl in her head, tears flow on and off because of the knowledge, not yet completely shut off, that life now has become incomprehensible and terribly cruel and she cannot change it and that she is drifting away.

"Do you think they can win?" my father asks me. It seems he has always asked me that, almost every summer when I came by to visit with him and my mother. It was a reasonable question then as it is now because the Red Sox always did seem to have a chance. But in those days if I said yes he would laugh at me and say, "You're crazy." A skeptic all his life, a skeptic about everything,

he came never to expect anything from the Red Sox. Rooting for the Red Sox over the years does reinforce one's basic nature if it leans toward the badness of mankind. But a summer earlier, when his health had not yet begun to deteriorate, he saw the Red Sox seven games ahead late in August and then collapse. So, once more, he is hedging his bet.

"They'll fold," I say smugly.

His passion flows. "No, they won't." He so very much wants them to win this year, for fundamental reasons.

The enemy loads the bases with two out and someone hits a long line drive that heads toward center field, toward that beckoning green wall. We watch the rookie, Fred Lynn, ride back to the wall, leap and come down with it in his glove. My father sighs and looks at me and says nothing, but the look flares like a drum roll.

In the bottom half of the same inning Carl Yastrzemski, a generation gapped from Fred Lynn, strides into a pitch, a scythe whipping at wheat, and a moment later the ball descends into the right-field bullpen, a home run that puts the Red Sox ahead. For the first time that day, my father smiles at me, a smile that disturbs my heart because a smile from him is such a rare thing; it always was, and it is rarer than ever now. It means that for the moment at least he has forgotten the pain that commands his body. I try to lock the smile in my mind. Behind it I imagine I see his dreams, all of his dreams over all of the years, and in that way I recall certain dreams of my own.

I was eight years old that October day when I walked alone toward Central Square, which was the bustling heart of Lynn in the 1930s. As I came closer to the square I saw a crowd, almost all men, teeming in the street. What was it all about? I didn't know, but I heard a voice from a loudspeaker and caught some of the strange names rippling through the air: Schoolboy Rowe, Mickey Cochrane, Charlie Gehringer, Goose Goslin, Hank Greenberg,

Dizzy Dean, Frankie Frisch, Leo Durocher, Pepper Martin. I saw people looking up at the building that housed the Lynn *Daily Evening Item.* I squeezed to the front and looked and there was this marvelous contraption hanging over the side of the building. It was in the shape of a baseball diamond, all green. On it a white ball was being propelled in whichever direction the action went. If someone hit a grounder the ball would move on a track out toward the infield, then over to first base, and disappear, which meant the out had been made. What an exotic way to watch a World Series. It moored me to baseball forever.

I tried never to miss a World Series from that time on. I would dash home from school, run downtown, go up on the train platform that overlooked the Lynn *Item* building so that I could watch the World Series without obstruction. Yes, *watch.* For that green diamond and the white ball moving in all directions still represents a vision to me of baseball as a pure and clean and demanding and inviolate sport, and of my boyhood at its most serene. Maybe television had the same effect on my sons, but I wish they could have been introduced to baseball the way I was.

That World Series of 1934 was one of the most thrilling of all World Series because of the nature of the one team, the Gashouse Gang of St. Louis. I discovered all that later, but it wasn't until 1936, when I had committed myself to the National League, that the World Series became an event for me. I couldn't wait to get up on the train station for that first game between the New York Yankees and the New York Giants. And what a joy it was—it is the first game in which I can recall details—when King Carl Hubbell beat the Yankees, 6–1. What I remember best is that white ball never once sailing to the outfield when the Yankees batted because Hubbell made DiMaggio and Gehrig and Crosetti and all those killers hit every ball on the ground.

I was back the next day and it

was awful. The Yankees scored eighteen runs. Lazzeri and Dickey murdered us and don't ask me what happened to Prince Hal Schumacher. I remember looking forward to the train from Gloucester pulling into the station so that the carnage would at least be temporarily blotted from my vision.

The Yankees won the third game, which I didn't mind as much because the winning pitcher was Irving "Bump" Hadley, who came from Lynn, Massachusetts, and you had to feel good about a hometown boy winning a World Series. Six games it took the Yankees but they were just too much for my Giants.

Not my Giants, actually. I wasn't a Giant fan. I was a National League fan second and a Boston Braves fan first. That happened, I think, because the first major-league game I got to see was a Braves game. (The truth is that becoming a Braves fan in those days was an act of defiance, the team was so bad. Everyone loved the Red Sox, and since I am given to occasional bursts of perversity, I attached to the Braves.)

It was my uncle who took me to my first baseball game. All I remember was that it was a Sunday doubleheader between the Boston Braves and the Pittsburgh Pirates, and that Babe Ruth was playing for the Braves. So it had to have been 1935, and early in the season, because Ruth lasted only twenty-eight games before he retired in bitterness, shaken by the knowledge that immortality has its boundaries, too.

This was my rich uncle, the only rich anything in our family. At least compared to everyone else he was rich. He was a surgeon and had a family reputation as a miser, and I believe he was mean of spirit, too, because he was also our landlord for a time and would not allow us to fall behind in our rent (which we were prone to do in those days). He had no particular interest in taking me to a ball game but my mother worked on him—she would never back off anyone—and finally wore him down. He drove with a friend to the game

and they sat in the grandstand and my uncle gave me money to sit in the Pavilion, which was what they called the left-field bleachers at Braves Field. The Pavilion seemed miles away from the infield but I didn't care. I was happy and I could see well enough. I loved sitting there, surrounded by open space, by sky and a sea of green grass, and clean smells and the camaraderie of the people around me. The Pavilion was hardly crowded, as I recall, but I loved the sense of relaxation and feeling of informality among the fans who were out there with me. They drank beer and ate hot dogs and reviled the enemy and continuously en-

couraged our players, especially one Wally Berger.

Berger was our hero that year, actually my first baseball hero. The Braves of 1935 won 38 games and lost 115, one of the worst baseball teams in history, and yet Berger led the league in home runs and runs batted in. If he could keep it up, maybe they could build a team around him. Alas, a couple of years later Berger was gone to another team and the Braves were still floundering. But I didn't care. They were all my heroes in those days: Deacon Danny MacFayden and Ben Cantwell one year, then Lou Fette and Jim Turner, a couple of thirty-year-old

Wally Berger, the author's hero, with Babe Ruth.

235

rookie pitchers in 1937 who each won twenty games. And the great non Hall of Fame players like Push-'Em-Up Tony Cuccinello, Debs Garms, Elbie Fletcher, Sibbi Sisti, Vince DiMaggio (yes, we even managed to get the least talented of the baseball-playing DiMaggio brothers). I knew in my heart I would never see them up on the board at the Lynn *Item* building but it almost didn't matter. Love was love.

I think the only other game I ever saw in those early years, at least until I was fourteen and beginning to travel into Boston alone, was with my mother. My father never once took me to a game. He couldn't afford to and he never had the time. It was the Depression and he was having trouble holding on to a job and he was disappointed in himself and, consequently, not completely at ease with us.

My mother's offer was an out-and-out bribe. She would take me and my younger sister into the Beth Israel Hospital in Brookline for allergy tests, and if we were "good" we would then go to the Red Sox game. I was very good. In those days they scratched your arm with all sorts of needles to see what you were allergic to and the response on my

part was spectacular in almost every direction. So Mom and my sister and I walked the two miles or so to Fenway Park. I don't remember a thing about the game except that my sister ate a lot of peanuts early on and got sick and we had to leave by the third or fourth inning.

By that time I was beginning to play baseball. When I was very young I would sit in the living room after school and listen to the Braves games on the radio and imagine myself as a Lou Fette or a Jim Tobin or a Sailor Bill Posedel. I had a small rubber ball and I would wind up and throw it as hard as I could into an old couch in our living room. If the ball stuck in the seam between the pillow and the back of the couch, it was a strike. If it bounced away, it was a ball. Walks and strikeouts constituted that exercise. Somehow, my mother always tolerated such nonsense. (I mentioned this youthful aberration to my wife recently and she said, "If my kids did that, I'd kill them.")

My mother, early on, instinctively grasped this thing I was having with baseball. Years later, shortly after my discharge from the navy, my mother went to some function and met Johnny Pesky, the Red Sox

shortstop who married a Lynn girl. She marched right up to him and said, "Mr. Pesky, I'm Mrs. Silverman and I want you to know my son is a fan of yours." Of course, she took away his autograph for me.

Anyway, my friends and I would go down to the playground adjoining Lynn Beach and play baseball all day long in the summer, and I shagged fly balls for hours on end and became a pretty good fielder. Strangely, in my best year—when I hit an even .300 for the YMHA team and played a cool center field—I stood out there not like a Johnny Cooney or a Tommy Holmes or one of the Braves procession of journeymen center fielders. I imitated the young Red Sox center fielder, Dominic DiMaggio. Dom had a graceful posture in center field, his body pointed not toward home plate but angled to the left or right, depending on whether the batter was left-handed or right-handed. And I did the same and when a lazy fly ball came my way I loped for it with a long, smooth, calculating stride, just like Dom.

Still, my connection was the Braves, always the Braves (though one year, out of desperation, they took the name Bees). The best of all years for me as a baseball fan came

Tommy Holmes' smooth cut.

236

Vern Bickford, left, John Sain and Warren Spahn, right, were Boston Braves' moundstays in '48.

in 1948. Ah, it was a wonderful summer. Worked a little. Spent a lot of time playing ball. Lolled some on the beach, listening to the games on the radio that summer when, day after day, the Braves kept pulling out victories in the late innings. Forgive my indulgence, but here were the boys of the summer of '48, who redeemed my years of frustration: Earl Torgeson, the bespectacled first baseman, with that huge wad of chewin' tobacco plugging his cheek; the kids, Ed Stanky at second base and Al Dark the shortstop (Stanky hit .320, Dark .322 that year); lantern-jawed Bob Elliott at third base (100 RBIs); Jeff Heath, Mike McCormick, and Tommy Holmes, all .300 hitters in the outfield; Phil Masi, the catcher; and those two pitchers, Johnny Sain and Warren Spahn, who inspired the immortal refrain "Spahn and Sain and two days of rain." In truth, the

two had some backing: Bill Voiselle from Ninety-six, South Carolina; Vern Bickford, Clyde Shoun, fat Red Barrett. That was the year—ninety-one wins and a pennant.

Luckily, my uncle Arky, a *good* uncle, an uncle I always admired, had helped install the lights at Braves Field. He was able to get me an ushering job for the first game of the World Series, the game won by the Braves, 1–0. I'm afraid I didn't perform very well that afternoon because the tension was so intense. Sain and Bob Feller were waging a brilliant duel. Nothing-nothing to the bottom of the eighth when, with Phil Masi on second base, Feller whirled, threw to second, and seemed to have Masi picked off. But the umpire called Masi safe, a decision that even some Braves fans (not me, however) found outrageous. A moment later Tommy Holmes lined one into the

outfield and Masi was home with the winning run.

I don't recall being terribly upset that Cleveland went on to win the Series in six games. The Braves had done it for me in almost every way. And provided, I see now, a coda for my youth.

It is a hot afternoon in early July of 1964 and my family is seated with me in a box down the third-base line at Shea Stadium. It is the All-Star Game and my three sons, Tom, who is ten, Brian, who is eight, and Matty, seven, have come to root for . . . the *American League.* We are living in New York now and my children know nothing of Boston, and they never heard of the Boston Braves, but have been told that the team in Milwaukee once represented my youth back in Boston. Yes, they could have loved the New York Giants or Brooklyn Dodgers before

Boston's Eddie Stanky sidesteps Cleveland's Larry Doby in the '48 Series.

those teams chose to leave town. But because of me, I'm sure, they chose the Yankees. Unlike me, they prefer winners and the Yankees, then, were still winning everything. So here we are at Shea Stadium. I have announced grandly that the National League will win and they have put their loyalties on the American League.

"Watch Mickey Mantle," one of them says.

"Watch Willie Mays," I say.

They watch gleefully into the ninth inning, the American League ahead 4–3, when Willie comes up and somehow works the Red Sox monster man, Dick Radatz, for a walk. Immediately, Mays steals second, which enables him to score the tying run on a bloop single by Orlando Cepeda. Johnny Callison hits a three-run home run and it is all over. Out of tact, I say nothing, my boys certainly say nothing, my wife allows how it has been such a nice after-

noon.

They all took to baseball, after their fashion, not with the intensity that I had back in the thirties when the world was somewhat different. They accepted distractions—television and the strictures of Little League baseball, and football, which meant at least as much to them as baseball. And they became a bit complacent because of privileges that other boys didn't have. I had become involved in sports in a professional

238

way soon after the 1948 baseball season, and the game took on much different shadings for me. Now that I earned part of my livelihood from the game I looked on baseball in a harder way. I met major-league players on the job and discovered that they were the same as you and I, except maybe less so. I also learned that the game itself was a business, and that some of the people I met in the business could be at least as mean-spirited as some in other businesses. The world turns the same way, no matter the environment. But the pleasure of the game, despite such disruptions as expansion and rules changes, remained essentially the same to me. I always loved being out at the ball park. The essence of the game was as I remembered it that day in 1935 sitting in the Pavilion in Braves Field. Of course, I wanted my children to share my experience.

And they did. One summer we spent a weekend at Cooperstown and listened as Bob Feller and Jackie Robinson made their Hall of Fame acceptance speeches. My oldest son was with me at Yankee Stadium the day Roger Maris hit his sixty-first home run, a historic event that he handled with considerably more aplomb and detachment than I did. There were other frolics, too, though by the time my sons were of prime rooting age the Yankees were through winning pennants. So there were no joyous World Series for them at the stadium. But they did go to Boston in 1967 for a World Series game between the Red Sox and the Cardinals. And afterward— the Red Sox had won that one—we went back to Lynn and my father asked his grandchildren how they liked the game and followed with his inevitable question—Do you think the Red Sox can win it? As I recall, being more strongly Yankee fans than American League fans, they said no.

Now my sons are out of the house, all in college, but they remain Yankee fans. They have already suggested to me that "next year," when the team moves back to Yankee Stadium, there will be an appropriate occasion for them to celebrate. Always, in baseball, there is a next year. I hope it happens to the Yankees so that I can join my sons in their celebration.

The game is not the same today as it was in my youth, but, then, nothing is. Yet here it is another October and I look forward to the World Series, even to watching it on television. My children will pay attention, too. And back in Lynn, I know my father will be sitting in his chair, time ebbing away, losing himself in the game, purging his pain for a while, even if one of the teams turns out not to be the Red Sox.

Once, another time at Cooperstown, soon after he was inducted into the Hall of Fame, Satchel Paige said to me: "I loved baseball. There wasn't no maybe so about it." He loved it for different reasons than I, my father, and my sons. But the sentiment is a good one. It pierces through memories and dreams and suffering, and it has helped us, at least, bind the generations together.

The ageless LeRoy Satchel Paige begins his windup.

CASEY STENGEL

BY JOE REICHLER

When the mighty New York Yankees announced on the afternoon of October 12, 1948, that they had signed Casey Stengel to succeed Bucky Harris as manager of the most successful ball club in the major leagues, most baseball writers concluded that the Yankees had hired Stengel to keep the audience amused while General Manager George Weiss rebuilt the team. Old age, they said, had caught up with the Yankees, and an odd character like Stengel was an ideal choice to hold the fort while reinforcements were being located and brought up to the stadium.

Win the pennant? How silly can you get? Not with Stengel. Why, the old man had managed nine years in the National League and had won more guffaws than ball games. Did not the Dodgers even pay him a full year's salary once not to manage the club?

Never were so many experts so wrong. Stengel not only won the pennant in 1949, his first year as manager of the Yankees, but he went on to direct the Yankees to ten pennants in twelve years. In seven of those years he won the World Championship. In the years he lost, his teams finished second and third. His record of five consecutive World Series triumphs has never been matched.

Stengel was not without his skeptics, however. There were some who insisted he was lucky to have such a wealth of material to work with. They pointed to his nine second division seasons with the Dodgers and Braves in the 1930s and 1940s and the four straight tenth-place finishes with the Mets in the 1960s. They cited his incoherences, his inconsistencies, his fracture of the English language. He was a clown . . . a buffoon.

Casey was a clown. Not a buffoon, but an authentic clown, with the gestures, the grimaces, the winks, even the pratfalls. He was also a skilled practitioner who could size up a comic effect as accurately as he could sense a pitcher's fading stuff. For all his weird shifts in strategy and weirder use of the English language, he was a genius as a manager. A superb baseball tactician, a master strategist, his manipulations of the players was based on sound, solid reasoning, the percentages, and his precise knowledge of every player in the league, his strength and his weaknesses. True, he had a wealth of material to work with, but he made the most of it.

In many ways, the old campaigner, this paradoxical personality christened Charles Dillon, but known throughout the world as Casey, was the most remarkable man ever to wear a baseball uniform. No one had

"The Perfesser," Charles Dillion Stengel.

Casey, the Professor, was not above trying to teach umpires a thing or two.

a more consuming devotion to baseball or knew more about the game. There was no one even remotely like him in the game. Not Connie Mack. Not John McGraw. Not Joe McCarthy. Not anybody. How could there be more than one Casey Stengel? How could there ever be another Casey Stengel?

His memory was unbelievable. After a game, he could play it back to the audience pitch by pitch. His physical endurance was astounding. He had the constitution of an ox. "Most people my age are dead," he was fond of saying. In addition he was a master of public relations which made him a daily target of not only his local writers but all visiting newspapermen, magazine writers, and broadcasters. He usually regaled them, telling different stories to different people. Nobody minded. Not all may have been newsworthy. But they were always funny. He was the most delightful and colorful character baseball has ever known.

Born in Kansas City, Missouri, on May 30, 1890, Casey entered Western Dental College in Kansas City after he graduated from high school. But baseball was his consuming interest, and it wasn't much of a

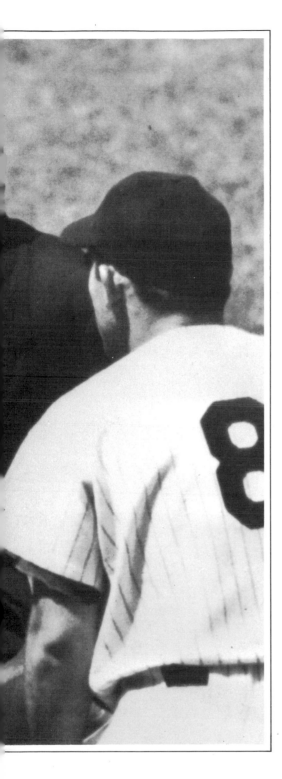

struggle for him to decide to quit college when he got a chance to sign with Kankakee and become a professional player. That was in 1910. Casey loved to talk about his days as a busher, earning seventy-five dollars a month. At age twenty, he was already a clown. He wore loud ties with his baseball uniform, and he insisted on practicing sliding while he trotted to his position in the outfield.

Stengel managed the New York Yankees to 10 pennants in 12 years.

"There was a lunatic asylum across the center-field fence," he recalled. "Them guys in the loony bin always cheered when they saw me slide. But my manager used to tap his forehead and point at the asylum and say, 'It's only a matter of time, Stengel.' "

By 1912, gags and all, Stengel made it to the majors. He was purchased by the Dodgers. "The Dodgers sent a scout to Montgomery in mid-season of 1912 to look me over, see?" he said. "It is a double-header and I have a pretty good day for myself, which you could look it up. I made six hits and a couple of tree-menjus catches in the outfield. I also make a couple of tree-menjus throws—except that I threw 'em to the wrong base. I am so fast that I overrun one base and am tagged out. I steal a couple of bases, which is embarrassing for me because there's runners already on them. So this scout wires back his report to Charlie Ebbets, which owns the Dodgers. 'Stengel is the world's greatest ball-player—from the neck down.' "

Lovable Wilbert Robinson was managing the Dodgers then and Stengel was a ballplayer after "Uncle Robbie's" heart. In 1916 he talked the Dodger manager into trying to catch a baseball dropped from one of those new-fangled flying machines. Robbie waited confidently on the bench, mitt poised, unaware that Casey had substituted a grapefruit for the ball. The plane passed overhead at four hundred feet. Uncle Robbie settled under the diving speck that dropped into his hands. But the big sphere slipped through his hands and burst into a wet, red mess on his chest. "My God, I'm killed, I'm dead. Look at that blood. My chest is caved in, somebody help me!" screamed the terrified manager. Casey roared with laughter.

Two years later, Casey was traded to Pittsburgh. Brooklyn fans, who had learned to love him, cheerfully razzed him the first time he turned up at Ebbets Field in an enemy uniform. Let Casey tell the rest.

Casey at bat.

244

1916 BROOKLYN TEAM

Stengel, top row, first on left, was a darling of the Dodger fans.

"Well, I'm in right field and alongside me is the Dodger bullpen, where I see our pitcher, Leon Cadore, chasing a sparrow. Now I'm not sure whether this is an old sparrow who ain't moving so good anymore or a young one who ain't yet learned how to fly so good. But Leon caught it. The inning is over, I asked him for the bird and stuck it under my cap. He scratched a bit but stayed quiet maybe from inhaling my dandruff.

"First up in the next inning, I came on swinging three bats like a Ty Cobb, and the crowd really gives it to me. I throw away two of the bats, take a bow, tip my hat, out flies the bird, who is now flying pretty good. Out of the Dodger bench comes Uncle Robbie who thinks the umpire should do something as I'm making a joke of the game. Says the umpire, 'Look, I always suspected this guy

had bats in the belfry. What's wrong with lettin' him prove it?' "

Casey's delightful assault on the English language came to be known as Stengelese. Nowhere was it better demonstrated than during the United States Senate Subcommittee on Antitrust and Monopoly hearings in July of 1958. Called upon as a witness, his answers to the senators' questions left them baffled and bewildered. When he was excused, they were still looking for the first direct answer.

"You want to know why the minors are in such financial straits?" he repeated. "I will tell you why. I don't think anybody can support a minor league when they see a great official, it would be just like if a great actor or actress came to town. If Greta Garbo came over there they would all go to see Greta Garbo but if you have a very poor team they

are not going to watch you until you become great and the minor leagues now with radio and television they will not pay very much attention to minor league players."

Once when Senator Estes Kefauver asked why Stengel thought baseball should not be under legislation, he replied: "I've always heard it could be done, but sometimes it don't always work.

"My opinion of baseball is that I've been in it for forty-eight years, there must be some good in it. It has been run cleaner than any business that was ever put out in 100 years, at the present time and the present company. You can retire at 50 and what organization in America allows you to retire at 50 and receive money? I don't happen to have children but I wish Mrs. Stengel and I had eight, I would like to put them on the bonus rule. If I was a ball

player and I was discharged and I saw within three years that I couldn't become a big league ball player, I would go into another business, or become a manager."

Casey touched all the bases, with the exception of first, second, and third. It remained for Mickey Mantle, who followed his manager to the stand, to bring down the house. One of his first remarks as he smiled blandly was, "My views are just about the same as Casey's."

Yes, Casey Stengel was a clown, a jester, a raconteur, a pantomimist, a funny man, a double talker, a master of the non sequiturs. But his wise old brain always whirred with wonderful precision on and off the field. He clicked out strategy that outraged strategists. His second guesses were right so often that it could hardly be called second guessing. He confounded rival managers, players, writers, and senators. He was bewildering but brainy. He fractured the language but was on speaking terms with presidents and kings. He dan-

gled his participles but manipulated his players like a master chessman. He could be irritating, he could be cranky, he could at times be downright rude. But he could also be kind, compassionate, and considerate. He had the heart of a lion, the soul of a Svengali, and the touch of a Midas. He was the most complex and at the same time the most intimate man baseball has ever known. The image he left behind will always endure.

Casey Stengel managed baseball teams for 25 years.

Casey called his Mets, "My Amazings".

JACKIE ROBINSON

BY JOE REICHLER

Unconquerable!

That's the word for Jackie Robinson.

No player in the history of baseball faced greater odds. No player endured more hatred and vituperation. In the beginning, he not only had to withstand threats and hostility from the opposition but open rebellion from his own teammates. He fought back the only way he could . . . with ringing base hits and brilliant base running. At the end, he had turned scorn into respect, hatred into admiration. Once there were players who threatened to go on strike rather than play with or against him. Today these same players recall with pride that they were contemporaries of the man who proved that a Negro ballplayer could compete equally on the major league diamonds of America with players of white skin.

Jackie Robinson was not the greatest player who ever wore a pair of spikes. More than a dozen players had a higher lifetime batting average than Robinson's best for any season. Lou Brock stole more bases in two seasons than Jackie did in all of a 10-year career. Numerous players hit more home runs, drove in more runs and scored more often. But no one, not even the fabled Ty Cobb, was more feared on the bases or more respected at the plate with the tying or winning run in scoring position.

Jackie Robinson was the only base runner of his time who could bring a game to a stop just by getting on base. His mere presence on the baselines was enough to upset the opposing pitcher. He was at his best when it counted the most. All these things make Jackie Robinson the most dynamic, the most colorful, the fiercest competitor, perhaps the

No one was more respected at the plate with men on base than Jackie Robinson.

Robinson came to the Dodgers from their Montreal farm club.

greatest all-around player Brooklyn, if not the entire National League, has ever known.

His consummate urge to win transcended all his skills on the ball field. He was combative. He was emotional. He was calculating. His aggressiveness and will to win lifted him above others of equal or greater ability. He gave no quarter, he asked for none. The point is that Jackie Robinson would not be defeated. Not on the baseball diamond . . . not in life.

There are many others of his race in major league baseball today. Several are in the front office. Others are on the coaching lines. And one is a big league manager. But of Jackie Robinson, it will always be said: He

was the first. He paved the way for the rest. And he did it not only with his speed and power but with his head and heart.

Jackie Robinson was unlike any other rookie when he first joined the Brooklyn Dodgers in April 1947. Few, if any, questioned his ability after he had torn up the International League, capturing the Most Valuable Player Award in his inaugural season at Montreal. What they did question was Jackie Robinson, the human being. Where others were measured on merit alone, Robinson was appraised on his behavior, his mental capacity, his actions on and off the field. As one rabble-rousing newspaper editor stated: "Robinson has to prove he deserves to live and

play with white men."

There isn't much use in recounting the insults, the indecent remarks, and unspeakable incidents that this gifted but muzzled athlete was forced to endure during most of that nightmarish first season. They were an ugly reality.

The seeds of dissension were sown from the first day Jackie joined the Dodgers, April 10, 1947. Certain Dodger players circulated a petition against Jackie. This news reached Branch Rickey, Robinson's benefactor, who called in his players and warned them they would be traded if they could not play on the same side with a Negro. Most of the players backed down. Two were eventually traded.

BARNSTORMING

By Ted Worner

For five-years Ted Worner promoted post season exhibition tours of Jackie Robinson's All-Stars. The following is one of his most vivid memories of that time.

Jack and I were a little worried that a team of blacks and whites barnstorming in the South might touch off incidents, but southern hospitality more than lived up to its name. We were even more warmly received in 1953 than the previous years, with one exception. This was Birmingham where I was advised to expect trouble from no less an authority than Sheriff "Bull" Connors, celebrated for his use of police dogs, hoses, and cattle prods—and for the immortal declaration that "whites and nigras ain't allowed to segregate together in this town." Connors sent two of his deputies to my room in the Tutwiler Hotel to see if some kind of compromise could be reached. The talks were informal.

"Listen, Jewboy," said the chief deputy, "if them whites show up at Rickwood Field on Sunday, you and 'Robbison's' gonna be in jail before the game starts. And Sheriff Connors might just shove that big seegar of yours up your —— while he's doin' it. He ain't afraid to lock up a U.S. Senator [Glenn Taylor of Idaho], and he sure as hell ain't gonna lose no sleep over you."

I phoned Jack in Chattanooga.

Although I was quite frightened, I didn't say so directly. Instead, I hedged, reminding Jack that Birmingham, after all, did have a local segregation ordinance on the books. I asked him if we'd really accomplish anything by tangling with Connors.

"Frig him," said Jack.

So I had to go ahead. I saw the local papers and asked for their backing. They told me to write the release. The story made the sports pages—with the names of the white players deleted. When I called the editors to protest, I could almost hear them shrugging on the phone. I had better luck with a local lawyer. Like many whites in Birmingham, he was ashamed of his sheriff. He told me that the U.S. Constitution overrode the city ordinance and that he'd personally take Connors to court if he tried to keep our white players off the field.

But Connors won. By now, the story had filtered back to the team. Hodges, Branca, and Young, all whites, were worried because their families were worried. Jack phoned.

"We'll just have to play without them, Ted. It's not fair to get them involved. Okay, so we'll take a loss at the gate, but I just don't want to see any of those fellows get hurt."

By a stroke of luck I was able to grab Willie Mays, on weekend pass from the army, with an offer of $1,500 for the game plus an extra

$500 for every thousand spectators over three thousand. Willie came out nicely ahead—there wasn't an empty seat in Rickwood Park. He and the others also enjoyed themselves by driving Connors' sixteen deputies up the wall with an unending barrage of Bronx cheers. The icing on our cake came when two of the cops stormed into the dugout and ordered Jack to remove the white kid playing center field. Maury Wills almost hemorrhaged from laughing.

Actually, our rather childish revenge on Connors gave Jack little satisfaction. In fact, to use an imprecise expression, he was almost white with rage throughout the game, and it took him quite a while to simmer down. I suppose I could cite his anger as a measure of his lifelong personal committment to the cause of equal rights, and of course, it was. But I think something even closer to Jack's nature was involved—he was beaten. Coming out second best in anything, whether a ball game or a golf match or a matter of principle, simply ran against his grain. Sure, he taught himself to lose gracefully, at least most of the time, but it always stuck in his craw. He was a competitor. He hated losing even more than Leo Durocher hated it.

The only difference was that Jack believed nice guys finished first.

Or ought to, anyway.

Jack and Rachel Robinson. This picture was taken shortly after Jackie was voted into the Hall of Fame.

Later in 1947, a report circulated that a rival team planned a strike in protest against Robinson. Ford Frick, then President of the National League, promptly issued a warning of quick retribution if the plan was carried out. There was no strike and eventually the opposition recognized that Robinson's presence on the diamond was good for baseball.

Robinson made his precedent-shattering invasion of organized baseball wearing an unnatural armor of quiet humility. A complete code of conduct was foredained for him before he ever stepped on a field. His deportment received more attention than the affairs of state. Hiding his true combativeness behind the armor carefully selected for him by Branch Rickey, allowed to vent his boundless competitive instincts only with his bat, glove, and flying feet, Jackie was the unresponsive target for barbs of humiliation that no man but Robinson could fully appreciate.

Despite his instant success—he concluded his first season batting .296, hammering 12 home runs and stealing 29 bases—Jackie could not be satisfied with things as they were. Within him welled a great resentment at being stifled, bound by restrictive do's and don't's that threatened his mental stability.

Jackie's beauteous and charming wife, who made a significant contribution to her husband's pioneering job in baseball, remembers:

"Along about mid-season of his first year," Rachel recalls, "I became extremely worried about Jack. I knew nobody could go along day after day, week after week, and month after month, bottling up his emotions. I knew what Mr. Rickey had advised but I also knew my husband and I expected him to break loose.

"He couldn't eat and at night he'd toss constantly in his sleep. I insisted that Jackie consult a doctor, who warned him about a nervous breakdown. But Jackie wouldn't give up. He continued to play with all he had, carrying the same problems around with him."

Despite his historic role, all Robinson ever asked, once he proved himself, was to be accepted as a player among other players. He didn't once whimper when the restrictions were placed upon him and the opposition began to test his courage and temper. He took every-

thing anybody had to give, and eventually he won the respect of his peers by doing everything better than they did, exchanging base hits for every insult and invective. No meek and humble man could possibly play baseball with the fire and dash Robinson exhibited, which he had to have, just as he had to restrain his emotions, in order to assure success.

Jackie threw off the shackles gradually. In 1948, he began to back-talk rival players. In 1949, he wrangled with the umpires. In 1950 he took the brakes off his feud with Leo Durocher and it burst forth into the open. Resenting bean balls being hurled at his head by the Giants' Sal Maglie, he laid down a bunt to force the pitcher to field the ball on the first base line where Jackie could collide with him. A typical Giant-Dodger rhubarb ensued.

The unrestrained Jackie Robinson was unstoppable. His heroics on the field have become Dodger legend. During the ten years he played with the Dodgers, they were the most exciting team in baseball and Jackie was the most exciting player. He batted over .300 in six of those years, leading the league in 1949 with a .342 average and winning the Most Valuable Player Award. Significantly, the Dodgers won six pennants and a World Championship in those ten seasons. Wherever the Dodgers played, great crowds came out to see Jackie.

Not since the heyday of Babe Ruth did a player have so profound an effect on baseball. Like Ruth, Jackie was both a player and a performer. He helped make the game more exciting, he helped swell attendance and he helped the other players in income earnings. In short, he helped baseball.

What Jack Roosevelt Robinson accomplished will last as long as the players of his or any other race send ringing hits onto green fields and flash speedy legs along smooth baselines.

Jackie Robinson will be remembered for lots of things. But above all . . . . . he was the first!

252

Robinson hookslides into home against the Giants.

THEY ALSO PLAY

BY JOE FALLS

My dream is simple enough. I want to stand at home plate in Fenway Park with a fungo bat and have someone about ten feet away, just off to the right, lob baseballs to me underhand.

Maybe Dick Tracewski, the first-base coach of the Detroit Tigers, would do it. Yes, he would understand. Dick's a good guy, a man of feeling. He would stand there and lob the balls just right, waist-high over the plate, and I would drill one after another off the wall, off the scoreboard, into the net, off the light towers, and—if I caught one right— over everything, the wall, the screen, the lights, all the way out into Kenmore Square.

I don't suppose it'll ever happen, but I think about it all the time. The sweet feeling of power, the exhilaration of lining one ball after another over that giant green barrier in left field. Frank Malzone? He never saw the day he could put one over the wall like I could. Bobby Doerr? I saw him hit the wall twice in one inning when the Red Sox were scoring thirteen runs off a pitcher named Carl Scheib of the Philadelphia A's. (I never understood why Connie Mack left him in for all thirteen runs; I suppose it had something to do with teaching the young man a lesson.) But I would hit them harder and farther than Doerr, Malzone, Dropo, Jensen, Stephens—yes, even farther than this new kid, Jim Rice. This is my dream; the dream of so many young boys.

We all dream of playing in the majors. Every last one of us who ever put on a mitt and went down to the field to play with the guys, a quarter a man, a dime, or just one-a-cat if there weren't enough guys around; we dreamed of the day we would do it in the big leagues. You just hoped the tape wouldn't come off the ball too much, and you'd better not get home too late for dinner, because if you did, your mom wouldn't let you go back to the field to play after dinner. You would have to do the dishes or some stupid thing like that.

We played on the sandlots and we dreamed.

Growing up in Brooklyn, I wanted to be Ron Northey.

Only the true baseball fan even knew Ron Northey existed. He was fat and out of shape but, boy, could he ever pound the ball in batting practice. He was with the Philadelphia Phillies, and whenever the team was in town to play the Brooklyn Dodgers, we'd go out to Ebbets Field early. Munching on salami and tomato sandwiches, we'd watch the Phillies take batting practice. Ron Northey was always good for half a dozen into Bedford Avenue, the street that ran behind the field.

I was a right-handed batter, except when we played softball in the schoolyard at P.S. 125 in Queens. Then I was Ron Northey. I'd turn around and bat left-handed, and that was difficult to do, since I never had any sneakers and it was hard to take a solid stance in the concrete with my leather-soled shoes. So I did the only thing I could. I spit on the ground and placed my left sole into the spit, taking dead aim at the right-field fence. One day I doubled off the wall and went standing up into second on my leather-soled shoes. I don't know when I was ever happier in my whole life.

Ron Northey.

Not all of us grew up to become major-league baseball players. But many dreams did come true. The fertile fields of organized and pickup baseball have nurtured and yielded the likes of Rod Carew, Carlton Fisk, and Pete Rose, to name only a few.

John Mayberry, the hulking first baseman of the Kansas City Royals, is another who lived and dreamed baseball on the sandlot. John played for big Ron Thompson on the fields of Detroit, around St. Martin's High School in Highland Park. When you say big Ron, you mean BIG RON. He goes about 350 pounds, and when it comes to the kids, he has a heart to match. He loves every one of

them. He loves it when they play "The Game."

Not organized baseball, as we know Little League and Babe Ruth Leagues, but when the kids just show up in the morning and start their games and keep playing all day long. Big Ron Thompson believes that baseball should be only one thing for kids who are ten, eleven, twelve, thirteen, fourteen, and even fifteen.

"It should be fun," he says. "If they want to get serious after that, they have plenty of time to get serious. Up until then, they should just go out there and enjoy themselves."

So every summer, when the

Big John Mayberry.

streets of Detroit start heating up and the tensions build in the community (this is the city that has the highest crime rate in the country; the one that has had the biggest, bloodiest, and costliest riot; the city that has had the longest strikes and can cripple an entire nation by closing down its assembly lines), Ron Thompson goes out at nine o'clock every morning with his few bats and his battered baseballs and gets his "Wildcat League" going.

He's got some shiny new baseballs back in his locker, and he'll bring them out from time to time, because who doesn't want to rub up a new baseball, or be the first one to take a good, clean crack at a white ball? But he'll bring along the tattered ones because he wants kids to tape them up so that they'll appreciate the new ones when he brings them out.

John Mayberry will tell you "the most fun I ever had in my whole life was in our championship when I was ten years old."

The game lasted four days.

The wisdom of Ron Thompson was at work.

"We had twenty kids on each side, and I figured they wouldn't know the difference at their age," he said. "So we put in a backup catcher, a backup first baseman, a backup third baseman, and about eight outfielders."

Everybody played, and everybody loved it.

"We went home at night arguing about the score," Mayberry recalled. "We didn't know a game was supposed to last four days, but it was all we talked about, all we thought about."

For four days, it gave forty young boys in Detroit a chance to involve themselves in something wholesome. For four days, forty young boys stayed clear of the trouble that can afflict youngsters on the streets.

"It wound up seventy to sixty-seven," Thompson grinned, and Mayberry grinned along with him. His team had the seventy.

"It's a strange thing with our

Little league world series action at second base.

kids," said Thompson. "We never have any trouble with anything being stolen. They all have respect for each other's equipment. We've never had so much as a bat or a cap stolen. The only time this happens is when somebody from the outside wanders by and gets jealous of these youngsters enjoying themselves."

Thompson's rules are pretty simple. When his tournament is nearing an end, he drives to the Eastern Market in downtown Detroit and buys one crate of oranges and one crate of apples. The winners get the oranges, presumably on the theory that they are sweeter and juicier, and the losers get the apples. The losers also have to clean the four helmets that the two teams share while playing.

Do not think that sandlot baseball is only for the young. Ray Herbert, the former major-league pitcher now in his late forties, is still pitching for the ITM (Inland Tool and Manufacturing) team in Detroit. He gets not a penny for his efforts, only the joy of competition he has known all his life. Billy Hoeft and Paul Foytack have also pitched for the ITM team, also for the sheer elation of getting out there one more time to see if they can get the best

of the batters.

The manager of the ITM team is a man named Larry Weiss, who has been involved with amateur baseball for much of his life. He will tell you about the nights—the endless nights —when his players would get out on the field after a rainstorm and spread sand around the field and then set fire to it with gasoline in an attempt to dry up the ground.

In the summer of 1975 Weiss' ITM team worked on the field starting at 4:00 in the afternoon, hoping to get it ready for an 8:00 P.M. play-off game. It was ready. So was ITM. It won the game. But that produced another problem: Due to the weather, another game had to be played—at 2:00 in the morning!

Weiss prepared to meet the worst from his players when he told them of the starting time. "I tried to figure out all the answers they'd give me when I told them we'd have to come back at two A.M. But not one of them offered a single comment."

Weiss then did what any good sandlot manager would do. He took his two pitchers home with him, bought them a pizza, and let them nap for an hour. ITM came back and won again, the game ending just before 5:00 in the morning.

The glory of scoring the winning run is the same everywhere.

Yes, baseball can be a love affair when you are older, when you can laugh at the thought of playing a game in the wee hours of the morning while other grown men sleep. But it is especially beautiful and appealing when you are young.

What does baseball mean to Tim McCamant, sixteen-year-old pitcher for the Sky Florist team in Detroit? Sky Florist played in the 1975 Babe Ruth League World Series in Pine Bluff, Arkansas. Tim was the best player on the team—a third baseman and left fielder—and got to be the best by simply working harder than anyone else.

He'd go to bed with his glove, wake up with it, and when school was out and practice was over, he'd come home and string up a tennis ball on the clothesline and—whack! whack! whack!—swing at it until the tennis ball spun around and became hopelessly snarled in the clothesline. He'd spend the next half hour untying it, and going through the whole thing again until it got too dark to see.

"The strange thing," said his mother, Irene McCamant, "is that he didn't want to go into baseball. He was very shy. He never talked to strange people. When anyone would come over to the house, he'd go up to his bedroom."

Down at the field, though, it was different. You'd better talk it up, baby, or you're not going to play. Let's hear some chatter! "Thataway-togo, Charlie, burn 'em in there! . . . No hitter up there, Charlie, boy, no hitter up there!"

Mrs. McCamant grew serious as mothers sometimes do.

"I think it's all been very good for him. It has taught him a lot of things. It has taught him to get along with others. It's given him discipline. If he's not there on time, he knows he's not going to play. And he's learned to compete; to win and to lose."

"All I know," said Tim's father, Bob, "is that I got so wrapped up in his team that I played less golf than I have in twenty years. Hell, I even went with the team to Pine Bluff for the play-offs."

A close play at the plate.

Ted Sizemore learned his baseball ABC's in downtown Detroit.

The McCamants are good people. They do what they can to help the team, offering encouragement and lemonade. That's beautiful.

At the Pine Bluff World Series, the players were not permitted to stay with their parents. They were taken over by "foster parents," the idea being that they had to live with strangers and —in a very brief time —establish a relationship with people they didn't even know. Smart folks there in Pine Bluff.

It is strange how this game of baseball can touch the minds of the young. Take Robby McCamant, Tim's nine-year-old brother. He hasn't figured out yet if Henry Aaron is Babe Ruth or if Babe Ruth is Henry Aaron. He has heard so much of these two men in the last few years of his life that they seem almost like one to him.

"Hey, Tim," Robby would say, "is Aaron the black one?"

"Yeah, Robby," Tim would answer, "Aaron is the black one."

"So we're going to watch Babe Ruth on TV today, right?"

"No, no, Robby. We're going to watch Aaron. He's the black one. Babe Ruth is white."

"Well," Robby would conclude, "you watch who you want. I'm watching Babe Ruth today . . . and I don't care if he's black or white. All I know is he's gonna hit one today."

Where else—O America— is there such understanding of life?

The ball diamond is the one common denominator in our land. Ted Sizemore, the second baseman for the Los Angeles Dodgers, lived in a Detroit suburb called Troy. But they didn't play very tough baseball in Troy in those days. So Ted would hitch rides into downtown Detroit (the menacing "inner city") so he could get in on some of the games they played down there. He knew

where the action was, and it didn't matter if he was the only white player on the field. He had to work hard to measure up, or they'd laugh him off the field.

It really doesn't matter what the kids' games are called—Little League, Babe Ruth League, Connie Mack, Mickey Mantle, Pee Wee Reese, Stan Musial, etc. They are playing . . . learning . . . and dreaming . . . in every part of the country.

I used to worry about the future of baseball. I'd worry a lot. I remember, after the war, there were something like sixty-five minor leagues. It was nothing for a team like the Yankees or the Dodgers or the Cardinals to have fourteen or fifteen minor-league clubs each. Sometimes they had three Triple-A clubs. But with the advent of television, minor-league baseball began to wilt. That worried me. I wondered where the players would come from. Would the game simply shrivel up and die? Heaven forbid if all we had to look forward to were zig-outs and options and zones and Howard, Giff, and Alex. Monday night isn't enough for me.

Baseball is a sport that is needed by our nation. I don't know Bill Vaughan, the associate editor of the Kansas City *Star,* but I must recall his thoughts and feelings for baseball.

"While many perceptive observers of the social scene are predicting a bleak future for baseball," Vaughan says, "I would like to go out on an opposite limb. I think baseball is going to grow in popularity. In fact it has to, unless this society is going to get as sick as the gloomier critics claim it already is."

"I went to the ball park the other day. It was in the afternoon, which is when God intended man to play baseball. The weather was beautiful and the game moved at its ancient and stately pace.

"There are those who contend that baseball is too slow. If it is, then the fault is with civilization which cries out incessantly for speed for speed's sake alone. We need something to slow us down. Most other sports are mining the box-office lode of continuous noise and action.

"Life was not meant to be lived at a constant hyped-up pitch.

"The spectator at a baseball game has time to unwind his nerves, contemplate eternal verities, and dissolve that hard knot which modern man carries around in the pit of his stomach.

"Of course baseball has its touch of boredom. What worthwhile human activity doesn't? To be slightly bored is to be more receptive to the periods of heightened emotion, a fact that the composers of great symphonies fully understand.

"Only baseball remains to remind us that leisure was meant to be spent in a leisurely manner and that we do not have to beat one another up in order to have a good time."

Baseball is something special—wherever it's played. Be it on a vacant lot in the cool of the early evening or at a regulation ball park under a blazing afternoon sun, the young and young in heart know this. Not all of those who play have a future in baseball, of course. But baseball and what it teaches will have an influence on the future of everyone involved with it. The people who play the game know this, too. But, most important, they know that—regardless of your shape or size, regardless of where you are in age or ability—baseball is fun to play. And that, in the end, is all that really matters.

All great hitters say concentration is the key to batting success.

BASEBALL FROM THE PRESSBOX

BY JEROME HOLTZMAN

John Drebinger set an Iron-Man record at *The New York Times*. Starting with 1929 and running through 1963, Drebinger wrote the page-one lead story on 203 consecutive World Series games. "They call it the Lou Gehrig record of baseball writing," Drebinger said, proudly. "I don't think anybody's going to bust it, not for a long time."

Finally, at the age of 73, and after 41 years of bouncing around the country with the Yankees and the old New York Giants, it came time for Drebinger to retire. He recalled then: "I couldn't have worked indoors. Look at the fun I had meeting all those people. Carl Hubbell. Mel Ott. John McGraw. Babe Ruth. Lou Gehrig. Casey Stengel. Ty Cobb. The Waner brothers, all the way back to Christy Mathewson. By God, it was a tremendous thing."

There is no question that baseball writers enjoy their work and some of this enjoyment, perhaps, is from the knowledge they are a breed apart. Whereas there are 600 major league players, themselves an elite corps, there are only 40 or 50 traveling baseball writers, one for every four to five million population. They are employed by big-city newspapers and are considerably more rare than brain surgeons. Some are just as talented.

Ring Lardner and Damon Runyon, two of America's greatest short story writers, were baseball writers. So were Grantland Rice and Heywood Broun. Walt Whitman of the Brooklyn Eagle was among the earliest baseball writers; his stilted reporting ("Mr. Johnson struck the ball well in the seventh inning,") gave no indication of his classic poetry to come.

Significantly, there doesn't seem to be any precise record of the first baseball player but history has identified the first baseball writer. He was Henry Chadwick of New York City, an Englishman by birth, the inventor of the box score (which has remained basically unchanged) and who, at the time of his death, was known, fondly, as "Father Chadwick."

Mr. Chadwick began his baseball writing career in 1856, at the age of 19, and during most of his life was the baseball editor of the New York Clipper. He attended and made records of games before the first Association of Base Ball Players was formed, wrote and edited many of the game's early annuals and guides, and for years, was the Chairman of the Committees on Rules for the leading Associations.

He was described as baseball's first "Chief Justice." Chadwick's un-

questioned authority can perhaps best be illustrated by an incident that occured on June 14, 1870 when he was the official scorer in a game matching the Cincinnati Red Stockings against the Atlantics of Brooklyn.

The Cincinnati nine, managed by Harry Wright, was virtually invincible and carried a 92-game winning streak embracing two seasons. After nine innings, the score was tied at 5–5 and the Atlantics, delighted with this unexpected success, walked off the field, eager to settle for the tie. Manager Wright appealed to Chadwick who decreed that the game be played into extra innings. The Atlantics won 8–7 in the 11th inning.

The most popular reading material, in Mr. Chadwick's time, were the so-called dime novels. Baseball, growing in popularity, was a constant subject in this form. So far as is known, the first baseball story to appear in a dime novel was published in 1885 and titled, "Captain of the Red Stockings, or The Last Inning of a Baseball Nine."

Then, as now, truth was better than fiction and novelists could take from real life. One of the most bizarre chapters in early baseball history had at its center, Oliver Perry Caylor, baseball editor, successively, of the Cincinnati Commercial Tribune, the New York Herald and the old Sporting Times.

Caylor, who wrote with a fiery pen and "who dealt out his opinions without fear or favor," climbed out of the press box to manage the Cincinnati Reds for the entire 1880 season, the only time in major league history a sportswriter descended onto the field and pulled on a uniform. As a manager, Caylor was a disaster. The Reds finished last with a 21–59 won and lost record, still the most embarrassing in Cincinnati history. Worse yet, at the season's end the Reds were "expelled from the National League (for one year) for violations of the rules, particularly those regulations forbidding the sale of liquor on grounds, or in buildings owned or controlled by owners of a Club."

Henry Chadwick, the first baseball writer, also devised the first box score.

Ring Lardner was voted into Baseball's Hall of Fame in 1963.

Baseball writers banded into a national organization as the Baseball Writers Association of America, in 1908, the year of Father Chadwick's death. According to popular legend, the genesis occured on October 8 of that year, the day of the famous playoff game between the Chicago Cubs and the New York Giants for the National League pennant, a game ordered re-played because of Merkle's Boner.

The playoff was scheduled for the Polo Grounds, the Giants' home

park. The Cubs, the story goes, were late in arriving and the correspondents accompanying the Chicago team, had difficulty finding seats in the press box. Hugh Fullerton of the *Chicago Tribune,* one of the star scribes of his day, was supposed to have a front-row seat, next to his telegraph wire but discovered his space was occupied by Louis Mann, a heavy-set actor then appearing on the New York stage. Mann wouldn't budge; apparently he had taken this seat many times before. The park po-

lice refused to intervene because he was a guest of the Giants' management.

Confronted with a deadline and with the knowledge he had to dictate a play by play, Fullerton plopped himself into Mann's ample lap and, despite this indignity, proceeded with and completed his assignment. Outraged, the baseball writers, 23 in number, met in Detroit six days later, on the morning of the final World Series game between the Cubs and Tigers, and gave formal birth to the BBWAA, which today is still easily the most prestigious of the various sports writing fraternities.

Among the charter members was Charley Dryden a native of Monmouth, Ill., and often described by his fellow Boswells as "The King of the Baseball Writers." Dryden had the equivalent of a grammar school education and had worked in a foundry before hooking on as a cub reporter in *1890* on the *San Francisco Examiner,* a Hearst paper.

In those days Hearst gave a weekly $5 award to the reporter who turned in the most original story. How Dryden won this prize was recently recounted by Abe Kemp, himself a long-time San Francisco sportswriter.

"Dryden's in a beer joint trying to think of how he can win that $5 prize," Kemp said. "This joint is run by a Dutchman who had a luxuriant beard. Trailed way down. And while the Dutchman was talking to him, Dryden got an inspiration.

"He lit a match, applied it to the Dutchman's whiskers and then walked down to the end of the bar and pulled an alarm that went to the fire department. When the firemen get there, the Dutchman's beard is smoldering and Dryden's squirting a bottle of seltzer water at the Dutchman's chin. Then Dryden went back and wrote the story how he put out this fire. He won the $5 prize." Much later, it was Dryden who first referred to the old Washington Senators as being "first in war, first in peace and last in the American League."

The Chicago press box was bulging with genius and housed three nationally-known scribes. I.E. (Cy) Sanborn, Hugh Fullerton and Ring Lardner. Sanborn and Fullerton were essentially analysts and specialized in writing about what Paul Gallico once described as the "inside of the inside." Fullerton was among the writers credited with "breaking" the 1919–20 Black Sox scandal.

Fullerton was a "dopester," an extinct breed and caught the imagination of the public by forecasting the outcome of the 1906 all-Chicago World Series. The Cubs were 3–1 favorites over the "Hitless Wonder" White Sox but Fullerton announced the Sox would take the Series and had the temerity to predict they would win the first and third games, and the Cubs the second. Legend has it that he also forecast a day of rain and that was his only guess that didn't come to pass.

Editors clamored for more predictions and Fullerton's analyses were syndicated. He correctly called the 1907 and 1908 series but his "dope" backfired in 1914. Growing bolder, Fullerton began predicting the scores of each game and in the eight-game 1921 Yankee-Giant series supposedly had the scores on the nose in five games. He met his Waterloo a year later when, contrary to his dope, the Giants won in five games, not the Yankees as he had predicted.

Flanking Fullerton in the press box but with a crystal ball that gave him a considerably different view was Ring Lardner of the *Chicago Tribune,* easily the best known of all baseball writers, embracing both ancients and moderns. When baseball's Hall of Fame began welcoming writers, posthumously, in 1963, Lardner was the first choice for enshrinement, by acclamation.

Lardner wasn't a dilettante ball writer covering an occasional game. He traveled with both Chicago teams for seven seasons before devoting full energies to fiction. That he was one of America's great writers, an original, there is no question. Critics have compared him to De-Maupassant and Chekhov as a master of the short story.

Long after Lardner had stopped writing baseball, he appeared unexpectedly at an annual meeting of the New York chapter of the BBWAA. Some of the writers began treating him with deference. "What's the matter with you guys," Lardner said. "I'm still a baseball writer and always will be."

Lardner was a pioneer in the "aw nuts" school of sportswriting, at the other end was the so-called "gee whiz" camp, telling it fair and square, but basically a cheerleading function nonetheless.

Through the ages, baseball writers had been divided into these two groups, both of which had stars of equal magnitude. Grantland Rice, John Kieran, Paul Gallico and Red Smith, in his early and middle years, were essentially "gee whiz" and played everything for high drama. Westbrook Pegler and Bill McGeehan were among the better-known practitioners of the "aw nuts" school.

But the style has been changing and today most of the baseball writers are somewhere in the middle, a position long championed by Jimmy Cannon who once said: "I don't want sportswriters being fans. I want them to be the guys who neither love nor hate the sport and who remember they are working newspapermen. Telling the truth—and writing it with vigor and clarity—that's what makes baseball and sportswriting exciting."

Close as he may be, a baseball writer never has been and never will be a member of the team, a circumstance best illustrated perhaps during the 1930 World Series when Bozeman Bulger, a famous New York scribe, was rushed to a hospital in St. Louis. An emergency operation was ordered and it was announced in the press box next day that Bulger's condition had necessitated surgery.

Irwin S. Cobb dispatched the following telegram to his fallen comrade: "Congratulations on being the first baseball writer to get a cut in a World Series."

Baseball was one of Damon Runyon's favorite beats.

ROBERTO CLEMENTE

BY JOE REICHLER

The way in which Roberto Clemente died on New Year's Eve, 1972, says more about the way he lived than all the Clemente memorabilia on display at the Baseball Hall of Fame in Cooperstown, New York.

He had become personally involved in a mission of mercy trying to relieve the suffering of strangers caused by an earthquake in a country he had previously visited only briefly. But his interest in Nicaragua and in the Nicaraguan people had been heightened by his experience in managing the Puerto Rican team that participated in the amateur World Series held in Managua in November and December, 1972.

Subsequent news of the earthquake affected him deeply, and he immediately spearheaded a relief committee in Puerto Rico to aid the disaster victims. Typical of Roberto, the program consumed him completely as he organized collection points, arranged publicity, and worked out the necessary transportation. Working 14 hours a day and rarely even taking the time to eat properly, he personally conducted a door to door campaign that collected $160,000 and tons of badly needed supplies.

Other athletes of Clemente's stature might have loaned their names or financial support to such a worthy cause, but his complete dedication to the task was typical of Roberto. "Honorary Chairmen" do not spend New Year's Eve aboard ill-fated DC7's which crash into the ocean carrying relief supplies.

This capacity for involvement characterized him as a ballplayer and helped create some of the misunderstandings that made him a contro-

versial personality. But in the end, his baseball skills remained the achievement of his life and the reason his personality mattered to so many people.

Clemente will be remembered, not only because he played the game so well, but because he played it with such total commitment, with such élan and flair, and with the insolence of a god. We recall the way he attacked the ball with a bat from his totally unorthodox stance taking that little step in the batter's box, and lashing the ball to right field. Others made diving catches—he made them one-handed, sliding across the outfield grass. Others deftly retrieved baseballs from concrete walls—he snatched them bare-handed and flung them like arrows to the proper base. Willie Mays made basket catches. Roberto Clemente made them matter-of-factly at his knees, so self-assuredly you never even considered he might drop one. The speed and abandon with which he ran the bases—these were peculiar to Roberto and to him alone. A lifetime batting average of .317, highest of any active player . . . 4-time batting champion . . . 12-time All Star . . . in the National League Top Ten in games, at bats, hits, singles, RBI's and total bases; and the All-Time Pirate leader in these same categories . . . 18 seasons . . . 3,000 hits . . . 13 times over .300 . . . 12 Gold Glove Awards . . . 1966 MVP . . . 1971 Babe Ruth Award. These are only the bare outlines of his genius. His style of play was a statement of himself—that he cared and cared deeply.

Dignity, honor and pride—these were the stuff of which he was made

The great Roberto Clemente.

—a consuming, dominating pride, fermenting and driving him in the headlong pursuit of excellence; a superior intelligence at terrible odds with a foreign tongue he battled but never mastered, a softly sardonic wit; a warmth that barely broke through the facade he painfully constructed because he was a private man; the satisfaction that flooded his face following the final game of the '71 World Series when after 18 splendid summers he had converted the final disbeliever to become an "overnight" sensation. Without him the game has lost some of its magic.

He was Puerto Rican, and he was black and fiercely proud of his identity. His status as a national hero in Puerto Rico stemmed as much from his outspoken expression of such pride as from his baseball feats. Other Puerto Ricans had won baseball glory, but none had made such explicit demands for respect and recognition.

Even at his peak moments on the ball field, Clemente related his baseball world to his world back home. After the Pirates had dethroned the Baltimore Orioles in the '71 Series, he was called to the microphone during the tumultuous locker-room celebration. He asked permission to include a few words in Spanish directed to his mother and father in Puerto Rico: "On this the proudest moment of my life, I ask your blessing."

Quotes from Roberto give an insight into the personality of this dashing figure who, along with Willie Mays, was perhaps the greatest all-round player since Ty Cobb and the greatest Pirate ever, with the possible exception of the immortal Honus Wagner. Roberto spoke the ballplayers' language.

"Any time you are not doing your best, you are stealing somebody's money and I don't consider myself a thief."

"I play the game as it was meant to be played. I don't think there is anybody who plays harder than I do and I play this way all the time. All season, every season, I give everything I have to the game of baseball.

One of the game's most feared hitters, Clemente compiled a .317 average over 18 splendid seasons.

I have a lot of pride and I think I am the best."

"I want to be remembered as one who gave all he had to give."

Few men, if any, played baseball better than Clemente did in his 18-year career with the Pirates, and few put as much passion into other aspects of life as he did. He had a wide variety of goals. He wanted to go into the big equipment business and provide bulldozers, tractors, graders and other earth-moving machines for small Puerto Rican towns which could not afford to buy their

own. He wanted to arrange a personal counseling service to aid and advise young Latin American baseball players. He was a firm believer in the benefits of chiropractic and after studying the profession in earnest, he planned to open a string of clinics in Puerto Rico for old people without money. Most of all, he was interested in children, and his fondest dream was of a "Youth City," a vast sports complex where the underprivileged of his native land would, through sports, be able to cultivate the finest human qualities.

Hopefully, this latter dream of Roberto's may someday soon become a reality. Through the establishment of the Roberto Clemente Memorial Fund, over half a million dollars has already been generated for a two-fold purpose: to continue his efforts on behalf of the Nicaraguan earthquake victims and to construct his Youth City. The Puerto Rican government has donated a 600-acre tract and the ground has already been broken for the development of athletic fields. The Pirates are playing a Ciudad De Portiva Series in San Juan,

meeting another major league team in a two-game series each Spring for five years, with all proceeds going to the Youth City project.

He was regal, intense, misunderstood, determined, proud, warm, sensitive, honorable, kind, considerate, and complex, but most of all, he was compassionate. He played from the heart, he did everything that way. Easily the most popular player on the ball club, he was a genuine humanitarian with a deep sense of involvement, who played the game with dignity and grace.

No man living is articulate enough to describe exactly how Roberto Clemente moved through the meadows of our land for 18 summers. But perhaps Baseball Commissioner Bowie Kuhn said it best, "He had about him a touch of royalty."

THE HALL OF FAME

Cap Anson
Grover C. Alexander
Luke Appling
Home Run Baker
Davy Bancroft
Ed Barrow
Jacob Beckley
James Bell
Chief Bender
Yogi Berra
Jim Bottomley
Lou Boudreau
Roger Bresnahan
Dan Brouthers
Mordecai Brown
Morgan Bulkeley
Jesse Burkett
Roy Campanella
Max Carey
Alexander Cartwright
Henry Chadwick
Frank Chance
Oscar Charleston
Jack Chesbro
Fred Clarke
John Clarkson
Roberto Clemente
Ty Cobb
Mickey Cochrane
Eddie Collins
James Collins

Earle Combs
Charlie Comiskey
Jocko Conlan
Tom Connolly
Roger Connor
Stanley Coveleski
Sam Crawford
Joe Cronin
Candy Cummings
Kiki Cuyler
Dizzy Dean
Ed Delahanty
Bill Dickey
Joe DiMaggio
Hugh Duffy
Bill Evans
John Evers
Buck Ewing
Urban Faber
Bob Feller
Elmer Flick
Whitey Ford
Jimmy Foxx
Ford Frick
Frank Frisch
James Galvin
Lou Gehrig
Charles Gehringer
Josh Gibson
Lefty Gomez
Goose Goslin

CHARLES L. GEHRINGER
SECOND BASEMAN WITH DETROIT A.L. FROM
1925 THROUGH 1941 AND COACH IN 1942.
COMPILED LIFETIME BATTING AVERAGE
OF .321 IN 2323 GAMES, COLLECTED 2839
HITS. NAMED MOST VALUABLE PLAYER IN
A.L. IN 1937. BATTED .321 IN WORLD SERIES
COMPETITION AND HAD A .500 AVERAGE
FOR SIX ALL-STAR GAMES.

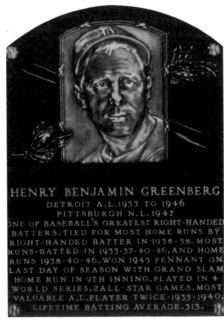

HENRY BENJAMIN GREENBERG
DETROIT A.L. 1933 TO 1946
PITTSBURGH N.L. 1947
ONE OF BASEBALL'S GREATEST RIGHT-HANDED
BATTERS. TIED FOR MOST HOME RUNS BY
RIGHT-HANDED BATTER IN 1938-58. MOST
RUNS-BATTED-IN 1935-37-40-46, AND HOME
RUNS 1938-40-46. WON 1945 PENNANT ON
LAST DAY OF SEASON WITH GRAND SLAM
HOME RUN IN 9TH INNING. PLAYED IN 4
WORLD SERIES, 2 ALL-STAR GAMES. MOST
VALUABLE A.L. PLAYER TWICE-1935-1940.
LIFETIME BATTING AVERAGE .313.

HAROLD J. (PIE) TRAYNOR
RATED AMONG THE GREAT THIRD BASEMEN
OF ALL TIME, BECAME A REGULAR WITH
THE PITTSBURGH N.L. TEAM IN 1922 AND
CONTINUED AS A PLAYER UNTIL CONCLUSION
OF 1937 SEASON. MANAGED THE PIRATES
FROM JUNE, 1934, THROUGH SEPT. 1939. HOLDS
SEVERAL FIELDING RECORDS AND COMPILED
A LIFETIME BATTING MARK OF .320. ONE OF
FEW PLAYERS EVER TO MAKE 200 OR MORE
HITS DURING A SEASON, COLLECTING
208 IN 1923.

Hank Greenberg
Clark Griffith
Burleigh Grimes
Robert Grove
Charles Hafey
Jesse Haines
Bill Hamilton
William Harridge
Gabby Hartnett
Harry Heilmann
Harry Hooper
Rogers Hornsby
Waite Hoyt
Cal Hubbard
Carl Hubbell
Miller Huggins
Monte Irvin
Hughie Jennings
Bancroft Johnson
Walter Johnson
Tim Keefe
Willie Keeler
Joe Kelley
George Kelly
Mike Kelly
Ralph Kiner
Bill Klem
Sandy Koufax
Nap Lajoie
Kenesaw Landis
Bob Lemon

Buck Leonard
Fred Lindstrom
Ted Lyons
Connie Mack
Mickey Mantle
Heinie Manush
Rabbit Maranville
Rube Marquard
Christy Mathewson
Joe McCarthy
Tom McCarthy
Joe McGinnity
John McGraw
Bill McKechnie
Joe Medwick
Stan Musial
Charles Nichols
James O'Rourke
Mel Ott
Satchel Paige
Herb Pennock
Eddie Plank
Charlie Radbourne
Sam Rice
Branch Rickey
Eppa Rixey
Robin Roberts
Jackie Robinson
Edd Roush
Red Ruffing
Babe Ruth

Ray Schalk
Al Simmons
George Sisler
Warren Spahn
Albert Spalding
Tris Speaker
Casey Stengel
Bill Terry
Sam Thompson
Joe Tinker
Pie Traynor
Dazzy Vance
Rube Waddell
Honus Wagner
Roderick Wallace
Ed Walsh
Lloyd Waner
Paul Waner
John Ward
George Weiss
Michael Welch
Zack Wheat
Ted Williams
George Wright
Harry Wright
Early Wynn
Cy Young
Ross Youngs

CARL HUBBELL
NEW YORK N.L. 1928-1943
HAILED FOR IMPRESSIVE PERFORMANCE IN
1934 ALL-STAR GAME WHEN HE STRUCK OUT
RUTH, GEHRIG, FOXX, SIMMONS AND CRONIN
IN SUCCESSION. NICKNAMED GIANTS
MEAL-TICKET. WON 253 GAMES IN MAJORS.
SCORING 16 STRAIGHT IN 1936. COMPILED
STREAK OF 46 1/3 SCORELESS INNINGS IN
1933. HOLDER OF MANY RECORDS.

GEORGE HAROLD SISLER
ST. LOUIS - WASHINGTON A.L.
BOSTON, N.L. 1915-1930
HOLDS TWO AMERICAN LEAGUE RECORDS,
MAKING 257 HITS IN 1920 AND BATTING
.4079 IN 1922. RETIRED WITH MAJOR
LEAGUE AVERAGE OF .341, CREDITED WITH
BEING ONE OF BEST TWO FIELDING FIRST
BASEMEN IN HISTORY OF GAME.

JOSEPH PAUL DI MAGGIO
NEW YORK A.L. 1936 TO 1951
HIT SAFELY IN 56 CONSECUTIVE GAMES
FOR MAJOR LEAGUE RECORD 1941. HIT 2
HOME-RUNS IN ONE INNING 1936. HIT 3
HOME-RUNS IN ONE GAME (3 TIMES). HOLDS
NUMEROUS BATTING RECORDS. PLAYED IN
10 WORLD SERIES (51 GAMES) AND 11 ALL
STAR GAMES. MOST VALUABLE PLAYER
A.L. 1939, 1941, 1947.

THE HALL OF FAME

BY CLIFFORD KACHLINE

Take equal parts of baseball, Americana, and nostalgia, mix well—and what do you have? Cooperstown, New York, and the National Baseball Hall of Fame and Museum.

Nowhere can one learn more about baseball's heritage—how it all began, who helped develop it, who its great stars were and are—than at the National Baseball Hall of Fame and Museum. The hundreds of displays and thousands of artifacts tell the story as no textbook could.

To a dyed-in-the-wool baseball fan, a trip to Cooperstown is something akin to a visit to Shangri-La. Even for a person only mildly interested in the sport, it can be a heartwarming experience, since a tour through the Hall of Fame and Museum is just a small part of the pleasant memories to be gained.

The village itself charms many visitors. Tucked into the scenic rolling hills of central New York, the town is located at the southern end of Otsego Lake, from which rises the north branch of the Susquehanna River. The quaint, nineteenth-century appearance of the tiny, pastoral community—population 2,500 when everyone is at home—serves as a vivid reminder of this nation's great past. "It's·so typically Ameri-

can" is a phrase often heard from those making their first visit to Cooperstown. The shrine attracts a quarter of a million visitors each year and is open every day except for Thanksgiving, Christmas, and New Year's Day. A three-story red brick building, it is located in the heart of town.

The museum depicts the colorful, exciting history of the sport through the relics, treasures, and other memorabilia making up the displays. The impressive Hall of Fame gallery houses the handsomely sculpted bronze plaques of the greats who have been voted into the game's most exclusive club. And a separate but related facility—the National Baseball Library—serves as a repository for baseball publications, documents, films, etc., and is a research haven for historians and scholars.

One feature of the museum is the merging of the past and present. Mementos of yesterday naturally predominate. Yet there are many contemporary displays linked to today's stars. During the baseball season tourists are even kept informed about how their favorite big-league teams fared in their latest games.

The Baseball Hall of Fame and

Museum consists of four floors with some seventeen thousand square feet of display space. Plans have been formulated for expansion in the near future. But even now most visitors take from two to four hours to go through the exhibition areas.

The first-floor exhibit rooms, the areas a tourist normally will explore first, contain mementos of approximately two dozen of baseball's all-time greats, ranging from Ty Cobb and Christy Mathewson to Ted Williams, Stan Musial, and the immortal Casey Stengel. Coincidentally, Cobb and Matty were among the five original Hall of Fame members, the others being Honus Wagner, Babe Ruth, and Walter Johnson.

Cobb, whose .367 career average remains unchallenged as the highest in history, donated many keepsakes to the museum, and friends contributed others. The most ancient of the Cobb artifacts is the contract he signed with Anniston, Alabama, of the Southeastern League in 1904, his first year in professional ball. It reveals the Georgia Peach was paid the then handsome sum of fifty dollars per month. Other items in the Cobb display include a warmup sweater and the last glove he used as a member of the Detroit Tigers in 1926 as well as the Philadelphia A's uniform, complete with the symbolic white elephant on the shirt front, that he wore in his farewell seasons of 1928.

Mathewson fared better financially than Cobb during his apprenticeship in the minors, according to a memento of his playing days. Matty's contract with Norfolk of the Virginia League for 1900, his second season as a pro, shows he was paid ninety dollars a month. Also decorating the Mathewson display are a Bible that he read while attending Sunday School in his hometown of Factoryville, Pa., the uniform he later wore as pitching ace of the New York Giants, and a score sheet of the last of his three shutouts in the 1905 World Series.

An entire showcase is devoted to Williams. Among the items in it are the uniform, shoes, and glove he

274

wore in his last game with the Boston Red Sox on September 28, 1960, together with the bat and ball with which he socked homer No. 521 in his dramatic farewell plate appearance. Visitors can also listen to a recorded broadcast of the actual event.

Musial likewise is well represented. Bats, autographed baseballs, and the official score sheets from many of his record-breaking achievements are on view. The locker he occupied during his days with the St. Louis Cardinals, complete with his uniform, glove, and shoes, is also a popular attraction.

The exhibit on Stengel features souvenirs from the starting point and a high spot of the Old Perfessor's career. One memento is a score book showing some games that Casey played in the Blue Grass League way back in 1910, his first year in organized ball. Another is the New York Yankee uniform he wore in 1953 while becoming the only manager ever to win five pennants and five World Series in succession.

Elsewhere on the first floor one can see such historic artifacts as Norman Rockwell's famous painting *The Three Umpires,* which graced a cover of *The Saturday Evening Post* in 1949; paintings of the minor leagues' first night game at Des Moines, Iowa, in 1930 and the first major-league night contest at Cincinnati in 1935; other works of art by William Medcalf; the century-old Abner Doubleday baseball; a lifelike statue of Roberto Clemente complete with his Pittsburgh Pirate uniform; Lou Gehrig's Yankee Stadium locker and his No. 4 uniform; the chair that Kenesaw M. Landis used in his office while serving as baseball's first commissioner; Mickey Mantle's Yankee uniform and the bat and ball with which he produced a 565-foot home run in Washington in 1953; plus dozens upon dozens of other items.

The Hall of Fame gallery, with its black marble columns and twenty-five-foot-high ceiling, is a particularly impressive and stately area. It is here that the immortals of the game are enshrined. Bronze plaques setting forth their credentials are in-stalled in alcoves along both sides of the eighty-five-foot-long room.

Election to the Hall of Fame is the highest honor attainable in baseball. While major-league baseball dates back more than one hundred years, the 1975 inductions brought membership in the Hall of Fame to just 151. Of this number, only 123 were chosen on the basis of their playing skills alone.

Each plaque features a sculpted likeness of the individual together with an inscription recounting the high points of his accomplishments.

On the lower level, the contemporary major-league scene is portrayed in the "Baseball Today" room. Each of the twenty-four major-league teams is represented by a separate 4½ x 5-foot display panel that contains the club's latest uniform, color photographs of the manager, several top stars and the home stadium, and current editions of the team's media guide, yearbook, and score book.

Another section of the same room has displays on many of today's standout performers, including Tom Seaver, Reggie Jackson, Pete Rose, Nolan Ryan, Lou Brock, and Vida Blue.

Other exhibit areas on this level feature such artifacts as an old bat-turning lathe, one of the earliest pitching machines used by a major-league club, the John D. Shibe collection of baseballs that was originally shown at the Philadelphia Centennial of 1876, Hank Aaron's Atlanta Stadium locker, the bat and ball with which Roger Maris hit his sixty-first homer in 1961, and the glove that Bob Gibson wore while striking out a record seventeen Detroit batters in the 1968 World Series.

The second and third floors of the museum are similarly crammed with memorabilia of baseball's greats. For most visitors, the Babe Ruth Room on the third floor holds special interest. The vast collection of treasures from the Bambino's career fills an entire room. Here you can see the Yankee Stadium locker he occupied in the 1920s and early 1930s, his famous pin-striped No. 3 uniform, the bat he used in hitting his sixtieth homer in 1927, and dozens upon dozens of other items. As an added thrill, there is a recording that enables visitors to hear the Babe's voice.

The National Baseball Library, located just across the lawn from the museum, also contains many exhibits.

The lower level of the library building houses a movie theater, while the second floor is the archives and research area. From mid-June through Labor Day, baseball films are shown throughout the day in the movie theater. The hilarious *Who's on First* short starring Abbott and Costello is worth seeing.

The busiest day of the year in Cooperstown is Hall of Fame Day. Traditionally this takes place on a Monday late in July or early in August. Two events highlight the occasion. In the morning, induction ceremonies are held for newly elected Hall of Fame members. Several thousand spectators usually attend. In the afternoon, two teams—one from each major league—play an annual exhibition game at historic Doubleday Field before a sellout crowd of around 9,970.

More than 10,000 visitors jam their way into the town that day. The result is a festive occasion. Many Hall of Fame members, some in their seventies and eighties, return each year for the festivities, and most of baseball's top brass, including the commissioner and the two league presidents, attend.

Although Cooperstown obviously is a resort town, it retains the serenity—except for a few brief hours on Hall of Fame Day—that marked an earlier period in American history. The quiet, treelined streets with their old-style lampposts and neatly kept homes are a far cry from the bustle of modern times.

It is this atmosphere, together with the village's many attractions—including three other fine museums—that has earned Cooperstown a special niche in the hearts of the millions who have visited there over the years.

CHRONOLOGY OF IMPORTANT BASEBALL EVENTS

1845—Alexander Cartwright drew up first set of baseball rules and formed first team, Knickerbockers of New York, who first tried rules in game against New York Nine at Elysian Fields in Hoboken, N.J., on June 19, 1846.

1869—Baseball's first completely professional team, Cincinnati Red Stockings, was formed by Harry Wright and enjoyed undefeated season, winning sixty-four games and tying one.

1871—National Association of Professional Baseball Players was organized and established what is now regarded as first major league—National Association—with teams in Boston, Chicago, Cleveland, Fort Wayne (Ind.), New York, Philadelphia, Rockford (Ill.), Troy (N.Y.), and Washington, D. C.

1874—Albert G. Spalding arranged baseball's first foreign tour, taking Boston and Philadelphia teams of National Association on fourteen-game trip to England and Ireland.

1876—National League was founded, replacing National Association, with teams in Boston, Chicago, Cincinnati, Hartford, Louisville, New York, Philadelphia, and St. Louis.

1888—First round-the-world tour, sponsored by Albert G. Spalding, saw teams of major-leaguers known as Chicagos and All-Americas circle globe, starting in New Zealand in December and ending in Ireland following March.

1890—National Brotherhood of Baseball Players, fraternal organization formed in 1885, staged revolt against reserve rule and formed Players League with teams in Boston, Brooklyn, Buffalo, Chicago, Cleveland, New York, Philadelphia, and Pittsburgh; approximately seventy-five players seceded from established major leagues to play in first and only season of Players League.

1892—National League expanded to twelve clubs by adding Baltimore, Louisville, St. Louis, and Washington following consolidation with American Association.

1900—National League reduced membership to eight teams by dropping Baltimore, Cleveland, and Washington and transferring Louisville club to Pittsburgh in consolidation move.

1901—American League claimed major-league status after expanding to East by placing teams in Baltimore, Boston, Philadelphia, and Washington to join holdovers Chicago, Cleveland, Detroit, and Milwaukee.

1903—Peace agreement was approved by American and National leagues, which agreed also to establish three-man National Commission, consisting of two league presidents and chairman, to govern baseball; New York Highlanders (later Yankees) replaced Baltimore in American League; first modern World Series was played with Boston Red Sox defeating Pittsburgh Pirates, five games to three.

—After one-year hiatus because manager John McGraw of N.L. champion New York Giants refused to play A.L. champion Boston Red Sox, World Series was resumed as annual affair with Giants defeating Philadelphia Athletics, four games to one, as Christy Mathewson pitched three shutouts in six days.

1906—Frank Chance's Chicago Cubs set major-league record by winning 116 games, but lost World Series to Chicago's Hitless Wonder White Sox, four games to two.

1914—Federal League, launched as independent loop a year earlier, raided A.L. and N.L. teams for players and, claiming major-league status, operated teams in Baltimore, Brooklyn, Buffalo, Chicago, Indianapolis, Kansas City, Pittsburgh, and St. Louis; George Stallings' Boston Braves, in last place in mid-July, won N.L. pennant by ten and a half games and then stunned Philadelphia Athletics by capturing World Series in four games.

1915—Federal League disbanded late in year following peace settlement with American and National leagues, part of which provided that two Federal League owners—Phil Ball and Charles Weeghman—could purchase St. Louis Browns and Chicago Cubs, respectively.

1917—In only double no-hitter in majors' history, Fred Toney of Cincinnati pitched ten hitless innings to win, 1–0, over Hippo Vaughn of Chicago Cubs, who had no-hitter until one out in tenth and lost on two hits.

1920—Kenesaw M. Landis, Federal District Judge in Chicago, was chosen as first commissioner following disbandment of National Commission.

1921—Commissioner Landis barred eight members of 1919 champion Chicago White Sox from baseball for life on charges of throwing that year's World Series to Cincinnati Reds.

1924—New York Giants, managed by John McGraw, became first team to win National League pennant four years in succession.

1927—Babe Ruth hit sixty home runs while New York Yankees were setting American League record (broken by Cleveland in 1954) of 110 victories.

1933—Majors' first All-Star Game, brainchild of Chicago *Tribune* sports editor Arch Ward, was played in Chicago.

1935—Larry MacPhail, Cincinnati Reds general manager, introduced night baseball to major leagues at Crosley Field.

1936—Ty Cobb, Christy Mathewson, Walter Johnson, Babe Ruth and Honus Wagner are the first players voted into the Baseball Hall of Fame.

1938—Johnny Vander Meer, Cincinnati Reds' southpaw, pitched consecutive no-hit, no-run games against Boston Bees and Brooklyn Dodgers.

1939—Lou Gehrig, New York Yankee first baseman, ended his playing streak of 2,130 consecutive games and never played again; Yankees, piloted by Joe McCarthy, became first team to win four consecutive World Championships.

1941—Joe DiMaggio, New York Yankee outfielder, established major-league record by hitting safely in 56 consecutive games.

1946—First pennant play-off in major-league history saw St. Louis Cardinals defeat Brooklyn Dodgers, two games to none, for National League flag.

1947—Jackie Robinson of the Brooklyn Dodgers became the first black ball player in the Major Leagues.

1953—Major leagues experienced first franchise shift in fifty years when Braves were transferred from Boston to Milwaukee less than month before season opened; New York Yankees set record by winning fifth consecutive American League pennant and fifth successive World Championship under leadership of Casey Stengel.

1954—Baltimore returned to majors as member of American League, having acquired St. Louis Browns franchise previous fall.

1955—Kansas City replaced Philadelphia A's in American League as Connie

Mack ended fifty-four-year association with club.

1956—Don Larsen pitched only perfect game in World Series history to help New York Yankees down Brooklyn Dodgers, four games to three.

1958—Major leagues expanded to West Coast as former Brooklyn Dodgers and New York Giants made debuts in Los Angeles and San Francisco respectively.

1961—American League expanded to ten teams with former Washington Senators moving to Minneapolis-St. Paul and new franchises being awarded to Washington and Los Angeles; Roger Maris hit sixty-one home runs for New York Yankees.

1962—National League played its first season as ten-team circuit by unveiling new franchises in New York and Houston.

1967—Atlanta joined National League through transfer of Braves from Milwaukee.

1968—Oakland became member of American League through shift of A's from Kansas City.

Denny McLain of Detroit became the first pitcher in 34 years to win 30 games by posting 31 victories.

1969—Both major leagues adopted two-division format after expanding to twelve teams each, American League by adding new franchises in Kansas City and Seattle and National League by adding Montreal and San Diego.

1970—American League shifted Seattle club to Milwaukee on eve of season openers.

1972—Texas Rangers made debut as member of American League following transfer of Washington Senators.

American League adopted "designated hitter" rule which allows an assigned hitter to bat for the pitcher.

1974—Lou Brock, outfielder of St. Louis Cardinals, established modern major-league record by stealing 118 bases.

Atlanta's Henry Aaron broke Babe Ruth's hallowed career home run mark by clouting his 715th four-bagger.

Roberto Clemente, who was killed in a plane crash, was voted into the Hall of Fame.

1975—Nolan Ryan, California Angels' pitcher, hurled his 4th career no-hit game—tying Sandy Koufax's mark.

1976—National League celebrates its 100th anniversary; American League commemorates its 75th.